Angela Tilby is the Vicar of St Benet's Church in Cambridge. A former Vice-Principal of Westcott House, a Church of England Theological College in Cambridge, she teaches Spirituality and Early Church History in the Cambridge Theological Federation. Before ordination, she was a producer for the BBC's Religious Broadcasting Department, working in both radio and television for over twenty years. She is the author of *Son of God* and *Soul*, and is in demand as a preacher, conference speaker and broadcaster.

THE SEVEN DEADLY SINS

Their origin in the spiritual teaching
of Evagrius the Hermit

ANGELA TILBY

First published in Great Britain in 2009
Society for Promoting Christian Knowledge
36 Causton Street
London SW1P 4ST

Scripture quotations are from the New Revised Standard Version of the Bible, Anglicized Edition,
copyright © 1989, 1995 by the Division of Christian Education of the National Council of the
Churches of Christ in the USA. Used by permission. All rights reserved.

Scriptures quoted from the Good News Bible (GNB) published by The Bible Societies/
HarperCollins Publishers Ltd UK © American Bible Society, 1966, 1971, 1976, 1992, 1994.

Extracts from The Book of Common Prayer, the rights in which are vested in the Crown,
are reproduced by permission of the Crown's Patentee, Cambridge University Press.

Extracts from *The Alternative Service Book 1980* are copyright © The Archbishops' Council
and are reproduced by permission.

The publisher and author also acknowledge with thanks permission to reproduce extracts
from the following:

New Patterns for Worship is copyright © The Archbishops' Council, 2002. Reproduced by
permission.

Alternative Services Second Series, Order for Holy Communion, 1966, 1967 is copyright ©
Central Board of Finance of the Church of England, 1978; The Archbishops' Council, 1999.
Reproduced by permission.

Dante, *The Divine Comedy*, translation by Dorothy L. Sayers. Penguin, Harmondsworth,
1949. Reproduced by permission of David Higham Associates Ltd.

Evagrius Pontus: Ad Monachos, translations and commentary by Jeremy Driscoll, copyright
© 2003 by Jeremy Driscoll. Paulist Press, Inc., New York/Mahwah, NJ. Reprinted by
permission of Paulist Press, Inc. www.paulistpress.com

John Cassian: Conferences, translation and preface by Colm Luibhéid, copyright © 1985 by
Colm Luibhéid. Paulist Press, Inc., New York/Mahwah, NJ. Reprinted by permission of
Paulist Press, Inc. www.paulistpress.com

Every effort has been made to seek permission to use copyright material
reproduced in this book. The publisher apologizes for those cases
where permission might not have been sought and, if notified,
will formally seek permission at the earliest opportunity.

British Library Cataloguing-in-Publication Data
A catalogue record for this book is available from the British Library

ISBN 978–0–281–05632–3

1   3   5   7   9   10   8   6   4   2

Typeset by Graphicraft Limited, Hong Kong
Printed in Great Britain by Ashford Colour Press

Produced on paper from sustainable forests

For Alison White

Jesus said, 'It is what comes out of a person that defiles. For it is from within, from the human heart, that evil intentions come: fornication, theft, murder, adultery, avarice, wickedness, deceit, licentiousness, envy, slander, pride, folly. All these evil things come from within and they defile the person.'

Mark 7.20–23

The deadly sins have become virtues: pride is 'self-esteem', envy is 'healthy ambition', sloth is an enviable ability to relax, anger is 'feistiness', greed and lust are regarded as full-blooded enthusiasm for life, and gluttony manifests itself as gourmet delicacy or neurotic diet-consciousness.

Libby Purves in The Tablet, *3 September 2005*

There are eight general and basic categories of thoughts in which are included every thought. First is that of gluttony, then lust, then avarice, sadness, anger, sloth, vainglory, and, finally, pride. It is beyond our control to determine whether we are disturbed by these thoughts, but it is up to us to decide whether they stay within us and whether or not they rouse our passions.

Evagrius Pontus, Praktikos *6*

Contents

Acknowledgements

I am grateful to a number of friends and colleagues who have helped me with this project. I am also indebted to Mother Joanna Burton who read the complete text and made some very helpful suggestions about the Orthodox understanding of sin, and to Fr Raphael Armour who gave me his insights into the Orthodox practice of confession. Finally I owe thanks to Ruth McCurry and SPCK for their patience and longsuffering in waiting for what started out as a little book about sin and has grown to be longer than expected.

Introduction

This book has its recent origins in a series of sermons I preached in Westminster Abbey at the invitation of the then Dean, the Very Revd Dr Wesley Carr, in Lent 2001. But its true origin goes back long before that. I had known about sin and temptation from the time at school when I had been taught the Ten Commandments. I realized that the commandments (solemnly memorized in the language of the King James Bible) spoke directly to my impulses and failings. By the age of seven I had become adept at stealing small bars of chocolate from the confectionery counter at Woolworths. Once I knew this was a sin, it had, of course, to stop. I had a strong sense that God looked down on all our deeds and thoughts, and that 'my sins would find me out' (Numbers 32.23) if I tried to conceal them. I also recognized that I routinely failed to honour my father as I should. This was rather more difficult and I am not sure that I ever managed it properly. Along with the Ten Commandments I had grown up imbibing something of the Roman Catholic faith to which my mother had converted in her young adulthood. She had lapsed when I was very young, but she remained convinced that Catholicism was what she called 'the perfect philosophy', and for many years she judged herself to have failed to live up to it.

In my teenage years I began attending church regularly and was deeply formed by evangelical teaching on the need for a personal relationship with Christ. As my commitment to Christianity intensified I found myself both fascinated and bewildered by certain evangelical teachings on sin, atonement and forgiveness. The theology behind these teachings was superficially so different from Catholic teaching and yet it was clearly based on very similar assumptions about what is wrong with human beings in relation to God. At my confirmation I was given a little book bound in pastoral green called *At The Lord's Table*, which took the Ten Commandments one by one, and suggested meditating on each one in turn to discover the old and new sins I had committed before my relationship with God was restored through the sacrament of Holy Communion. When reviewing my life in the light of the commandments it was important not to be limited by the literal meaning. I discovered that 'Honour thy father and thy mother' referred not only to having proper respect and care for one's parents, but also to those in authority, including the clergy. 'Thou shalt do no murder' was a command to avoid feelings and attitudes of hatred, which were the root of violence. There was a lot of emphasis, too, on avoiding idolatry, which meant putting God first in one's life, and not being intoxicated by wealth or ambition or admiration for others. Self-examination was a key element in the spiritual life. It was impressed upon me over and over again that sin cut us off from God and we needed to confess and be forgiven before we could pray freely or live our faith with conviction and confidence. There was much to be said for this pattern, and it is still ingrained in me. When I go to a Prayer Book Communion Service, I find the intensity of the language both arresting and strangely consoling. It is a language of the heart, both urgent and passionate.

But there were, and are, problems with this way of understanding sin. Self-examination is useful, but it does not always bring one to accurate self-knowledge. Though I prayed for the Holy Spirit to bring my sins to light, the judgement over what was and was not a real sin was often quite difficult to make. It was easy to overlook sins of speech and deed which may have been obvious to those who had to put up with me every day. On the other hand it was easy to get weighed down with a neurotic guilt which no amount of repenting and believing could take away. The practice of confessing to a priest or discussing the issues with another person could have helped of course, but in the end a great deal depended on how well we knew ourselves. And because even *thinking* an evil thought was itself a sin there was a tendency not to search very deeply into one's inner motivations and desires. Being too scrupulous was a recognized danger in the spiritual life. As for sins of neglect or omission, there was always plenty of scope to agonize over good deeds not done, prayers skipped over, obligations unfulfilled. How could it be otherwise since in the Gospel of Luke Jesus tells his disciples that even 'when you have done all that you were ordered to do, say, "We are worthless slaves; we have only done what we ought to have done!"' It was natural to take such apparently harsh texts at face value, not to see any irony or exaggeration or humour in Jesus' words. The consequence was that it was difficult not to feel constantly guilty before God, not to be burdened by the sense that there was always something more to be done. Times of self-questioning inevitably became times of self-accusation.

In 1969 I went up to Cambridge to read theology. I soon found myself falling in love with the world of early Christianity and particularly with the teachings of Irenaeus of Lyons and the Greek fathers of the fourth century. It seemed obvious to me that their understanding of the human condition was rather different from that which I had absorbed through home, school and church. There was a freshness and vitality about their teaching; a confidence in the innate worth of God's creation and the dignity of human persons made in God's image, which seemed quite different from what was expressed in church.

Many years later, when I came to preach on the deadly sins in Westminster Abbey I had identified Evagrius as a major figure of the early Christian spiritual tradition and had become intrigued by his analysis of the harmful passions which make us vulnerable to sin. I had also discovered why his name was virtually unknown in the West and began to see that there was a story to be uncovered about how his most interesting insights had been overlooked by those who used his teaching to formulate the seven deadly sins. Since then there has been an explosion of academic interest in Evagrius and a spate of new English translations of his works.

It must be said from the outset that Evagrius is far from being an obvious soulmate. He writes in a highly compressed and poetic Greek style, often in the form of proverbs or maxims which are not always easy to understand.

He held beliefs which are difficult for us to grasp, such as that the world is infested with legions of demons. His spiritual practice would never be recommended today – he fought temptation by standing all night in a freezing well and lived on an appalling diet for years without washing. But in spite of this there is a surprising freshness, realism and even humour in his writing. He does not come across as churchy or moralistic, nor does he seem to belong to a neurotic, introverted religious 'elite' with no experience of the real world.

What I am attempting in this book is to rehabilitate Evagrius and introduce his spiritual teachings to those who share my sense that the Church's teaching on sin does not quite reach to what is really wrong with us. The problem of sin is deeper than a disorder of the will. Evagrius shows us that it lies in the very instincts which enable us to survive, those instincts which are at the basis of our appetites and emotions and which can drive us to inordinate lengths to protect ourselves against danger. What needs to be altered in us lies very deep, beyond the reach of words, concepts and memory. Only images reach so far and they remain dimly in us, the blurred imprint of unimaginable suffering and anxiety. There is bad news and good news in this. The bad news is that the problem of what we call sin may lie far beyond the reach of the will, and of our capacity to *choose* to be good, even after 'conversion', and with the help of God's grace. The good news is that our sheer helplessness and vulnerability is accepted and known to God in all its complexity. Those unknown images, laden with inchoate emotions more powerful than words, are where we are most vulnerable, but also where our healing begins.

Part 1

SYMPTOMS

1

Before the deadly sins:
the relevance of Evagrius

Most of us have heard of the seven deadly sins. We can even remember some of them. The lists are not all consistent, but all the ones we are likely to have heard of include *pride, anger, lust, gluttony, avarice and sloth*. Some early lists include a sin called *vainglory*, which is an overdose of self-esteem to the point of delusions of grandeur, *avarice* is sometimes replaced by *covetousness*, and in many lists there is *envy*.

The deadly sins have been an important part of the Christian spiritual tradition since they were characterized by Pope Gregory the Great (540–604). This was the pope who sent Augustine to England to convert the inhabitants from paganism to Christianity. But the deadly sins did not originate with this notable pope. He was in fact drawing on spiritual teachings from two centuries earlier, when thousands of Christians withdrew from the cities and towns of the eastern part of the Roman Empire to live lives of solitude, poverty and silence in the deserts of Egypt, Palestine and Syria. We know about these desert ascetics from contemporary historians who found their lives fascinating and awe-inspiring. We also have some of their sayings and teachings which were treasured, collected and handed down. These sayings and teachings put us in touch with the roots of Christian spirituality, the first experiments in radical Christian living, which began as Christianity emerged from the shadows of three centuries of persecution.

The monks and hermits of the fourth and fifth centuries were driven by an urgent sense that the world was hopelessly corrupt. They believed that human nature itself was in a state of disintegration. Monks saw themselves as Christ's 'athletes', spiritual successors to the early Christian martyrs who had contended for Christ in the theatres and arenas of the Roman Empire before that world had become Christian. The monks believed that though Christianity was becoming influential and even popular throughout the empire, many of those who flocked to church were Christian only in name. True salvation required extreme resistance to the world, and the Church, with its new-found wealth and the opportunities it offered to the career minded, shared the world's corruption. It was clear to them that the gospel demanded the abandonment of earthly ties and responsibilities after the pattern of Christ's response to the rich young ruler: 'If you wish to be perfect, go, sell your possessions and give the money to the poor, and you will have treasure in heaven: then come, follow me' (Matthew 19.21). Only in the desert, the monks believed, could authentic discipleship be brought to fruition. Only through prayers and tears could human nature be re-created. The desert became the 'laboratory' of Christian spirituality. Though

3

some of the experiments conducted were judged excessive both at the time and later, the desert was the crucible in which the spiritual tradition was formed.

Many of the men and women who went out into the desert came from the peasant classes and were not educated. But there were also sophisticated men and women who combined their austere lifestyle with study. One such is the subject of this book, Evagrius of Pontus (*c.* 345–399). He was the first Christian thinker to attempt to analyse the psychology of sin. Evagrius was born into a Christian family in Ibora, Pontus, a city in what is now Turkey. He was a provincial country boy but he received a good education. He became interested in the monastic experiments that were going on at the time and he developed a skill for theological argument. After a brief career as a theologian in the imperial city of Constantinople, he became a monk in the desert of Upper Egypt where he lived until he died. He was a prolific writer and a spiritual guide to many who valued his gentleness and discretion. He knew that sin was neither a joke nor a matter for a cosy after-church chat. But he was not what we might call a fundamentalist either. He did not think we were born in a state of utter corruption, damned by inheriting the guilt of Adam and Eve for their disobedience in the Garden of Eden. For Evagrius sin was a sickness that required careful diagnosis and appropriate therapy. In this belief he speaks to our age in which we are much more aware of the psychological roots of human motivation and behaviour.

Until recently Evagrius has hardly been known about in the West because after his lifetime his theology was judged to be heretical. His main interpreter in the West, John Cassian (*c.* 365–*c.* 435), never mentioned him by name and changed key elements of his teaching. Even in the Eastern Church, where his spiritual teaching survived and continued to be influential, there were enough doubts about his theological soundness for his name to be problematic. Much of his work disappeared and some was only preserved by being attributed to others. As a result his memory more or less faded out of history. Where he was remembered it was as a speculative intellectual whose beliefs about God and Christ and the world fell short of Christian orthodoxy.

In recent years scholars have turned their attention to this long-forgotten figure and it is now becoming possible for the first time to retrieve and reassemble his writings. As a result of this his reputation is being reassessed.

Although Evagrius is credited with being the first Christian thinker to codify the teaching that became the seven deadly sins, he did not speak of deadly sins at all but of evil thoughts, which he called in Greek *logismoi*. The term is ultimately derived from the Greek word *logos*, 'word' or 'reason', which carried a great deal of theological weight in the early Christian centuries. Here, Evagrius seems to be suggesting that *logismoi* are false rationalizations, the kind of compulsive, twisted logic that can lead to spiritual disaster. But before examining the history of sin and Evagrius' role in its development I want to explore in more detail why the notion of sin is such a problem today.

The problem of sin in contemporary Christian life

The Bible, our hymns and inherited patterns of Western Christian morality teach a clear difference between good and evil, and speak of God rewarding the faithful and punishing the wicked. We are descendants of Adam and Eve and we share the guilt of original sin. Much of the traditional language used in the discussion of sin comes from the law court. Sin itself is a form of trespass. It involves the breaking of a law. God is the judge, we are guilty. God passes sentence, we are condemned. Christ is innocent of sin yet receives the sentence of death. We are imprisoned by sin, yet Christ was punished for our sins and sets us free. He is still our advocate and pleads for us in heaven. At the end of our lives we will come before the judgement seat of God. All this forensic language of law and crime and sentence and judgement has its roots in scripture. The prophet Isaiah speaks of the Servant of the Lord being 'wounded for our transgressions, crushed for our iniquities; upon him was the punishment that made us whole' (Isaiah 53.5). That prophecy has been seen in Christian interpretation as an explanation of the role of Christ as the promised Messiah, and in particular of his saving death on the cross. As the hymn puts it, 'He died that we might be forgiven, he died to make us good, that we might go at last to heaven, saved by his precious blood.' The Church interprets the death as a substitutionary punishment for our sins. The liturgical language of the Church emphasized the awfulness of sin as an offence to God. In the Church of England we knelt to admit, 'we have erred and strayed from thy ways like lost sheep'. The picture would come into mind of those terrified sheep, wandering in the dark, falling into ditches, a prey to wild beasts. At Holy Communion we confessed our sins in words of anguished emotional intensity, 'the remembrance of them is grievous unto us, the burden of them is intolerable. Have mercy upon us, most merciful Father . . .' The sense was always that forgiveness was not to be taken for granted; God was angry with human sin and needed to be constantly reminded of Christ's sacrificial death in order to extend his forgiveness to us.

Until very recently in the Roman Catholic Church personal confession before a priest was expected as a norm before communion, and there were queues outside the confessionals before Sunday Mass. In the Protestant churches the call to worship was nearly always followed by an act of confession and absolution in which all participated often with heads bowed and eyes closed, each person indicating by their posture that they were in a sense alone before the judgement seat of God.

The forensic view of sin is not the only way sin is understood in Western Christendom, but it has been immensely influential. Yet in the last fifty years or so there has been a revolt against it. The traditional liturgical language has come to be felt by many to be too oppressive, too guilt-ridden, too grovelling. People have come to find it difficult to believe in a God who responds to our sinfulness with wrath, even just wrath. The traditional language of sin simply feels unreal and overdramatic. People today do not *feel* that they are that wicked as individuals. They look to their own experience and though they can see that they have sometimes made terrible mistakes, they can also see that these mistakes have helped them to learn and grow as people. Most of us are not as afraid of judgement after death as were our forebears in faith.

Today it is only in very conservative churches in the West that there is much emphasis on God as the one who rewards and punishes, on God the judge, to whom we must all give account. I am writing from the limited perspective of English Anglicanism, but I don't notice much difference with Roman Catholics and Reformed Christians, either here or in other parts of Europe, North America or Australia. There *are* churches where you can still expect a genuine hell-fire sermon, especially when it comes to sexual sin, but the stress is generally much more on God as one who is all-forgiving and all-loving. In parts of Africa, Asia and Latin America it is often different. There is a more vivid sense of the supernatural, and preaching and teaching about sin assumes a more straightforward link between sin and punishment.

The problem with the traditional language of sin and forgiveness has led to new liturgical forms for corporate confession. These reflect attempts to extend the notion of sin to cover what we now call structural sins, in recognition that many of our global problems are due to harmful attitudes which go beyond the individual. There has been a search for a liturgical language in which to express our own complicity in, for example, corporate avarice, or racism, sexism, ageism and causing harm to the environment. But this attempt, worthy as it is, throws up yet another problem, which is that these 'structural' sins depend on a view of society which is, arguably, politically loaded. Structural sins have to be *agreed* to be sins. There has to be a common standpoint on what is sinful and what is not. Of course it is possible to interpret the Ten Commandments and other such texts in a 'structural' way. For example, we could say 'Thou shalt not steal' is a prohibition against capitalist exploitation in countries of the developing world and I engage in it every time I choose not to buy Fairtrade bananas. But it is one thing to extrapolate meaning for an individual, it is another to do so for a whole community of faith, because to do so requires a degree of political and moral consensus which may not be available. (Does it matter if I happen to prefer the taste or size of other bananas? What about the arguments of some economists that schemes such as Fairtrade actually inhibit trade justice rather than encourage it?)

Traditional texts could help us to confess to avarice as individuals, for example, but once avarice becomes a structural sin it is not clear how it can ever be repented of or forgiven. We end up with banalities that are so general as to be almost meaningless.

For example:

> We confess to you
> our lack of care for the world you have given us.
> Lord, have mercy.
> **Lord, have mercy.**

We confess to you
our selfishness in not sharing the earth's bounty fairly.
Christ, have mercy.
Christ, have mercy.

We confess to you
our failure to protect resources for others.
Lord, have mercy.
Christ, have mercy.[1]

In recent years people have been encouraged to think that these 'big' general sins are the really important ones, while the old-fashioned sins with which earlier generations of Christians struggled, like impure thoughts and petty dishonesty, are unimportant. The result is that we find ourselves confessing in language that is mildly provocative and guilt-inducing but not necessarily effective. People go through the motions, but it is not always clear that either the heart or the brain is engaged. Meanwhile the unease and guilt which we habitually carry around with us finds no expression and no relief.

The consequence of this is that people who are really concerned about their spiritual growth tend to take their real concerns elsewhere and not bring them to church. *Feelings*, say, of guilt, or worthlessness; *problems*, such as compulsive behaviour; *disordered thoughts* of limitless power or revenge tend to be endured in silence or shared, if at all, with a therapist or counsellor. We want to be heard by someone who will take us seriously but not condemn us, and the fear may be if we take such problems to a priest, or express our feelings to a group of fellow Christians, that we will either find that our concerns are made light of or that we are rebuked in some humiliating way.

Evagrius: a voice from Christian antiquity

It was to this dilemma that I found Evagrius' writings spoke. Evagrius came across to me less as a moralist than a profoundly insightful psychologist. His concern was to deal with the roots of sin within the human person, not merely with the symptoms, as they manifest in sinful behaviour. As John Eudes Bamberger wrote:

> We cannot be perfected merely from action that proceeds from the exterior to the interior. We must be altered even in the depths of our spirits, where there lie hidden in the furthest recesses of our being unknown images, inaccessible to the external world save by some long-forgotten, distant paths which still exert their influence on our attitudes and ways.[2]

In other words Evagrius knew that the roots of sin lie so deep within the human heart that they pre-date our ability to use language. Our inner world is full of images laden with emotion, compressed into particular drives and compulsions, over which we can exercise little conscious control. There is no original innocence, if by that we mean that the human child is essentially free of compulsive and violent reactions and desires. Babies need lungs and fists to survive, to express hunger and discomfort and frustration. The primitive emotions which accompany these horrible sensations are not simply outgrown. They remain in our memories, even though most of us are taught to behave in a more measured and considerate way. Yet they remain as 'cracks in the heart', not in themselves sinful, but features of our inner landscape which sometimes break through in our conscious thoughts and behaviour.[3] Their location in the self is at points of our greatest vulnerability. They need our own merciful recognition and acceptance before they can be healed and transformed.

This process of recognition and healing is where Evagrius can most help us. He was more optimistic than most spiritual thinkers and writers came to be in the Western Church. He believed without reserve that the most important truth of human beings was their creation in God's image. In this sense there is an 'original innocence'; there is the nobility and beauty of the human person as held within the mind of God. On the other hand he was fearlessly realistic. He knew that those taking the monastic path of integrity must expect many years, even a lifetime, struggling with inner chaos and outer temptation. The spiritual life requires individuals to become familiar with their drives and compulsions and to recognize the effects these have on themselves and others. Only in this way can healing take place.

In this Evagrius was thoroughly in tune with the Christian gospel. Again and again in the Gospel accounts, Christ encounters individuals who are suffering the consequences of sin. It is not always their own fault. Sometimes the main issue is what has been done to them; the sins of others, including the structural sins of exclusion and cruelty. Sometimes the main focus is on their own wickedness or cruelty. Often it is both, because we tend to repeat what has been done to us. Jesus deals with all of this, by, for example, both pronouncing forgiveness to the individual and healing the disease or insisting that the individual reports to the priest and so comes back into the community from which he or she has been excluded. The gospel shows us that these are not separate issues; the personal and the social are intimately linked. We do, not always as we *would be* done by, but as we *have been* done by. Healing for myself is inextricably linked with healing for my neighbour. In a wider sense, the integration of the individual is inseparable from the advance of justice and well-being for all. The rift that we have made between personal and structural sin is fundamentally false.

This flaw does not appear, I believe, in the writings of Evagrius. He believed that with patience, discipline, trust in God and ceaseless prayer, the individual could find healing for the turbulent passions of the heart and would eventually reach a state of inner freedom. He calls this *apatheia*, passionlessness, an inner serenity which was marked by an unpossessive love for the whole creation: 'Happy is the monk who views the welfare and progress of all men with as much joy as if it were his own.'[4]

2

A brief history of sin

Sin and virtue in the ancient world

The notion of deadly sins does not begin with Adam and Eve and the Garden of Eden. Its roots are rather in ancient classical and Jewish literature. According to Diogenes Laertes, a Greek writer of the early Christian era, the Stoics believed that human beings were prone to four *passions*: grief, fear, craving and pleasure.[1] He cites the Stoic teacher Zeno who used the word *pathos* to describe 'an agitation of the soul alien from right reason and contrary to nature'. *Pathos* usually means suffering, being passive to or subjected to something. Passion is a word which has positive overtones in our culture; it suggests inspirational energy and enthusiasm. But in the ancient world passions were often thought of negatively, as compulsions, drives beyond the control of the mind which threatened the individual's equilibrium. In Zeno's teaching the four basic passions gave rise to many others. Grief, for example, produced 'pity,[2] envy, jealousy, rivalry, heaviness, annoyance, distress, anguish and distraction'. Fear produced 'terror, nervous shrinking, shame, consternation, panic and mental agony'.[3] Here lie the origins of the belief that deadly sins have their roots in the common soil of our instinctive life, in the vulnerabilities that belong to our nature. The basic passions give rise to others. This recognition, that in the world of instinct and emotion one thing leads to another, was echoed by the Christian writers who took up the theme of trying to manage, deal with or conquer the passions. The Roman writer Cicero, who was well acquainted with Zeno's teaching, preferred the word *perturbatio* to *passio*, the Latin equivalent of *pathos*. It suggested to him a disturbance of spirit, a disorder of the emotions.[4] Cicero's Latin refinement of a Greek idea is interesting and might even suggest that there is something in the Latin language and temperament which, when it takes up a Greek idea, brings a tone which is both more moral and more concrete than the more neutral and open Greek. This is a theme to which we shall return.

A second influence on the understanding of sin and virtue in the ancient world came from the Greek philosopher Plato and his successors. Plato taught that behind the world of appearances was a transcendent world of perfect 'forms', originals or archetypes of what exists in our world. Later Platonists were monotheists. Plato's highest form, the form of the Good, became identified with God as the source of all being. Platonic philosophy assumes that human beings are attracted to this transcendent world even though it lies beyond the experience of the senses. We are, however, able to participate in it by contemplation. Bodily asceticism is an aid to the contemplation of the ultimate Good, and the practice of virtue flows from such contemplation. Platonism provides a model for reaching through and beyond the experiences of the senses to the unknown dimension of pure being. Prayer is, in such a model, a return to simplicity and unity, the perfection in which we are held in the mind of God. The deadly sins prevent this ascent, entangling us in addictions and habits which make true contemplation impossible.

Another major influence in the emergence of the deadly sin tradition, at least in its early forms in the practice of the desert ascetics, comes from the teaching of the Greek philosopher Aristotle (384–322 BC). Aristotle did not have a direct influence on the Christian ascetic movement; the early Christian monks were at least in practice as far away from his 'golden mean' as might be thought possible. But his understanding of the point of virtue and how it is acquired has proved pervasive. Aristotle believed that virtue was a rational choice directed towards human fulfilment. Human beings are essentially social, so it benefits individuals to practise the virtues that will lead to the formation of a good society. By doing so, they will themselves find a measure of happiness, though he was realistic enough to realize that things beyond the control of the individual, such as good or bad health, are enormously important in determining how happy we are. Aristotle did not believe that virtue was innate, but that it could be acquired by practice. A person becomes virtuous by continually choosing virtuous actions over less virtuous ones. The accumulation of virtuous choices leads to the formation of a virtuous character. Aristotle's virtues were not identical to those later identified as Christian ones; but his belief that practice of the virtues forms virtuous character would be echoed in the Christian monastic tradition, particularly in the Rule of St Benedict.

It is important for us in trying to understand the Christian deadly sin tradition to recognize that its classical origins were not in a moral code of right and wrong so much as a quest for wisdom, in which various social and spiritual practices were directed at bringing peace, balance and harmony to individual lives, while contributing to the creation of an ordered society. The purpose of philosophy in the ancient world could be summarized as learning to live and learning to die. Learning to live involved a kind of spiritual conversion to authentic living, living with reason and harmony with oneself, other people and the natural world. In order to attain this, the individual has to learn attentiveness to the present moment and to the flow of feelings and thoughts which arise spontaneously in human consciousness. Meditation, memorization and repetition of helpful proverbs and phrases were an aid to spiritual concentration. At the same time the bad habits of mind and heart which led away from authentic living were exposed through dialogue, either with another person or in conversation with the self. It is this kind of conversation that the emperor Marcus Aurelius (121–180) had with himself in his *Meditations*.[5]

Dialogue provided therapy for the passions and enabled the individual to fulfil the ancient Greek maxim '*Gnothi seauton*', 'Know thyself'. This famous phrase, which has been ascribed to Socrates, Pythagoras and a host of other figures from Greek antiquity, was according to the ancient Greek travel-writer Pausanias inscribed in the forecourt of the temple of Apollo at Delphi. The Roman writer Juvenal simply claimed the phrase came from heaven. It certainly has a universal resonance which is still recognized today. Evagrius of Pontus quotes it in a Christian context: 'You want to know God? First know yourself.'[6] The quest for happiness, fulfilment and freedom from pain is a human constant and most people recognize that the way we choose to behave has an effect on our own happiness and that of other people. The virtuous life is a good life, but it is also a wise life. Wisdom requires us to overcome our vices, not so much as a heroic exercise of overcoming the temptation to do things we really want to do, but more as a way of becoming truly fulfilled as human beings. Learning to die was also important in ancient philosophy. Life gives us the opportunity to transform ourselves in such a way that we are no longer trapped by bodily desires and mental habits which turn us in on ourselves. By such practices we begin to realize that what is essential to our nature are not the hungers and ambitions which drive us, but immaterial values. These are the business of the soul and constitute what is immortal about us.

So philosophy is spirituality, therapy for the passions. Overcoming our vices means first being able to recognize them. The Roman poet Horace, who died just before the birth of Jesus Christ and wrote celebratory lyrics for the first Roman emperor, describes some of the destructive vices to which humans are prone. Horace was a love poet, and he claimed in this work to be giving up his frivolous employment for the serious life of a philosopher: 'To flee vice is the beginning of virtue, and to have got rid of folly is the beginning of wisdom.' The vices he names are avarice, covetousness, ambition, envy, anger, sloth, wine (drunkenness) and lewdness. They are not so far from later Christian lists of vices. Horace seems to have believed, perhaps over-optimistically, that all these could be tamed by study and learning.[7]

Sin in early Christianity

Christianity was born from Judaism and inherited the Ten Commandments as the basis of its personal and social ethic. The commandments prohibit idolatry, murder, theft, covetousness, slander. The Wisdom literature of Judaism, which includes the books of Proverbs and Ecclesiastes, Ecclesiasticus and the Wisdom of Sirach, offers extended reflections on virtue and vice which parallel in some respects the insights of classical culture. But Judaism differs from classical wisdom in that trust in God, prayer and alms-giving are regarded as the foundations of the virtuous life. God has given his law, Torah, which rules heaven and earth and guides human behaviour. The law is not an iron system of right and wrong, but a gift and a blessing which brings life to those who follow it. Because in Judaism God is personal and accessible it is appropriate to confess sins to God and express sorrow for them. God forgives those who repent of their sins and make amends for their past wrongs.

Early Christian writings reflect a blend of Jewish and classical culture, a blend which had already taken shape within Judaism beyond Palestine. The letters of Paul, both those generally considered authentic and those which may have been authored by others claiming his authority, include a number of lists of vices and opposing virtues which show both Jewish and classical roots.[8] Although the vices are set out as wrongs which individuals commit, they are not just private issues; they clearly also have social consequences, and the early Christian lists of vices and virtues are particularly concerned about their communal effects. The *Didache*[9] lists the following vices as 'The Way of Death', which is contrasted with 'The Way of Life'. In the way of death are 'murders, adulteries, lusts, fornications, thefts, idolatries, witchcraft, sorceries, robberies, perjuries, hypocrisies, duplicities, deceit, pride, malice, self-will, avarice, foul language, jealousy, insolence, arrogance and boastfulness'. Christianity is not an individualistic religion, though it is deeply concerned for individuals. In general its spiritual teachings locate the well-being of the individual within the well-being of the whole people of God. Paul longs for the new Christian communities he is founding to be harmonious communities, filled with the Holy Spirit, and not a rabble torn apart by rivalry or dissent.

Behind Paul's teaching lie the remembered teachings of Jesus which are reflected in different ways in the four Gospels. Jesus' teaching shows a balance between the individual and social dimensions. Many of his parables, wise words and teachings are about the ways and byways of the human heart, and show an acute sensitivity to individual human psychology. Yet the orientation of his teaching is towards the Kingdom of God, the social reality of God's rule. In Mark's Gospel Jesus described the 'evil thoughts' which come from the human heart, using the word *dialogismoi*. This is a significant word, for it anticipates the word *logismoi* which Evagrius would later employ. The 'thoughts' Jesus identified were fornication, theft, murder, adultery, covetousness, wickedness, deceit, licentiousness, envy, slander, pride, foolishness. These, Jesus said, 'defile' a person. The context of this teaching was the extensive grip of Jewish purity laws on the communities to which Jesus preached. Impurity, for the Jews, was all around, in the air, in the different kinds of animals, in natural processes, in sex and death. It was a kind of spiritual pollution which cut people off from God. Jesus was revolutionary in that he sat light to the purity laws and challenged individuals instead to look within themselves to the source of 'defilement' in terms of the social evils that come from personal disharmony.

The Jewish purity laws have their own context in the ancient world of the Middle East. The Jews were not alone in believing that there were supernatural forces which could cause people to sin. Ancient Persian religion assumed a constant battle between the forces of good and evil in which the human heart was a battleground. Babylonian mythology reflects a belief in seven evil spirits. Judaism was influenced by these beliefs and absorbed some of them into its own teachings. There is evidence for the emergence of seven as a significant number in the *Testament of Reuben*, part of the *Testaments of the Twelve Patriarchs*. This work is modelled on the Testament of Jacob in Genesis. It is not clear whether it is Jewish or Christian in origin, and it has proved difficult to date, with suggestions varying from the second century BC to around AD 200. Reuben describes seven spirits given to human beings in creation along with seven opposing spirits of error.[10] The first of the good spirits is the spirit of life and the last is the spirit that enables us to procreate. In between are the senses: sight, hearing, smell and taste and the spirit of speech. Against these are the spirits of error: lust, gluttony, anger, vanity, arrogance, lying and injustice. There is also an eighth spirit which is created with all that entrances and seduces human nature, and is described as 'the image of death'. This is a spirit of 'sleepiness' – an anticipation of 'sloth', the paralysing reluctance to perform the tedious tasks necessary for normal living.

Two of the most influential texts in the development of the Christian notion of sin were the Gospel accounts of Jesus' temptation in the wilderness (Matthew 4.1–11; Luke 4.1–12). Early Christian writers saw the three temptations as archetypal. The conquering of temptation was seen as a key event in the redemption of humanity. By the fourth century they had become in particular a model for the temptations an aspiring monk was likely to confront in the desert. The accounts describe how Jesus after his baptism was led by the Holy Spirit into the wilderness where he fasted for forty days and nights. Both Matthew and Luke speak of the devil initially tempting Jesus to break his fast by turning the stones of the desert into bread. The order of the second and third temptations are different in Luke and Matthew. Luke has as the second temptation the devil producing a vision of all the kingdoms of the world simultaneously, and promising them to Jesus in exchange for his submission. Matthew puts this temptation last. The third temptation in Luke was for Jesus to test his own vocation as Son of God by taking a heroic plunge from the pinnacle of the Temple. This is the second temptation in Matthew's account. Evagrius would later understand these as the three most fundamental temptations, to gluttony, to avarice and to vainglory.[11] Augustine identified them with the three worldly loves referred to in 1 John 2.16: 'the desire of the flesh' (gluttony), 'the desire of the eyes' (vainglory), 'the pride in riches' (avarice).

The Letter of James, which assumes that Christianity is continuous with Judaism, echoes the teaching of Jesus in Mark's Gospel by insisting that the roots of temptation lie within the human person. 'One is tempted by one's own desire, being lured and enticed by it; then, when that desire has conceived, it gives birth to sin, and that sin, when it is fully grown, gives birth to death' (James 1.14–15). Here is a causal link between desire, sin and death which would prove important in the development of the notion of deadly sin. James does not say that the human heart itself is the cause of sin, or that desire itself is necessarily sinful, though he comes close to doing so. But what he identifies is a process. Temptation is spurred by desire for what is evil, but that desire is dormant unless it is 'conceived', entertained by the mind, and then made actual. When it is made actual its consequences are death. The whole line of thought is Jewish, though it parallels classical notions.

The author of the Letter to the Hebrews is insistent that 'those who wilfully persist in sin after having received knowledge of the truth' (Hebrews 10.26) can look forward only to 'a fearful prospect of judgement'. To persist in such sin is to have 'spurned the Son of God, profaned the blood of the covenant by which they were sanctified and outraged the Spirit of grace' (10.29). There is no way back even for those who repent. The author cites Esau as one who sought with tears to recapture the blessing he had lost to his brother Jacob. Yet he was unable to do so, the opportunity had passed (12.17). The author did not believe a second repentance was possible. This attitude was taken up by a number of other early Christian writers who argued that no repentance was possible after baptism.

The beginning of the idea of 'mortal' sin

In the First Letter of John we find a distinction made between sins which are 'mortal' and sins which are 'not mortal': 'If you see your brother committing what is not a mortal sin, you will ask, and God will give life to such a one – to those whose sin is not mortal. There is sin that is mortal; I do not say that you should pray about that. All wrongdoing is sin, but there is sin that is not mortal' (1 John 5.16–17). The distinction John makes here is not the same as the classic Roman Catholic distinction between mortal and venial sin where venial sin does not endanger the sinner's immortal life whereas mortal sin does. But John regards both kinds of sin as dangerous. Both call into question the immortal life of the sinner. The distinction is that the first kind can be helped by intercession; the second, 'the sin that is mortal, is beyond such help'.

This distinction is the subject of analysis by the North African theologian Tertullian, the most important of the early Christian theologians to write and think in Latin (c. 200). He reckons that there are some sins which we all tend to commit on a daily basis; sins of anger, hitting out, badmouthing others, swearing and lying: 'In business, in official duties, in trade, in food, in sight, in hearing, by how great temptations we are plied! So that, if there were no pardon for sins as these, salvation would be unattainable to any.'[12] Tertullian believes that these daily examples of less than perfect behaviour are precisely the sins which John says can be forgiven by prayer. But then, he goes on, there are 'the graver and destructive ones (sins), such as are incapable of pardon – murder, idolatry, fraud, apostasy, blasphemy, and, of course, adultery and fornication'.[13]

For these latter sins, he teaches, even the prayer of Christ cannot prevail. Tertullian here is clearly echoing John's suggestion that prayer is inappropriate in cases of very serious sin. To justify this teaching further he recalls a verse from Jeremiah (7.16), in which God positively forbade the prophet to intercede for his people because they are beyond forgiveness and therefore subject to his wrath. Tertullian contributed to the Church's understanding of deadly sin in other ways too. He believed that the human soul is a kind of shadowy substance which is produced with the body in the act of conception. Every soul and body is descended from Adam, like a cutting from a plant, and therefore in some sense every soul inherits Adam's tendency to sin. Tertullian sees this as an irrational tendency, echoing Stoic teaching that it is the passions which prevent us living in harmony with nature and reason. The 'stain' of our inheritance from Adam is what is washed away in baptism. Tertullian was also the first Christian theologian to suggest that our sins put us in some kind of relationship of debt towards God which required satisfaction, though he was thinking in terms of compensatory good deeds rather than linking this to the death of Christ as later Christian thinkers did.

In spite of the importance he attached to baptism Tertullian initially believed that there could be just one opportunity for repentance for sins committed after baptism, though it would be much better not to count on it. This was while he was still part of the mainstream Church; he later joined the strict Montanist community, which took a more rigorist view. Origen adds to biblical evidence for the difficulty of any second repentance a verse from 1 Samuel: 'If someone sins against the Lord, who can make intercession?' (2.25). Yet he himself reports as widespread the practice of bishops forgiving certain sins,[14] while regarding idolatry, fornication and adultery as sins for which there can be no repentance. Of 'mortal' sins in the early Church the most fundamental was apostasy – the betrayal of Christian faith. This was seen as idolatry, a rejection of the true God for a deceitful substitute. Homicide and fornication were also regarded as 'mortal' sins. The singling out of these particular sins may go back to the decrees of the Council of Jerusalem (Acts 15.29), which listed idolatry, unchastity and 'blood' (homicide) as vices that Gentile Christians should abstain from. Until the end of the second century there was a virtual consensus that these three sins could not be forgiven. Whether pastoral practice always followed this consensus is another question.

Where sin was serious but forgivable, it was within the authority of the Church to declare forgiveness. This authority belonged to the Church by virtue of Christ's promise to Peter in Matthew 16.19: 'Whatever you bind on earth will be bound in heaven, and whatever you loose on earth will be loosed in heaven.' The Church took this to mean that it had received the power to remit sin and declare God's forgiveness. Until at least the fourth century confession of sins and restoration was always a public event. There was no such thing as private confession, though individuals inevitably sought out others for counsel and advice.

The severity of the discipline of the primitive Church could not last. Christians were never very good at living sinless lives. Over time sexual sins in particular came to be treated more leniently than they had been previously.[15] Callistus, who was Bishop of Rome from 217 to 222, was known for his kindness to those who fell short of perfection in their personal lives. He was much criticized for his leniency. But he argued that the Church should always find room for sinners, citing the parable of the wheat and the tares (Matthew 13.24–30) as justification. He also suggested that the Church, rather than being a gathering of the pure, should see itself more as being like Noah's ark, a refuge for all kinds of creatures.

Persecution and apostasy

The issue of who could be forgiven for what was hammered out under the pressure of persecution. In the middle of the third century the emperor Decius initiated a pogrom against Christians. As a key part of his campaign everyone was required to obtain a special certificate proving that he had sacrificed to the Roman gods. In spite of strong encouragement to stand firm even to the point of death, many Christians lapsed rather than face imprisonment, torture, loss of property and possible execution. The Church regarded as lapsed not only those who had actually taken part in sacrifices, but those who had managed to buy a certificate from an official source.

The persecution and its aftermath provoked a crisis in the Church. Some continued to believe that such apostasy could never be forgiven, and some were inclined to forgive it a little too readily. The Bishop of Carthage, Cyprian (248–258), who himself later died as a martyr, believed that the lapsed could be restored after a suitable time of penitence. Cyprian also anticipates later lists of deadly sins and shows how one sin might lead to another:

> Our warfare is with immodesty, with anger, with ambition, our diligent and toilsome wrestle with carnal vices, with enticements of the world. The mind of man besieged, and in every quarter invested with the onsets of the devil, scarcely in each point meets the attack, scarcely resists it. If avarice is prostrated, lust springs up. If lust is overcome, ambition takes its place. If ambition is despised, anger exasperates, pride puffs up, wine-bibbing entices, envy breaks concord, jealousy cuts friendship; you are constrained to curse, which the divine law forbids; you are compelled to swear, which is not lawful.[16]

Interestingly, he also cites the Carthaginian church's understanding attitude to sexual sin as providing a precedent for the re-admittance to the Church of those who had betrayed their faith: 'We allow adulterers an opportunity of penance and grant them absolution.'[17]

The last great persecution, which began in 303 under the emperor Diocletian (245–313), once again raised the issue of whether apostasy could be forgiven. The problem was that there was no consensus about what constituted apostasy. In the Eastern part of the Church attendance at pagan sacrifices was a proof of betrayed faith, but suspending acts of worship and surrendering liturgical books were not. Such divisions led afterwards to bitter schism, as many continued to hold to a strong line. In North Africa the issue was never settled, and led to the argument being carried on in different forms until Muslim invasions of the seventh century swept away the Christians with all their disputations.

Christian empire

The conversion of Constantine (*c.* 312) guaranteed freedom and safety to the Church throughout the empire. It also changed the nature of the Church. Constantine accepted the major tenets of Christian belief, but he delayed his baptism until he was near the point of death. Since in the course of his reign he arranged for the murder of a number of his relatives and behaved with considerable duplicity to maintain his power and inheritance, he may have also reckoned that he would be better off committing all the sins he regarded as politically necessary *before* being forgiven in the baptismal font. He died in 337, having firmly established Christianity as the favoured religion of the empire.

Evagrius, then, was a Christian child of Constantine's empire, born around 345, the son of an itinerant bishop in Ibora, Pontus. When Evagrius was a teenager Julian the Apostate reigned briefly as emperor (November 361 to March 363) and in that time attempted to implement anti-Christian policies. But his measures were deeply unpopular; it was too late to turn the clock back. Christianity was from that time free from persecution, but was still struggling to define its key doctrines. Evagrius grew up in a world of passionate theological dispute, in particular about the nature of Christ and the Trinity. It was also a world in which the sheer popularity and success of Christianity in the cities and towns of the empire triggered a spiritual revolt. Many lamented the passing of the heroic age of the martyrs, and tried to imitate their sacrifice by taking up what became known as 'white martyrdom' – lives of extreme poverty and hardship. Evagrius had a good education and he became associated with a religious community in Annisa, near Pontus, where he came under the influence of some of the leading theologians of the day. He then spent some years in the imperial city of Constantinople where he played a significant role in the build-up to the Council of Constantinople (381), where the orthodox faith was endorsed by the Creed,[18] which the churches still use to this day. From Constantinople he went to Palestine and eventually he withdrew to the Egyptian desert. It was there that he made his particular contribution to the formation of the Christian spiritual tradition.

The early ascetic movement

Evagrius and the other early ascetics tried to live in an extreme way the renunciations and promises of the baptized life. They believed that the coming of Christ involved a fundamental renewal of human nature, a restoration of the image of God in humankind; and that through ascetic practice and the grace of the Holy Spirit they could train themselves for immortal life. This training involved bodily disciplines and mental exercises. Like the Stoic and Platonist philosophers, the desert ascetics aimed at healing the passions and thus transforming the self, learning to live and learning to die. But although they shared some of the assumptions and methods of Greek philosophy the template for their spiritual exertions was entirely Christian, based on the mystery of the death and resurrection of Christ. Life was repentance, a constant dying to sin; death was a happy exodus to eternal life with Christ. In the meantime there was a battle to be won. In the desert human beings were directly exposed to the assaults of the demonic realm. The desert was the new arena where the successors of the martyrs struggled and prevailed.

It is probable that there were Christians drawn to some form of disciplined, ascetic lifestyle from earliest times. Jesus and Paul both spent time in the remoteness of the desert. But the ascetic movement really began with the experiments of Antony and Pachomius in Egypt in the first half of the fourth century. Antony had not been a city-dweller; his exodus was from village life, and his journey into remoteness and solitude took place in stages. The first Christian monks and hermits aimed to live the Christian life as perfectly as possible; to imitate the struggles of the martyrs by training their bodies and minds for unrelenting warfare against spiritual forces. Although the desert ascetics prized solitude and silence their life was never as isolated as it might be thought. Pachomius founded a monastery in which the life of prayer was lived communally. The hermit Antony made journeys to Alexandria and was frequently visited by those hoping for spiritual guidance. The fascination that his strange life evoked in others ensured that he had a fairly constant stream of visitors. He moved deeper into the desert but the troubled and the curious and the devoted still managed to find him. In the Nitrian desert a pattern emerged of monks living near to a spiritual father and gathering at weekends for teaching and common prayer. Evagrius trained for the monastic life by spending two years in a structured community of monks in Nitria in Lower Egypt. He then withdrew to a more remote area and it was here that he developed his spiritual expertise and began to codify his teaching in elegant and poetic Greek. Evagrius, though known as a theologian with a particular skill for upholding the orthodox faith against heretics, was valued in his lifetime for his *discretion*, his understanding of the human heart and skill at spiritual direction. He developed practical guidelines for dealing with day-to-day temptation, and it is this part of his legacy which has survived and been transmitted in different ways in the East and West of the Christian world. At the core of Evagrius' teaching is his identification of what he calls 'eight thoughts'. These represent the vulnerabilities to which all human beings are prone, the weaknesses that express themselves in image-laden fantasies and compulsions. As Evagrius saw it, these 'thoughts' were inspired by the presence of evil demons whose mission was to deflect monks from their spiritual quest, and hence away from God. Andrew Louth, the Orthodox scholar, describes Evagrius' eight thoughts as 'eight cracks in the heart'.[19]

The eight thoughts, *logismoi*,[20] are gluttony, lust, avarice, sadness, anger, acedia (sloth), vainglory and pride. Evagrius' treatment of the eight types of thoughts reveals a penetrating insight into human nature, which is as fresh as it is unexpected. Evagrius speaks with a voice which is observational, experiential and non-judgemental. He does not moralize, nor does he sound like the spokesman either for an infallible Bible or for an authoritarian Church. He knows that the spiritual life has to be lived rather than taught and that those who seek to come close to God must get to know themselves, as well as accepting and learning from the judgement of others.

Gluttony, for example, has nothing to do with the gross demonic caricatures of the compulsively overfed that are familiar from medieval Catholicism. It begins rather in a demonic assault on the monk's attempt to live a disciplined life, in which fasting and abstinence have a part to play. *Lust* targets those who try to be chaste and attempts to persuade them that it is futile. It arouses erotic fantasies which are so vivid as to be almost real and 'bows the soul down' in such a way that sufferers feel almost as though they have already sinned merely by entertaining the thought.

Avarice is not about misers greedily hoarding wealth while living with spectacular meanness towards others. It is about the very obvious fear of poverty and old age and the way in which this fear can imprison the spirit. *Sadness* does not appear in later lists, but for Evagrius it was a crippling form of nostalgia which prevented the individual from living in the present. *Anger* for Evagrius was the fiercest of the passions and can become an obsessive habit leading to paranoia.

Acedia is a kind of listless boredom which saps vitality and paralyses the will. *Vainglory* afflicts the virtuous, encouraging them to believe that their virtues deserve admiration from others. Last of all, in Evagrius' list, comes *Pride*, the demon which tempts the successful monk to turn away from God altogether.

In the West, Evagrius' teaching on the thoughts became the seven deadly sins; in the East, it became the foundation of spiritual practice and warfare against temptation. Yet neither the Christian East nor West has recognized its dependence on Evagrius, for reasons which we will consider in the next chapter. In the West, many of his insights were lost and his therapeutic approach to the problems of the human heart were transformed into our familiar forensic code of sin, guilt and punishment. The central chapters of this book will attempt to uncover Evagrius' lost teaching and offer an interpretation of it and its relevance for today. But at this stage it is important to understand how we got to where we are; what, in other words, the fathers of the Western Church did with Evagrius' desert teachings.

After Evagrius: Cassian to Augustine

One of Evagrius' disciples was a young man called John Cassian (*c.* 360– *c.* 442), a creative and enquiring personality from Central Europe. In his youth he visited the desert hermits of Egypt, observing their way of life and collecting samples of their teaching. Later, he travelled west, finally reaching Marseilles. Here he was made a priest and he founded two monasteries, one for women and one for men. At the invitation of the Bishop of Apt, who was himself planning to found a monastery, Cassian wrote down the teaching he had remembered from his encounters in Egypt. His *Monastic Institutes* was intended for beginners in monastic life. In his *Conferences* he attempts to pass on the teaching he received in Egypt in the form of discourses from some of the spiritual fathers of the desert. Both works have been influenced by Evagrius' teaching on the evil thoughts. The major part of the *Institutes* comprises an expanded Latin version of Evagrius' spiritual theology. Cassian's list of faults is almost identical to the thoughts of Evagrius, and many of his insights are borrowed from him. But Cassian never acknowledges this fact; in fact he conceals his debt to Evagrius entirely. Moreover his list is of vices, not thoughts – he begins the transformation of Evagrius' psychological and diagnostic approach to temptation into the more familiar list of sins. Why he did this will be considered in the next chapter. Cassian was not the only source of Evagrius' teaching in the West. Thanks to translations of some of his works into Latin by his friend Rufinus his teaching circulated in a rather more direct form.

Contemporary with Cassian was the greatest theologian of the Western Church, Augustine of Hippo (354–430). Augustine was attracted to monastic life and inspired by Athanasius' famous life of Antony of Egypt. Augustine was steeped in Latin literature; he was never at home in the world of Greek thought. The capacity of the Greek language to convey abstract ideas is not matched in Latin, which is much more concrete in its forms of expression. It is to Augustine that the Western Church owes its primary definition of deadly sin as something which is said, or thought, which is against divine law.[21]

Sin is a matter of the human will, a preference for something other than the will of God. This at first sight is an entirely reasonable definition, which echoes scripture and reminds us of the Jewish roots of Christianity. It reinforces the notion of sin as transgression, which is, after all, based in the Lord's Prayer where we pray for our transgressions, 'trespasses', to be forgiven. But Augustine's definition also contributes to the development of the forensic and moralistic account of sin which would later dominate the West.

Augustine was concerned from an early age with issues of human happiness and fulfilment. Long before his conversion to Christianity he struggled with notions of vice and virtue. Augustine saw pride as the most fundamental of human sins. His reflections on this go back to the period shortly after his conversion. In his treatise on *The Happy Life*,[22] he describes happiness in terms of a blessed destination for those who pursue it through philosophy. Those spiritual pilgrims are like seafarers in search of a safe harbour. Almost in sight of harbour stands a great mountain, an almost insuperable obstacle for the travellers. This, for Augustine, is pride. The seafarers can only reach their destination if they accept help from those who inhabit the blessed land. The need for others punctures the tendency to self-sufficiency. There is no salvation through one's own unaided efforts.

Years later Augustine preached a homily on 1 John 2.16, verses which, to him, reflected the three fundamental temptations of gluttony, avarice and vainglory (which here he interprets as pride). Augustine uses this text to discuss whether pride or avarice is the more fundamental sin. He is aware that scripture gives some support to both views. According to Ecclesiasticus 10.13, 'The beginning of all sin is pride', but according to 1 Timothy 6.10, 'the love of money is a root of all kinds of evil'. Returning to his original text Augustine tries to draw connections between pride and the grasping tendencies that lead to avarice. He concludes that the worldly attractions which draw people away from God are related to one another by what he calls *concupiscence*, an ardent, lustful longing both for physical enjoyment and power over others. At the heart of concupiscence is pride, the fundamental rebellion against God. This connection of thoughts in Augustine's mind was crucial, for it meant that pride is prior to all other sins. It was from this position that he came to assume that it must have been pride that led to Adam's fall.

It was in his arguments with Pelagius that Augustine refined his views on pride. Pelagius was a British-born ascetic who believed, as most early Christians did, that human beings had the God-given capacity to collaborate with the grace of God. Augustine saw Pelagius' teaching as a denial of the need for God's grace. This was not entirely fair, but as the controversy proceeded both sides were guilty of the classic Christian tendency of distorting their opponent's views and hardening their own in response. While Pelagius was convinced that children are born innocent and can, with God's help, fulfil his will, Augustine came to see the fall as the point in time at which the whole human race, through an act of pride, lost its capacity to do God's will. Because of the fall our wills are warped away from God's. Pride, then, separates humanity from God. All human efforts to live a virtuous life are in vain because they spring from our own corrupt inclinations. Only by the grace of God are we able to please him. There was no room in Augustine's later thought for any collaboration between God's will and human effort. Sin for Augustine is, literally, a sexually transmitted disease, from which all human beings suffer, simply by being conceived.

The identification of Adam's sin with pride was not universally accepted. It was possible as late as the eighth century for Alcuin, the scholar and liturgist, to teach that gluttony had been the sin of the Garden of Eden. In the thirteenth century Thomas Aquinas argued that gluttony had some part in Adam's original sin. A good case could also be made out for avarice, on the grounds that Adam and Eve's seizing of the fruit arose from a greed for what they did not have. But Augustine's teaching laid the groundwork for the fall to be seen as a cosmic tragedy in which humanity, just by being what it is, falls subject to God's just condemnation.

This development took Christianity a long way from its spiritual roots. The early Christians had believed in the reality of free will; they treasured the example of the martyrs who had freely died for Christ and for the faith. They were aware of human vulnerability, both to natural weakness and demonic attack. Evagrius' analysis of the evil thoughts followed centuries of patristic precedent in seeing sin primarily as a matter of sickness and vulnerability to demonic deception. Christ was the Saviour of humankind because he was the healer of sin, the one who restored us to fullness of life and opened up the eternal destiny which God always intended for Adam and Eve. In general the early Christians understood temptation as the assault of the devil intended to lure people away from virtue, rather than as a punishment for vices already entrenched in the human spirit. Most critically they held that any claim the devil might have on humanity was fundamentally unjust. The death of Christ was not a righteous punishment for sin so much as a completion of God's mission to humanity in Christ which culminates in the defeat of death.

But after Augustine the problem of sin is no longer the result of demonic attack stirring human vulnerability. Sin is part of what it means to be a human being whether or not actual sins have been committed. It was this conviction that lay behind Augustine's teaching that babies who died unbaptized could not enter heaven. The Catholic Church has recently distanced itself from the teaching that such babies ended up in an unspecified condition known as 'limbo'. But the underlying beliefs about sin remain, and are at the heart of Western Christian moral teaching, Catholic and Protestant. Sin is not just what we do, but in some sense what we are. We begin in the wrong place as enemies of God and subject to his just wrath. Augustine characterized humanity as *massa damnata* – humanity as a whole lies under condemnation, and 'if the deserved punishment of condemnation were rendered to all, it would without doubt be righteously rendered'.[23] The fact that any are saved is a testament to God's abundant mercy and overwhelming grace. The salvation of the elect is determined by the will of God, and only some are chosen for reasons which lie beyond human understanding. Augustine's views were controversial and his most extreme arguments were not wholly accepted in the Latin Church. John Cassian was horrified at his teaching and feared that if it was widely promoted it would undermine any attempt to live a virtuous life, especially monastic life. What was the point in sacrificial living if salvation and damnation were already determined?

Cassian's thirteenth *Conference* is a spirited and scriptural defence of the part played by free will in responding to God. He claimed that God's grace and human free will are not opposed to each other, but work together for our salvation. In this way he hoped to hold together Augustine's stress on the primacy of grace with a recognition of the importance of the human response.

In fact, the Second Council of Orange (529), while upholding Augustine's views on the centrality of grace, rejected any notion that human beings could be pre-ordained by God to commit evil. The idea that human beings were in some sense predestined for heaven or hell did, however, become part of Catholic belief, even though it was also recognized that no one could know the divine mind, or be ultimately sure either of their final salvation or damnation. It was the insecurity generated by this teaching which reinforced the incipient legalism of the Western view of sin. When the divine choice is inaccessible to human beings it provides motivation to avoid sin as much as possible. Cassian's fear that predestination would demotivate people turned out not to be true, though it may well have promoted despair among those who believed their sins were beyond healing or forgiveness, and that they were therefore counted among the damned.

Cassian's writings had a considerable influence on St Benedict (d. *c.* 550), who is regarded as the founder of Western monasticism. Benedict recommended that his monks read a daily portion of Cassian's writings, but he makes no mention of Evagrius, even though it is probable that translations of his work were still circulating in the West during Benedict's lifetime. Through Benedict, Cassian's teaching on sin came to the attention of Pope Gregory the Great (d. 604) and became a keystone of the Western moral tradition. Meanwhile, as we shall see, during the sixth century Evagrius' name dropped out of history as Cassian, Gregory and his successors used his categories of evil thoughts for quite different purposes from those he had intended.

After Evagrius: Gregory the Great

Gregory was an immensely capable pope with a passion for monastic life and an acute sensitivity to the paradoxes of the human condition. As chief pastor of the Church in a desperate time of economic decline and social disorder he came to an understanding that the universe of God's creation was a tightly interconnected whole in which good and evil were locked in war with one another. Yet this war was contained within the good providence of God, who allowed the devil space to inflict suffering on human beings both as a just punishment and warning against sin. Gregory was insistent that wrongdoing would always incur judgement. His vivid belief in hell was related to this strong belief in ultimate justice. Sin could be forgiven, but it did not go unpunished. So human beings lived under constant tension, drawn to the goodness of God but pulled to and fro by their own desires. The providential creativity of God was mirrored and parodied in the ingenious destructiveness of the devil, who was capable of all kinds of trickery and deceit. Cassian had written of sin as though it were some sort of plant with roots and seeds, and Gregory developed this idea in a manner reminiscent of Cicero,[24] showing how the principal vices had generative power; they gave birth to others, as to variants on themselves. While living as a monk in community Gregory delivered a series of lengthy reflections to his fellow monks on the book of Job; these were the basis of his great work the *Moralia in Job*. Here Gregory described 'seven principal vices',[25] which, he says, are the offspring of pride, 'the leader of the devil's army'. Gregory argued that it was because these seven vices had humankind helpless in their grip that the Redeemer, Christ, came to rescue us, bringing in exchange the sevenfold gifts of the Holy Spirit. Gregory tried to show how the seven vices are related to one another. Pride is the initial sin which gives rise to vainglory, which, because of its essential emptiness, gives rise to envy which then produces anger, and so on.

For Gregory, then, all that is wrong with us can be traced to pride. Pride then generates the seven principal sins, producing vainglory, envy, anger, sadness, avarice, gluttony and lust. Each of these principal sins comes with its own 'army' as Gregory puts it, a whole cohort of additional sins lined up to attack humankind.[26] So from vainglory come disobedience, boasting, hypocrisy, quarrelling, wrangling, discord and novelty-seeking. From envy come hatred, gossip, scorn, rejoicing in a neighbour's bad luck, or being upset when they succeed. From anger come scowling, big-headedness, detraction, rowdiness, indignation and blasphemy. From sadness come aggression, rancour, cowardice, desperation, lack of self-care, restless thoughts, and other illicit things. From avarice come treachery, fraud, lying, perjury, lack of calm, violence, callousness towards the wretched. From gluttony, false jollity, dirty jokes, slobbishness, talking too much, and dulling of the intellect. From lust, blindness of mind, lack of consideration, inconstancy, rashness, self-love, hatred of God, an obsession with the present moment and despair about the future.

Gregory's list, when pride is included, makes up eight, though the attraction of seven as a symbolic number was already influencing the way the tradition was passed on. Through Gregory the term 'seven principal vices' came into the vocabulary of the Church. Gregory goes further than Evagrius and Cassian in showing how the vices relate to one another so as to produce recognizable patterns of behaviour. It is not difficult to *see* the fruits of gluttony in 'false jollity, dirty jokes and slobbishness' – the combination is already forming a kind of human caricature. The scowling big-headed rowdy who is the result of anger is also recognizable. With Gregory we have moved quite a distance from a diagnosis of the symptoms that can lead to sin to a full-blown account of various human perversities.

Gregory has no difficulty in seeing that wickedness has become a fundamental part of human nature. He accepts Augustine's theory that Adam's guilt is transmitted through sexual intercourse. But he refines this idea in a way which tightened the link between sex, sin and guilt beyond anything which Augustine could have intended. The struggle to attain a virtuous life is not, as it was for the desert fathers, a return to a original virtue; it is a battle against what human nature has become, requiring constant and heroic effort, a scrupulous tracking of thoughts, and an iron discipline of the body.

In this he was even more suspicious of the body than Augustine. Where Augustine had seen sin as a disease of the will, Gregory believed that disordered desire came first and perverted the will. He noted that the fall of Adam and Eve began with concupiscence, a gluttony towards the apple, which also conveys the shadow of incipient lust. Temptation comes from outside in and attracts the eyes and the stomach before the will is involved in giving consent. For Gregory the trouble with human beings was that they were addicted to pleasure, and in particular to the pleasures of the body. Pleasure could not be enjoyed without independence from God. So the impetus to pride comes from our bodily nature, our desire to be free from God so that we can indulge the life of the senses. Pride is displayed in Adam's act of independence and we all follow him in the proud self-sufficiency which denies our true dependence on God. It is not surprising that Gregory saw pride as a parallel to male lust. Pride and lust both involve a vaunting of human autonomy: lust involves 'an open lapse of the body'; pride, an inner swelling of the heart. Indeed, when the heart swells with pride it is described by Gregory as being 'secretly erected', even though it may later become publicly evident.[27] The catch in all this is that Gregory sees our sinfulness as its own punishment. Human beings have looked for freedom to indulge themselves, and it is precisely this freedom which has been granted them. But the freedom turns out to be no freedom. It is to live tormented by the changing desires of the flesh, to be incapable of any constancy or stability in the service of God.

Augustine and Gregory differ on the form that our rebellion against God takes, and where in the human person its consequences are most felt. Both were aware that human desire is mutable and that some at least of our desires are beneath conscious awareness. For Augustine this is proof that our will is divided; we love God and evil at the same time and it is the conflict of desires which is the main cause of our spiritual and moral struggle. The healing of the fractured self is a long process for Augustine, in which we continue to be drawn by the grace and beauty of God, while becoming more and more aware of our capacity for self-deception. For Gregory the effects of the fall undermine any feelings and intuitions that might move us towards the love of God because 'after the adversary has once invaded man's inmost parts, through man's consent, it will now cost great effort to drive out the conqueror'.[28] Carole Straw, who has written a masterly analysis of Gregory's thought, comments on this that 'The Fall has given the devil possession of man's inmost being . . . Gregory is convinced that devils *do* [my emphasis] enter the human heart . . . to reject this is Pelagianism, a denial of man's inborn sinfulness.'[29] In Gregory's thought, the last defence of the soul is reason, and it is through reason and bodily discipline that the moral struggle must be attempted. For Gregory, the spiritual life involves unrelenting effort. There is no place of rest or stability. Our constantly changing thoughts cannot be innocently observed because they betray our fundamental sinfulness; we are responsible not only for conscious evil, but for the spontaneous thoughts themselves. 'Who can comprehend how many evils we commit each moment through the inconstant motions of our thoughts?'[30] Or, as Carole Straw comments, 'The sinner is responsible not only for the evil that he chooses, but also for unconscious thoughts and inadvertent sins.'[31]

It is important to realize that for Gregory God's justice is absolute. Humans live in constant tension between the demands of God's justice and their own weakness, desire and wilfulness. Because sin involves the transgression of divine law, it is offensive to God and results in inevitable retribution both in this life and beyond. The justice of God demands satisfaction. According to Gregory, Christ was the supreme mediator who on the cross bore the punishment of sin on behalf of humanity and thus 'both reproved man so that he would not sin, and he resisted God so that he would not smite man dead'.[32] Christ's death propitiates God's anger, and also leaves humanity with a model of sacrificial living and dying. Prayers, penances, attendance at Mass, good works and the patient bearing of suffering in this life are the ways in which individuals may take up and actualize Christ's work in their own lives. But the most important way of actualizing the redemption of Christ is by the Eucharist: 'The daily sacrifice of the mass recapitulates Christ's sacrifice and reconciliation of the cosmos and offers man the opportunity of sharing concord and harmony through union with Christ's body.'[33] The Mass is absolutely central for Gregory because it is open to everyone and infinitely repeatable. It is efficacious for individuals and communities, for the living and the dead. It offers a fixed point at which sin is effectively dealt with and salvation becomes possible. Gregory set the pattern of the Western understanding of the cosmos as a gigantic moral machine built on the principle of God's retributive justice.

Other theologians commented on the theme of principal vices, included Gregory's contemporary Eutropius of Valencia (d. 610), who identified eight sins to be resisted with all the strength of will and faith of which the individual was capable. His list, like Gregory's, is derived from that of Cassian. A similar list was produced by Isidore of Seville (560–636), who asserted that there are seven principal vices of which the queen and mother is pride.

After Evagrius: penitence and penance

Meanwhile the practical knowledge of the vices was spreading to the extreme West. In the Irish church of the late sixth century the Deadly Vices as set out by John Cassian form the basis for the penitentials, manuals of discipline for use by monks which include tables of punishments for particular sins. Irish monks who followed the teaching of Columban, the missionary and founder of monasteries (d. 615), were expected to confess to a senior monk on a daily basis, and this was the first time confession became regularly used as a private discipline, a move which would eventually greatly increase the power and status of the priesthood. The penances for particular sins given in the Irish Penitentials involve contrary disciplines; so the sins of the body are dealt with by various regimes of fasting. The principle here is that 'the eight principal vices contrary to human salvation shall be healed by the eight remedies that are their contraries'.[34]

The practice of individual confession was brought into the early medieval Church in the Frankish kingdom by Celtic missionaries. There were attempts during the reign of Charlemagne (c. 742–814) to make it mandatory, though this was resisted by some who still believed that confession and penance should be a public act, or that it could be put off until death was near.[35] The teaching of the penitentials was made the basis of new handbooks for those hearing sins, with penances graded appropriately to match the seriousness of the sins confessed. Many of the penances involved fasting or abstinence, from wine or meat for example. The use of the penitentials brought some of the insights of the desert tradition into the lives of ordinary Christians of the early medieval world. They raised questions about the roots of sin, about the underlying motives and attitudes which led to an infringement of God's law. In this way they helped to shape the prayer and sense of self that individuals brought to the practice of religion, encouraging reflection and self-examination. At the same time the system of graded penances must have also impressed on individuals the injury done to God through sin; an injury not so much to God's person but to his honour and majesty. Doing an appropriate penance restored something real to God, something God required for his honour to be intact.

Anselm of Canterbury developed this theme in his theory of the meaning of the death of Christ. He set out to show that earlier theories of why Christ needed to die on the cross, such as the patristic view that Christ's death was a kind of ransom paid to the devil, were unsatisfactory. For Anselm every created being lives in debt to God, a debt which is paid by a righteous and holy life. The sting of sin is that it robs God of the honour due to him. This creates a moral deficit which human beings are unable to pay. The death of Christ on the cross is the solution to this moral deficit. Christ's death satisfies God's honour, it pays the debt that all owe to God. The implication of this is that God lacks something; he has been robbed of his honour and requires that human beings restore this to him. But once it became part of the Church's teaching that God needs repaying by human beings the possibility then arose that this real debt could perhaps be commuted or provided by someone other than the person who had committed the original offence. 'Merit' became transferable from one person to another, or from a saint to a sinner. Penance became part of a deal between the sinners on earth or in purgatory, who were hopelessly in debt to God, and the saints in heaven who had merit in abundance. Transfers of merit were mediated and overseen by the Church.

What made the deadly sins part of the landscape of the medieval mind was the Fourth Lateran Council of 1215, presided over by the reforming Pope Innocent III. The Council made the practice of confession to a priest mandatory for all: 'Everyone who has attained the age of reason is bound to confess his sins at least once a year to their own priest, and to receive the Eucharist at least at Easter' (Summary: Canon 21). There was provision for confessing to a priest other than one's own parish priest as long as the parish priest gave permission. The important point was, though, that the parish priest knew who had confessed and could check up on any who failed to do so. In this way he became the guardian of the conscience of each individual soul in the parish.

It is also important that the decrees of the Council linked the confession of sins more formally than it had been previously to the requirement to receive the Eucharist. The seriousness of doing this was reinforced by the fact that this Council was the first to state in unambiguous terms that the bread and wine was changed (transubstantiated) into the body and blood of Christ and received as such by the faithful. Spurning the blood of Christ by an inadequate confession or a failure to perform a perfect penance became a real and dreadful possibility. Yet the aim of the Council was not so much to oppress people's souls so much as to bring them into an ordered relationship with a God of supreme mercy and justice. The Council instructed priests to treat penitents 'after the manner of a skilled physician, carefully inquiring into the circumstances of the sinner and the sin, from the nature of which he may understand what kind of advice to give and what remedy to apply, making use of different experiments to heal the sick one'. It is interesting that the canon uses the language of medicine to refer to the process of confession and penance, even echoing the parable of the Good Samaritan to describe the ministrations of the priest to the individual penitent: 'Let the priest be discreet and cautious that he may pour wine and oil into the wounds of the one injured.' Yet, though healing may have been the intention, the confessional is also referred to as 'the tribunal of penance', suggesting that forensic language had established itself as the more determinative element in the Church's understanding of sin. Mercy was always present, but justice came first.

The rule of annual confession could only be implemented with any degree of integrity if it was accompanied by a teaching programme for the clergy and laity to ensure that the most serious sins were recognized and not committed out of ignorance. So during the next century we begin to find teaching about the Seven Deadly Sins in medieval catechisms designed for everyday parish use. No longer for monks only, the deadly sins provided a checklist for everyone, as well as a warning of the danger of persistent sin.

After Evagrius: Aquinas

Meanwhile, in his compendium of theology, the *Summa Theologiae*, the Dominican Thomas Aquinas (1225–74) considered the nature of the seven capital vices. Like Gregory, he saw pride as standing alone as the fundamental cause and root of sin, and the source of all the others. He also surveyed the whole tradition of the fathers, considering insights from East and West and subjecting both to a rigorous logical analysis. While accepting the legacy of Augustine and Gregory, Aquinas brought to the issue a measure of detachment and rationality which has been of huge benefit to the Western moral tradition.

Aquinas also articulated what had become the Church's belief about sin in terms of guilt and punishment, developing the thought of Anselm in such a way as to strengthen the forensic view of sin in the Western Church. For Aquinas, the problem of sin was not so much that it robbed God of honour, but that it infringes God's justice. Where Anselm believed that human beings could never pay the debt they owed, Aquinas taught that we *can* contribute something by accepting some part of the punishment owing to our sins. For Aquinas sin had two components: the act itself and the moral guilt that leaves a mark on the sinner. There are four stages in the remission of sins. The first is *compunction*, a genuine awareness of having sinned and a sense of appropriate guilt. The second is *confession*, owning and taking responsibility for one's sins. The third is *contrition*, a heartfelt recognition of the effect of one's sins on oneself, others and God, a willingness to accept punishment as a just outcome, and a determination to avoid future occasions of sin. And lastly, *satisfaction*, some action designed to restore to God or others what sin has taken from them. This involves accepting whatever loss or punishment may be involved in restoring the moral balance, and making appropriate compensation to the injured party. These four terms found a permanent place within the moral and spiritual vocabulary of the Catholic Church.

The educational programme which followed the Fourth Lateran Council ensured that a great deal of power was put into the hands of the clergy. In effect, the clergy were those responsible for making judgements about the nature and seriousness of individual sins. At the heart of this system was the formal distinction between lesser sins and deadly sins. Lesser (or 'venial') sins could be forgiven without a formal priestly confession, though confession of them was generally considered to be prudent. Deadly sins, on the other hand, would lead direct to hell if they were not confessed, repented of and absolved in the sacrament of confession.

After Evagrius: deadly sins as education in virtue

In this way, the deadly sins became part of the landscape of the medieval imagination. They formed the conscience of clergy and laity. They depicted the terrible consequences of unrepented sin and how, in a universe founded on retributive justice, these consequences were inescapable even beyond this life. They also promoted as their antidote the seven opposing virtues: faith, hope, charity, justice, prudence, temperance and fortitude. The first three of these are derived from Paul's teaching in 1 Corinthians 13, and are hence known as the 'theological virtues'; the others have roots in classical culture and are named the 'cardinal virtues'. Alongside this were two other medieval lists of seven, designed to encourage moral and spiritual growth in virtue. The seven corporal works of mercy are acts of compassion which alleviate the suffering of others: feeding the hungry, giving drink to the thirsty, clothing the naked, giving shelter to the homeless, visiting the sick, ransoming captives and burying the dead. The spiritual works of mercy are particularly enjoined on clergy and religious. They are to instruct the ignorant, to counsel the doubtful, to admonish sinners, to bear wrongs patiently, to forgive offences willingly, to comfort the afflicted and to pray for the living and the dead. The contrast of virtues and vices gave plenty of opportunity for illustration and vivid and imaginative teaching. It also enabled something of the older, therapeutic understanding of the roots of sin to flourish in a new climate. Particular sinful tendencies could be healed by concentrating on their opposing virtues; those tempted to gluttony could concentrate on temperance while consciously making efforts to ensure that the hungry were fed. We can assume that the therapeutic approach was never lost to sensitive spiritual guides who were naturally able to empathize and encourage those who came to unburden themselves to them. Even in the terms laid down by the Fourth Lateran Council, confessors were instructed to treat sin diagnostically, to be 'skilled physicians'. The therapeutic understanding would find an English and female voice in the writing of Julian of Norwich (*c.* 1342–1416), who questioned the Church's teaching on hell and insisted that God looked on his human creatures 'with pity and not with blame'. The theology that arises out of her visions, the *Shewings of Divine Love*, moves away from the notion that the universe is founded on retributive justice. For her, Love is supreme and will prevail. She accepts the Church's teaching on hell, but distances herself from it.

After Evagrius: *The Divine Comedy*

Within a more conventionally orthodox theology it was still possible to express an understanding of sin in terms of motivation and attitude, albeit within a forensic framework which assumed a hierarchy of punishments for different kinds of sin. Dante's threefold work of imagination, *The Divine*

Comedy, shows how hell, purgatory and heaven are linked by the will and purpose of God. God's desire is for human beings to reach the Paradise for which they are created. In spite of the theme of the afterlife, retributive justice does not play a central part in this great work; not for nothing is it called a Comedy. Dante gives us two contrasting pictures of sin in the Inferno and Purgatorio. In the Inferno the poet is taken on a tour of hell by the Roman poet Virgil. Hell is a gigantic funnel which descends in nine layers, becoming narrower as it approaches the centre of the earth. Here, the consequences of sin are played out in eternity. Punishments are graded in order of the seriousness of the offence, with the worst offences being punished in the lower and narrower regions. Dante's image of hell is derived only in part from the deadly sins, but more from classical sources, which include Aristotle's analysis of the vices. Hell consists of nine concentric circles which grow narrower towards the base of hell, which is located at the centre of the earth. The first circle of hell is reserved for the unbaptized and for virtuous pagans. Sin proper begins one level down. The first three circles are allocated to those whose sins arise from incontinence: the lustful, the gluttons and the avaricious. In each circle it is clear how persistence in sin brings its own eternal punishment. The lustful are blown about in perpetual storm, the final outcome of their physical and emotional incontinence. The gluttons lie as though in oozing garbage composed of black slush and hail. The avaricious and profligate push great weights against each other in a perpetual competition.

The next series of layers depict the consequences of more violent sins. The permanently angry struggle with each other on the surface of the River Styx, while the slothful lie perpetually drowning as they gurgle beneath the water. Heretics are trapped for ever in flaming tombs. In the seventh circle, the violent are inundated in burning blood, equivalent to the amount that they have spilt. Next come the suicides, and those who recklessly misused their property or possessions and so destroyed themselves. Further into this circle lie those whose violence was intellectual or ideological in character; those who attacked God, nature and art.

In the last two circles of hell are the corrupt and deceitful, with traitors condemned to the last and lowest circle, an icy domain beyond any possibility of relationship. Terrible as Dante's hell is, the well-known figures from the past who end up there have not been *sent* there. There is no judgement scene with God consigning people to eternal punishment. As Dante sees it, persistent sin creates its own hells. Character is formed through the exercise of the will, and those who are condemned to hell are simply living out the consequences of accumulated evil choices. On the other hand, Dante echoes Gregory the Great by affirming that hell was created because of the justice of God. Indeed, on the gate of hell are inscribed the words,

> Justice moved my great maker; God eternal
> Wrought me: the power and the unsearchably
> High wisdom, and the primal love supernal.[36]

30

In hell there is no hope and no possibility of redemption. Yet, and this is important, Dante's hell is a vision, not a theological treatise. No living person is condemned to hell because the possibility of repentance is always open in this life, though Dante allows for some cases in which the will becomes so hardened that repentance becomes impossible.

If hell is proof of God's justice; purgatory is proof of God's love and redemptive purpose. Purgatory is a mountain; the way to redemption is an ascent. The mountain consists of a series of terraces. The gate to purgatory proper is positioned above two preliminary terraces, where those who have repented at the last minute and those who have died excommunicate prepare for the remedial treatment that will enable them to be saved. The way through Peter's gate involves the discipline of the Church as laid down at the Fourth Lateran Council and as expounded by Aquinas. Compunction, confession, contrition and satisfaction prepare the errant soul to rise through the appropriate stages of 'treatment' in which sin is progressively purged. The mountain above this point is modelled very closely on the seven deadly sins. The way up and into Paradise is obviously slower and longer for those whose sins are more grievous. Purgatory is not a prison; the point is not just to 'do time' for sins committed but to undo the damage that sin has caused. Accepting the justice of punishment for sin is part of the remedy.

At this point it is fascinating to see how Dante's vision recalls the wisdom of the desert. The reformation of character which Dante sees as possible after death was exactly what the desert fathers and mothers were attempting in this life. They *chose* near starvation to heal the wounds of the flesh, they *chose* extreme poverty to cure themselves of avarice, extreme humility to purge the sins of vainglory and pride. Dante, like the desert fathers, was interested not so much in the guilt of sin, but in its roots, in the vulnerabilities of the heart, which, if indulged, harden the heart and stain the soul. The therapies that Dante imagined in purgatory consist either of suffering the effects of the sin, or of practising an opposing virtue, or of a combination of both. He, like Evagrius, understood how the demonic realm represents fragmentation and works to divide us from ourselves and from one another. But the love of God is the binding principle of the universe. Love is just, but it remains love, a love which calls all things together in a symphony of praise. At each level of Dante's purgatory a bell rings as each soul is liberated to the next level, and each soul is given a prayer to sing in thankfulness for the divine mercy.

The deadly sins in the art of the English medieval Church

The medieval Church intended to protect the faithful from sin and its consequences: education was the key; individuals must understand the vices and the virtues and be aware of the seeds of vice in themselves. There are many examples in which the sins are portrayed as illustration in manuscripts, sometimes alongside the contrasting virtues. They also appear in the form of wall paintings in English churches. For example, in the Church of St Ethelbert in the village of Hessett in Suffolk the sins are shown in a fourteenth-century wall painting emerging from the branches of a deep red-coloured tree. The roots of the tree are in hell and each branch buds with a monstrous mouth from which a personification of one of the sins is vomited out. The sins in these wall paintings are shown in a hierarchical order, but the exact order varies from place to place. At Hessett, the trunk of the tree grows straight out of the mouth of hell and produces at the top a handsome male figure with a long, jaunty feather in his hat. This is pride. Just below are an embracing couple representing lust, and on the other side a well-dressed figure wielding what looks like a sword, or a whip. He also appears to be holding a dagger with which he is stabbing himself – violent anger is self-destructive. Below lust is sloth, leaning backwards as though with exhaustion and almost falling off his branch. Avarice is below sloth holding a bag of money. Gluttony is on the opposite branch to avarice, with envy above and anger at the top, opposite lust.

There is a rather different arrangement at St Peter's Church in Raunds, Northamptonshire. Here pride is shown as a crowned and glamorously dressed woman, the 'Queen' of sin. She is being pierced with a great lance by a demonic figure, and the puncture is forcing eruptions from her body in the form of monsters, which vomit out the other deadly sins. This, like the painting at Hessett, is on the north wall, so it made a great impact when people entered church from the south side. It is probable that the virtues were painted on the opposite wall at Raunds.

Visual representations of the sins are often accompanied by related themes. At South Leigh in Oxfordshire, where a deadly sin mural is now reduced to almost abstract form, there is a very well-preserved painting of doomsday above the chancel arch. Other themes include St Michael weighing souls at the judgement and the good deeds which can undo the poison of the deadly sins, the seven corporal works of mercy. In this way the whole church became a visual warning of the seriousness of sin, its deadly consequences and the available remedies. To go into one of these medieval churches was to be mirrored and exposed, both as a guilty sinner and as a potential saint. It was brilliant and exuberant, guilt-inducing and liberating.

By the end of the Middle Ages the seven deadly sins were successfully embedded into the didactic and moral programme of the Church. Priests were advised to use the opportunity of confession to teach about the deadly sins and to encourage the practice of the virtues. There was no doubt where spiritual power lay. It was the clergy and not the laity who made spiritual judgements, and that these were based on instruction which could be handed down in words and texts rather than communicated person to person. Preparation for confession and communion was based on a response to set questions which are usually accusatory in tone. Have you sinned in this particular way? How? Against whom? And how often? If an answer was positive the response was a prescribed penance. The whole system was extraordinarily sophisticated and rigorous and yet it could be easily under-stood by the simple and uneducated. Meeting the sins, the saints, doomsday and heaven every time you entered a parish church meant that you were always part of a community of saints and sinners in your progress towards salvation.

St Ethelbert, Hessett, houses not only one of the best preserved of medieval murals on this theme, it also has the Reformers' contribution to our understanding of sin: the Ten Commandments inscribed with simple formality and dignity on the east wall. The commandments functioned in the Reformation age as the deadly sins had done previously. They provided a standard by which people measured their closeness or distance from God. The Reformers dropped the distinction between deadly and venial sins. They also dropped the whole apparatus of priestly confession, penance and absolution (though private confession and priestly absolution was permitted in times of sickness or grievous doubt). But in other ways the forensic approach to sin survived intact, and was, perhaps, even strengthened by the teaching of those Reformers who particularly stressed the total depravity of human beings. In Calvin's teaching, the death of Jesus on the cross satisfied God's wrath by paying the moral penalty incurred by the specific sins of each individual. In this branch of Reformation thought Christ's death does not win merit that could be transferred to the penitent, so much as pay the required penalty for particular sinful acts. By being the just punishment for actual sins, Christ enabled the Father to show mercy. But his sacrificial death was therefore of limited effectiveness – only those predestined to be saved had the price of their sins paid for them.

Moral appraisal was still at the heart of Christian life, though this was now internalized. The commandments encouraged the churchgoer to exercise rigorous *self*-examination. Have you failed to honour your father and mother? How, how often, how about others in authority over you? The conscience of the individual became both counsel for the prosecution and judge, since it was no longer to an external authority that people looked for direction as to whether or not they have infringed the divine law. Only the Bible stood higher than the reasoning conscience. The struggle against temptation was driven inwards. Where the Calvinist theology of election was preached the real question for the individual worshipper was 'Am I saved?' The most rigorous attempt to practise virtue was no guarantee that there was a positive answer to that question, since the Reformation Church drove a wedge between faith and works. Satisfaction could not be achieved by any individual sinner; all was the work of Christ on the cross and must be received by faith alone. Human merit availed nothing at the divine tribunal. In a sense this marked the end of asceticism as the choice of a distinctively radical response to the call of Christ. Withdrawal from the world, celibacy and extreme poverty were no longer seen as necessarily virtuous choices. Yet all Christians were encouraged to live their faith deeply and for the glory of God. Daily work and family life were the setting for a new kind of Christian ascetic effort in which good works and moral purity were seen as *proof* of the salvation given through Christ's death; though good works could never contribute anything to the attainment of salvation.

The Calvinist soul could only hope that by constant self-appraisal, repentance and confession to the Lord, the reality of election might be manifest in a deepening, personal assurance of salvation. As for the rest of humanity, there was a sense in which, at least in the strictest Calvinism, it was only divine justice that it should go to hell. Strictest Calvinism of this kind is much less common in the contemporary Church of the West than it once was. But it still has a powerful impact on the Christian imagination. Particularly important is the belief that on the cross Christ paid the penalty for our sins to God the Father. God's righteousness is satisfied by the shedding of Christ's blood. This is in some ways an extraordinary doctrine, and one which many Christians find emotionally and morally repellent. Yet, for others it goes right to the heart of the human problem of sin. The legal language reinforces the seriousness of the issue; the satisfaction afforded by Christ's death gives immense intellectual, moral and emotional satisfaction to those who find this approach compelling. If the universe is indeed, as Gregory the Great appears to have believed, a gigantic machine built on the principle of retributive justice, then the death of Christ is indeed the only possible answer. Nothing less will do to save us. Although I would not want to give the theological weight to the doctrine of penal substitution that it has in some Christian circles I can't help but be struck by its forcefulness. It speaks to the desperate in a language which is deeply shocking and hence has transformative power. It confirms our worst fears that we are simply unacceptable to others, ourselves and to God. Yet the cruelty God imposes on his Son paradoxically speaks of the depths of his love. The sickness of humanity requires the most radical surgery imaginable and this is what God undertakes to bring us back to himself.

And yet, even for those who are compelled by this understanding of the cross, the human problem of sin is not finally solved. People go on sinning; not living up to their expectations, falling short of the Christian ideal. Salvation may be once for all, but we have to go on living with ourselves and with others in the present and the future. The question of how to live virtuously is a real one for all of us.

Can a rediscovery of the thought of Evagrius of Pontus help us with this? Can he give us guidelines for a deepening process of moral and spiritual integration? This is the point at which to explore who Evagrius was and what he stood for, and to engage with the enduring problems that surround his name. His legacy was lost because he came to be regarded as a heretic. The historical reasons for this need to be understood and his reputation reassessed if his insights are to prove useful for our time. So to Evagrius himself.

3

Evagrius lost and found

'If you are a theologian, you will pray truly; and if you pray truly you will be a theologian.'[1]

The life of Evagrius

Evagrius was born in Ibora, Pontus, in the region of Cappadocia in about the year 345. The principal source for his life is a short sketch by Palladius (*c.* 364–430), who was a disciple of Evagrius in the closing decades of the fourth century. This sketch is one of a series of short 'lives' of the 'friends of God', holy men and women whom Palladius had met or heard of in his time in the Egyptian desert. He wrote this history some twenty years later, dedicating the work to Lausus, the chamberlain of the emperor Theodosius II. The *Lausiac History*, as it was called, proved to be a very popular work and was widely translated into Latin, Syriac and Coptic. It exists in many different versions. Two other historians, Socrates (*c.* 380–450) and Sozomen (early fifth century), add important information about Evagrius' life, though they probably both used Palladius' work as a source. Some sayings of Evagrius are preserved in the various collections of the Sayings of the Fathers – compilations of nuggets of wisdom which were circulated in the early Christian world and have come down to us through the medieval Church.

Evagrius was the son of an itinerant local bishop. Palladius tells us that he was well educated and in his early adulthood was introduced to some of the greatest theologians of his day in the Christian East. His first significant mentor was Basil, the Bishop of Caesarea (*c.* 330–379), who had retired to found a monastic community in nearby Annisa. Basil made him a *lector*, a reader in the Church, and may have introduced him to religious life. It is likely that it was through Basil that Evagrius was introduced to his second mentor, Gregory of Nazianzus (*c.* 329–389), who ordained him a deacon. It was through Gregory that Evagrius became acquainted with the writings of the third-century theologian and Bible scholar, Origen of Alexandria.[2] As Evagrius is regarded as a proponent of Origen's teachings it is worth saying something about him at this stage.

Origen (*c.* 185–254) was born into a Christian family. His father died as a martyr in the reign of the emperor Severus. Origen became head of a famous academy of Christian instruction in Alexandria before moving to Palestine where he established an academy in Caesarea. Origen loved scholarship and advocated learning in the widest sense. He believed that God was always reaching out to his creation not only through the Bible but also through the best insights of classical Greek philosophy. He was not uncritical of such philosophy and always subjected it to what he took to be the teaching of the Bible. For him, the Bible was divine revelation which unfolded on various levels; the literal meaning was the outer husk for the spiritual meanings which lay within and pointed to the mystery of Christ. One of his best known works was in the form of a dialogue with the pagan philosopher Celsus. In it Origen explored both the ideas he held in common with the Platonist Celsus and the point at which Christianity moved beyond the insights of Platonism.

Origen was a hugely influential figure in early Christianity. It was largely because of his endeavours to present Christianity as a credible and life-changing philosophy that it began to be taken seriously by the cultured and educated of the Roman world. With men of his calibre arguing the case for Christianity it became impossible to dismiss it as no more than a superstitious cult for the poorly educated and oppressed. Evagrius absorbed Origen's approach to the Bible; many of his later comments on biblical texts would assume their truest meaning was allegorical. He also shared some of his more speculative beliefs, for example in the pre-existence of souls and the final restoration of all things. Like Origen, he was ultimately optimistic about the triumph of God's purpose for the human race.

In around 379 Evagrius moved to the imperial city of Constantinople. He says in a letter[3] that he was motivated by 'a certain longing for godly teachings, and for the philosophy pertaining to them'. He has found 'a vessel of election', 'the mouthpiece of Christ', and this is none other than his former teacher Gregory of Nazianzus who had become the Bishop of Constantinople, a post which carried formidable responsibilities and considerable difficulties. The orthodox faith, as defined at the Council of Nicaea in 325, was under siege, both from followers of the thought of the heretic Arius and from extremists whose theology challenged orthodoxy from other perspectives. If Evagrius' motive in coming to Constantinople was to learn at the feet of Gregory, Gregory was glad to have the support of an energetic young man with a keen mind and a love of good argument. Evagrius proved useful in the run-up to the Council of Constantinople in 381, and 'he was in all probability involved in the drafting and editing of the great orations which earned for Gregory the sobriquet "the Theologian"'.[4] He certainly proved himself to be a useful assistant. When the Council was over, Gregory was forced to leave the city by his opponents. He was succeeded as Archbishop by Nectarius who appointed Evagrius to be his archdeacon. Evagrius flourished in the cosmopolitan hubbub of the imperial city where he built on his reputation for challenging and refuting various heresies. But his time in Constantinople came to an abrupt end as a result of an unfortunate love affair and he left the city for Palestine.

In 382 he arrived in Jerusalem and was welcomed by a remarkable holy woman, Melania, who, with her friend Rufinus of Aquileia, had set up a double monastery for men and women on the Mount of Olives. Both Melania and Rufinus had scholarly interests. They were both fascinated by the teaching of Origen and saw the committed religious life as a reflection of his spiritual theology. Melania persuaded Evagrius, who by this time was having some kind of nervous breakdown, to commit himself to monastic life. Accordingly he received the monastic habit from her at Easter in 383 and departed for Nitria to the west of the Nile Delta in Lower Egypt. Here he enrolled in one of a large number of monastic foundations which had formed around various renowned spiritual teachers. Members of these small communities probably lived, prayed and worked separately during the week, gathering at weekends to share the Eucharist and for a time of teaching and discussion. For over a year Evagrius learnt the rhythms and disciplines of monastic life. Then, as others had done before him, he went deeper into the desert, into a more remote region known as Kellia, where he became the disciple of Macarius the Great. Here he was more isolated, the monastic dwellings were further apart and the monks were too remote from one another to meet except at weekends. Most would have several miles to walk to come together in the church at Kellia. Here Evagrius remained until his death in 399. He practised an austere lifestyle, making enough money to provide for his needs from copying manuscripts. He kept in touch with Melania and other friends through letters. He studied scripture and wrote notes on scriptural passages, he taught and gave spiritual guidance. In time he became a renowned spiritual director in his own right and attracted interest from pilgrims, as well as having his own followers. One of these was John Cassian who would later produce the version of his teaching which would inspire the Deadly Sin tradition in the West. Evagrius wrote substantial works on religious life, of which the best known, and the one which is central to this book, is the *Praktikos*. This is concerned with *praktike*, the practice of disciplines to purify the soul from harmful passions. For Evagrius, *praktike* was the first and vital stage of religious life. When the monk had made some progress at *praktike* he was ready to embark on *gnostike*, the overcoming of ignorance by contemplation.

Over the years, the clever young cleric turned monk acquired a reputation for gentle holiness, discretion and practical wisdom. He was never simply an intellectuals' monk. His shrewd insights and humane judgements commended him to those who needed practical advice particularly about dealing with demonic temptations. His teaching on the evil thoughts is at the heart of this advice. But he also came up with a practical weapon to help in the fight with temptation. This was a formidable collection of scripture sayings called *Antirrhetikos*, which could be translated as 'Refutations', or perhaps more colloquially, 'How to Answer Back'. Here Evagrius suggested a range of biblical texts which could be quoted to quell each one of 487 dangerous or obsessive thoughts, which the devils might inspire in struggling monks. Evagrius' skill at combating heresies was here deployed against the demonic powers. The texts were organized into eight categories representing the eight areas of temptation. As he himself put it, it was by 'starving and battling with foul thoughts' that Evagrius came to a new and vivid understanding of the ways of the human heart.

Evagrius' regime of asceticism took its toll. He not only lived on a very restricted diet, he also believed in limiting his intake of water. Later in life he suffered from poor digestion and had to alter his diet. He died at 55, a young age even for his own time, shortly after receiving communion on the Feast of the Epiphany, probably in 399.

The reputation of Evagrius

Until very recently Evagrius has not been well known. It has been difficult to read what he wrote, not only because there have been few translations of his works but because much of the original has been lost, destroyed or attributed to other writers. It is one of the successes of modern scholarship that his literary legacy is now being recovered. There is now a reasonable consensus about what can genuinely be ascribed to him. There are English translations available of his major Greek works; those that survive only in Syriac are quoted by contemporary scholars, but have not yet been disseminated more widely. It is likely that we shall soon be able to see his work as a whole and come to a much more accurate judgement about his standing as a theologian of the spiritual life than has so far been possible.

One thing to note at the outset is that Evagrius never regarded himself as anything other than an orthodox Christian. He had spent his youth refuting heresy and he continued to engage in argument on behalf of the orthodox cause. The aspect of his theology which is perhaps most difficult for us to assimilate is its sheer integrity. For Evagrius there was no distinction between thinking theologically about God and the life of prayer: 'If you are a theologian, you will pray truly; and if you pray truly, you will be a theologian.'[5]

For Evagrius the goal of theology is contemplation, where the mind and heart are brought to rest in the vision of God. For us in the West this is a difficult goal to aim at because our whole intellectual tradition has taught us to keep our critical sense separate from what we might call our appreciative sense. Spiritual experience and theological rigour exercise different parts of us. This does not mean that the two are disconnected. The part of us which might revel in the study of Christian doctrine might well find that such study moves us to prayer. It is perhaps less likely that an insight received in prayer might move us to further study. We certainly struggle to think of thinking and praying as the same thing. Yet for Evagrius thinking and praying were part of one another; prayer was an activity of the *nous*, the mind, and the mind, when purified, 'is an intelligible height resembling the colour of heaven, to which the light of the Holy Trinity comes in the time or prayer'.[6]

The persistent criticism of Evagrius, which seems to have begun in his own lifetime, is that he was over-intellectual, a 'hewer of words' as he was described by one contemporary.[7] More seriously he was, and still is, regularly accused not only of having absorbed the metaphysical speculations of Origen but of making them central to his spiritual purpose, transforming them into a rigidly dogmatic theological system far removed from scripture and closer to pantheism than Christian orthodoxy. Hans Urs von Balthasar claims that Evagrius, as Origen's disciple, even lacks the virtues of his master, having 'sacrificed Origen's versatile thought to an iron-clad system to which he holds fast, come what may to its final consequences'.[8]

The twentieth-century Benedictine scholar John Leclerq also claims that 'we have in Evagrius a sort of extreme "Origenism", which is not without its dangers, for according to this viewpoint a man can unite himself directly to the Trinity without the mediation of the Incarnate Word'.[9] Owen Chadwick, in an introduction to selections of John Cassian's writings, suggests that 'the God to which he [Evagrius] aspired was rather like Plato's One or Essence'.[10] Von Balthasar seems to have regarded him as more Buddhist than Christian.[11] The implication of these criticisms is that there is something vaguely sub-Christian about Evagrius' theology, and that at the very least it is dangerous enough to lead the unwary astray. A recent specialist on Evagrius' work summarizes the problem by saying that 'Evagrius's mystical theology has been variously characterised as apophatic, iconoclastic, and even as questionably Christian'.[12]

The one irrefutable fact is that from 553 onwards Evagrius was condemned as a heretic and regarded as such by both Greek and Latin Churches, though he continued to be revered in other parts of the Christian orient. His condemnation was linked to that of Origen himself and another learned Bible scholar and theologian of the fourth century, Didymus the Blind (c. 313–398). What led to this condemnation needs to be unravelled, as does the way modern scholars have used it to interpret Evagrius' teaching. It is certainly true that there are passages in Evagrius' writings which have been judged as falling short of Christian orthodoxy. However, very recent scholarship, reflected in a book by Augustine Casiday,[13] suggests that the interpretation of these passages is not as clear cut as has been thought, and has possibly been prejudiced in a negative direction by the condemnation passed on him by the sixth-century Church. Circular logic is in operation: *because* Evagrius was condemned, heretical doctrines are expected in his work, and unsurprisingly are found there.

It has not helped that Evagrius has an occasional maddening habit of appearing to withhold what he really thinks on an issue, as though, as one scholar suggests, he 'has something to hide'.[14] This is quite possible – theological controversy over the legacy of Origen may well have been boiling up during Evagrius' later years in Kellia. It was in this period that he wrote an important letter (the *Great Letter*, as it is called) summarizing his beliefs about the relationship between God and creation. In this letter Evagrius states his unwillingness to express himself fully for fear of who might later read the letter.[15] Some scholars have seized on this as evidence that Evagrius was trying to conceal the eschatological speculations which later led to his condemnation. But the passage does not require such an interpretation. A more obvious way of reading it would suggest that he is simply anxious to maintain a distinction between foundational and more advanced teaching. It was fairly common in early Christian writing to make such a distinction, and, indeed, has biblical precedent.[16] Evagrius himself follows this practice in a passage in the *Praktikos*, complete with scriptural justification: 'We shall veil some things, and obscure others, lest "We give holy things to dogs" and "cast pearls before swine" ' (Matthew 7.6).[17] It is perhaps because the majority of scholars have simply *assumed* that Evagrius is guilty of the charges made against him in 553 that they tend to see a sinister purpose behind his reluctance to express himself fully in the *Great Letter*. So what was this more advanced teaching? Was it secret teachings about the soul's ultimate destiny to be 'equal to Christ', or some other weird doctrine ascribed to Origen?

Casiday thinks such questions are misplaced. Central to his argument is the fact that Evagrius has no qualms in the *Great Letter* of speaking of human minds returning to God, as 'the mingling of rivers with the sea',[18] a passage which could certainly bear a pantheistic interpretation, though it need not necessarily do so. If he was really trying to conceal his suspect tendencies why would he have written in these terms? Casiday has another suggestion. It is possible that Evagrius did not want to distract individuals inclined to pursue the ascetic life by burdening them with more theoretical material than they needed. He cites Basil of Caesarea and Origen himself who made similar provision for different levels of interest in their teachings about liturgical practices. The point is that all take part in the same practices, but not all need to have a sophisticated grasp of their meaning. It is participation which counts; some will be helped by advanced study, others will be distracted by it. The pursuit of deeper levels of interpretation is open to all who desire it but it is not to be forced on people. Casiday's suggestion is given weight by the fact that an important theme of the *Great Letter* is the way in which the whole cosmos can itself be 'read' as a letter from God, a letter which reveals the meaning and purpose God has for his creation, and can be 'read' on different levels.

So Casiday thinks that modern scholars have been far too uncritical in their interpretation of Evagrius' condemnation, which they have used as a criterion for their own assessment of him, reading into his work (or supposed work) a judgement which was unfair to start with. In particular he questions a consensus which emerged following the publication in 1958 of a newly discovered version of Evagrius' *Gnostic Chapters* by the scholar Antoine Guillaumont.[19] Guillaumont claimed that this new version of the work contained the precise heretical teachings that led to Evagrius' condemnation in 553. (A version of the *Gnostic Chapters* discovered earlier which did not contain the dubious passages was published by Guillaumont alongside his own edition. He claimed that this was a later version from which the heretical passages had been removed in order to allow it to continue to circulate.) Guillaumont's claims were accepted wholesale by both Eastern and Western scholars as proof of Evagrius' heretical leanings. John Meyendorff, the Orthodox scholar, stated simply that 'the authentic text of his *Gnostic Chapters* with their quite heretical Christology explains his condemnation by the Council in 553'.[20] John Eudes Bamberger agrees, 'the version recently discovered is more faithful to the original text', and that the text discovered earlier had been 'purged of much of its objectionable Christology'.[21]

Casiday claims the consensus that Guillaumont's text satisfactorily explains Evagrius' condemnation depends on stringing together rather atypical comments that Evagrius makes in this work in a particular way, a way determined by the terms in which he was condemned. A more 'innocent' reading is possible – that these passages were not necessarily central to Evagrius' thought or to his purpose, and do not require an interpretation consistent with the terms in which he was condemned.

What was the heresy for which Evagrius was condemned and which Guillaumont claimed to find expressed in the original version of the *Gnostic Chapters*? The obvious place to look is in the decrees of the Second Council of Constantinople, better known as the Fifth Ecumenical Council, which has 15 anathemas directed against 'Origenist' teachings.[22] Among the beliefs to be condemned are:

- belief in the pre-existence of souls
- belief that material existence is somehow evil
- belief that the resurrection is not physical
- belief that Christ as a rational being is separate from the *logos* who is part of the Holy Trinity
- belief that at the final *eschaton* matter will disappear
- belief that all rational beings, including demons, will become *isochristoi*, 'equal to Christ'
- belief that everything will finally return to the simple divine unity that there was in the beginning.

Guillaumont's reconstruction of these teachings through the text he produced of the *Gnostic Chapters* comprises the cocktail of esoteric christological and eschatological thoughts which were indeed condemned here. But it is an open issue whether or not they are truly to be found in Evagrius' work. It is certainly true that Evagrius believed in something like the pre-existence of souls. But at the same time he did not think of the fall in straightforward historical terms, and so even this belief may be open to differing interpretations. He did not believe that matter was inherently evil, nor did he separate Christ from the Trinity. It is true that he assumed the final restoration would be non-material. It is also true that he believed that redemption was always possible. His writings show that he thought that even the punishments of hell have a potentially therapeutic purpose.[23] But that is not necessarily the same thing as believing that all evil can or will be redeemed.

So how do we look beyond the prejudices of history? It is impossible to do this without some deeper understanding of the controversy over the legacy of Origen and the way Evagrius' reputation was influenced by this. This controversy was rumbling away in the monasteries of Egypt towards the end of Evagrius' life. It finally broke out in violence, which brought to an end the golden age of Egyptian monasticism and set the Church on a path of argument about the nature of God and the practice of prayer which has never quite been resolved.

The Origenist controversy: episode one

According to the historical sources the main point at issue was Origen's view of God. Origen was convinced, as were many early Christian thinkers, that the true God must transcend all merely human images and concepts. Because of this he saw Christian prayer as a form of spiritual, emotional and intellectual purification in which the soul, progressively freed from its material and emotional encumbrances, found its true home in God. In this respect Origen, and his like-minded contemporaries, were in debt to the philosophical tradition of Plato. In a very general sense their view of God can be described as *apophatic*, which means 'without or beyond speech'. There were more controversial aspects of Origen's teaching which had never been universally accepted, like the pre-existence of souls and his beliefs about the end of the world. But underlying a suspicion of these was a conviction among his most persistent detractors that he was, at heart, a Platonist rather than a biblical Christian. Even before Evagrius moved from Constantinople to the Egyptian desert Epiphanius, the Bishop of Salamis (*c.* 315–403), had written a refutation of various heresies, in which he roundly and unfairly condemned Origen's teachings and complained about the influence of Origenists in the monasteries of Nitria. Epiphanius was a fanatic with an overwhelming drive to root out unsound doctrine. His cause against Origen received support from Jerome, the famous Bible scholar (*c.* 345–420) who translated the Bible into readable Latin. Jerome was a brilliant but argumentative character who had tried desert life and found it extremely difficult. He had originally been an admirer of Origen's, but under Epiphanius' influence was drawn into a campaign of denunciation. From 393 Jerome was an adamant and vituperative opponent of Origen's theology.

It is hardly surprising that the less-educated Egyptian monks of Nitria and Kellia were not particularly sympathetic to Origen's teachings. The sources suggest that there had always been tensions between these simple devout men, and the more worldly, cosmopolitan seekers after truth, like Evagrius, who joined their way of life. There was a much-loved saying among the monks, 'You have seen your brother, you have seen your God', which spoke of humility and service between the brothers and sisters of the desert, of serving Christ in one another. Yet it could also be taken in a more literal sense as the historian Socrates (*c.* 380–450) points out: 'Very many of the more simple ascetics asserted that God is corporeal, and has a human shape, but most others condemn their judgement and contended that God is incorporeal and free of all form whatever.'[24] The 'simple' ascetics, if we accept the distinction as made here by Socrates, certainly had a point. Had not God made himself known in Christ in human form? And did that not imply that in some sense the human form *was* the shape of the divine? Surely the fact that the Bible spoke of human beings being made in God's image must imply, conversely, that God really was a larger version of man. Against this, the followers of Origen insisted that God could not be limited by human categories. God by definition was beyond what could be thought or imagined.

Such a picture of an emerging dispute between simple pious monks and learned intellectuals has an obvious appeal. Socrates had some of the skills that we would recognize as belonging to lively journalism and he was building his story towards a dramatic denouement which I shall come to shortly. But the story as he tells it sets the scene for what later became a deliberate exaggeration of the divide between the monks. Casiday argues that there was no clear-cut division along ethnic (Greek versus Coptic) lines, and that the picture of 'simple monks' versus 'learned intellectuals' has been somewhat overdrawn: 'It does not do to imagine that the monasteries in the desert were inhabited by an uneasy mixture of Coptic bumpkins and Greek philosophers.'[25] No doubt there were some rough-mannered Copts who had no time for scholarship and some fastidious scholars, but the tensions might well have remained dormant had it not been for the skilful political machinations of the Bishop of Alexandria, Theophilus (d. 412). He brought different views on the legacy of Origen to the surface, thus producing a picture of a long-running dispute which historians would follow. The first thing he did, just a year after Evagrius' death, was to issue an Easter letter in which he condemned anthropomorphism, that is, the tendency to see God in human terms. This would seem to have justified the followers of Origen in the way they interpreted scripture. But, in the communities of the less educated monks, the Bishop's Easter letter provoked a crisis. John Cassian describes being present when a deacon called Photinus came from Cappadocia to visit a group of monks living in the desert of Skete under the instruction of 'the blessed Paphnutius'. The Bishop's letter had already been introduced to the brethren, but a revered older monk, Sarapion, had refused to accept it. Photinus explained that the entire Church was agreed that the image and likeness of God was not a literal but a spiritual likeness. Sarapion, finally convinced, accepted Photinus' arguments. Yet in the rejoicing that followed, Sarapion 'sensed that the human image of God which he used to draw before him as he prayed was now gone from his heart'. He broke into weeping, throwing himself to the ground, and sobbed, 'They have taken my God away from me. I have no one to hold on to, and I don't know whom to adore or to address.'[26] John Cassian would have agreed with the Bishop's letter and had no qualms about Photinus' argument, and yet to his youthful eyes it must have seemed a tragic assault on the holiness of a vulnerable old man. Perhaps this incident played a part in the way that in later years he felt he should subtly alter Evagrius' theology to make it more acceptable to those whose faith demanded more concrete and literal expression.

Theophilus' letter did not end the dispute. Socrates tells us[27] how a rabble of distressed and angry monks left their monasteries and went to confront him, threatening him with violence if he did not recant. Trying to placate them, Theophilus assured them that 'to see them was to see the face of God himself'. But this attempt at a diplomatic response, while it probably saved his life, only provoked the monks to insist that if their faces really *were* the face of God to him, then he must immediately condemn the writings of Origen and all who accepted them. This Theophilus did, making a complete episcopal U-turn. He began to engage in a campaign against Origen's thought, caricaturing his ideas and reinforcing the view that the monasteries were being torn apart by conflict between two groups, the austere intellectual Origenists and the pious, if sometimes rather credulous, Copts. Both sides clearly needed his correction.

In fact Theophilus was playing a thoroughly shady game. His change of views reflected his changing priorities. He now found it expedient to position himself against the followers of Origen. The reason for this was that he had become involved in a row with four Origenist monks, known as the Tall Brothers. He had earlier inveigled one of them, named Dioscorus, into becoming the bishop of the city of Hermopolis in Lower Egypt.[28] He had also persuaded the others to leave their monastery to work for him as city administrators. The Tall Brothers had gone along with this out of obedience, but had become rapidly disillusioned with Theophilus' leadership. Eventually they had left and attempted to return to their monastic life. Furious at being thwarted, Theophilus provoked the anthropomorphists to rise up against the Tall Brothers, not only in Alexandria but in the Nitrian desert where they had returned to live.

In the year 400, a year after Evagrius' death, Theophilus summoned a Council at Alexandria at which the teaching of Origen was condemned. The resolution of the Council was followed up by a campaign attempting to demonstrate that Origenism was the source of all heresies. The Tall Brothers were expelled from their monastery and over three hundred of the supporters of Origen fled their desert communities, some going to Palestine, others taking refuge in the imperial city of Constantinople. Among them were Evagrius' disciples, John Cassian and Palladius.

Theophilus' attack on Origen needs to be seen as part of a wider campaign to purify the Church. In the last two decades of the fourth century Catholic Christianity began to be promoted as the sole faith of the empire. Pagan sacrifice was forbidden in 391. In the same year Theophilus destroyed the temple of Serapis in Alexandria. In the year of Evagrius' death in 399, an imperial decree instructed that temples to the gods in the countryside should be destroyed. The assault on paganism perhaps exacerbated the tendency to attack Christian intellectuals who were thought to have compromised with paganism by accepting some of the tenets of Platonism.

Jerome's was by now the most influential voice in the attack on Origenism, though he also employed his passionate invective against a raft of other heresies. He mentions Evagrius disparagingly in a letter, describing him as a fraud, who 'has published a book of maxims on apathy, or, as we should say, impassivity or imperturbability; a state in which the mind ceases to be agitated and to put it plainly, becomes either a stone, or a god'.[29]

Jerome's concern here is with Evagrius' teaching on *apatheia*. From the evidence of his letter he seems to regard this as an attempt to suppress emotion; though this is not what the word means in Evagrius' writings. Evagrius speaks of joy and tears in prayer. He even uses a form of imaginative contemplation, inviting the monk to 'groan and weep' at the judgement of sinners and to 'rejoice and be glad and happy' at the good things awaiting the saved.[30] But the really significant point is that Jerome does not condemn Evagrius on the grounds of his being an Origenist. Jerome certainly could have seized the opportunity to do so, and in this passage he names him among others who have been attacked on the basis of their supposed support for Origenism. Luke Dysinger suggests that Jerome saw Evagrius more as a crypto-Pelagian than as an Origenist,[31] and this may well be right. Further evidence that Evagrius was not thought of as any kind of extreme advocate of Origen's thought at this stage is that his disciple Palladius, while describing a number of his biographical subjects as followers of Origen, does not describe Evagrius in this way.

John Cassian, having fled from the desert with other followers of Origen, found refuge in Constantinople, where he was made a deacon by the bishop, John Chrysostom. Chrysostom was not an advocate of Origen's thought, and it may well be that he influenced Cassian away from too uncritical a support for Origen's theories. But in about 403 John Chrysostom fell from favour (he upset the empress) and in the aftermath Cassian left Constantinople on his journey westwards. Meanwhile, Theophilus made up his quarrel with the Origenists and some of them returned to the desert. The first phase of the Origenist crisis was over. But the split had gone to the heart of desert life and the intensity and power of the witness of the monks would never be quite the same again. Meanwhile, to Jerome's regret, Evagrius' writings were being widely read, in the East in Greek, and in the West in Latin, thanks to the translation of some of his works by Jerome's former friend Rufinus. A second translation was made towards the end of the fifth century by the priest and historian Gennadius of Marseilles (c. 470). Various collections and anthologies of Evagrius' work also circulated from Palestine. He became further known in the West through Latin versions of Palladius' *Lausiac History* and the maxims attributed to him in the Sayings of the Fathers. His work was enthusiastically translated into Coptic and Syrian and inspired commentaries from Syrian spiritual teachers. By the end of the first Origenist controversy it seems that Evagrius' reputation as a spiritual teacher of distinction was fairly intact.

The Origenist controversy: episode two

The second phase of the Origenist controversy began in the sixth century. Casiday pinpoints the first skirmish in the new battle as resulting from a question raised in correspondence between an ascetic teacher Barsanuphius and his disciple John as to whether it was permissible to read the works of Origen, Didymus the Blind and Evagrius.[32] This is evidence that the three names were now being put together and all were being regarded with suspicion. Barsanuphius condemned all three writers, but John was more discriminating. He suggested that it *might* be permissible to read Evagrius with profit, but that considerable care was required.

By the third decade of the sixth century the imperial assault on the remnants of pagan thought and practice was continuing with vigour under the guidance of the emperor Justinian (c. 483–565). His intention was to create a Christian society purged of heresy and idolatry. The heresies associated with the name of Origen had not gone away. The correspondence between Barsanuphius and John was only the first stirring of a new wave of opposition to Origenism. According to Cyril of Scythopolis (b. 525) a monk called Kyriakos denounced a raft of dangerous teachings which, he said, Origen, Evagrius and Didymus the Blind had propagated. These teachings were not Christian at all, Kyriakos claimed, but were taken from Plato and Pythagoras. He cited belief in the pre-existence of souls, the belief that at the final restoration all rational beings will have equal powers with God, and the curious belief, ultimately derived from Plato, that bodies will be raised at the resurrection as perfect spheres. What lay behind these accusations appears to have been a revival of wild ideas circulating in the monasteries of Palestine. This was made worse by the arrival of a monk from Edessa, one Stephen bar Sudaili who had become notorious for promoting a form of mystical pantheism including the kinds of teaching condemned by Kyriakos. The disturbance in the monasteries resulted in a letter from no less than the emperor Justinian himself, condemning Origen by name. This was the prelude to the Council of 553 with its 15 anathemas.

The decrees of the Council were not accepted by the Origenists in Palestine and there were violent reprisals against them. The Origenist monks were forced out of their monasteries and replaced with those whose views were considered sound. This was really the end of the road for Origenism. Just to make sure, the condemnations were repeated at the Sixth (680–1) and Seventh (787) Ecumenical Councils and also at the Eighth Council of 869 (though this is not given the same degree of authority as the previous seven in the West). The result of all this was that, as Casiday puts it, 'for a period of some three and a half centuries, Evagrius's reputation was roundly trounced'.[33]

At the same time as this was going on there was a good deal of interest in the monastic 'golden age' of the previous century. Sixth-century chroniclers and editors, as Casiday puts it, 'were busy re-imagining a history of monasticism in which intellectual culture was irreconcilably at odds with God-given sanctity'.[34] So the context in which Evagrius was remembered was highly unsympathetic – he was on the wrong side of this fundamental divide.

Condemnation and disappearance

The condemnation of 553 was enough to bring about the loss of the major part of Evagrius' work. Many of the Latin translations of his work were destroyed; Greek versions were destroyed or suppressed. The erasure was not complete: Evagrius' name was preserved in the brief biography of the *Lausiac History* and some of his maxims were passed on in the Sayings of the Fathers. Rufinus' translations were still available to a select few and continued to have influence in Western monastic circles throughout the medieval period. Only in the Syrian Church was his memory revered and his writings preserved. Translations of the Syrian versions were made for the Armenian Church.

These writings are now being slowly reconstructed by scholars. The Syrian and Armenian translations are the basis for most of their work. These groups were less affected by the Origenist and Pelagian controversies and so had less reason to be suspicious of Evagrius – he is regarded as a saint in the Armenian Church. Although it is too early to assess whether or not Evagrius really did hold the views for which he was later condemned it is worth noting that if he did hold these views they must have been in stark contradiction, whether conscious or not, with views he had earlier vigorously upheld, both about the uniqueness of Christ – the Creed of Constantinople asserts that 'his kingdom shall have no end' – and about the nature of God as Trinity.

The condemnation of Evagrius by the Greek Church played out in what theologians of the spiritual life had to say about him. John Moschos (c. 550–619) expressed the belief that he had always been a heretic, insisting that even in his lifetime he had lived in a cell haunted by a demon.[35] John Climacus (c. 570–649) refers to Evagrius as 'outstandingly foolish' and suggests that he thought too much of himself.[36] He particularly criticized his teaching on keeping to a rigorously simple diet, though this teaching was commonplace among the desert ascetics. Yet in spite of the condemnation, the Byzantine Church did not entirely extirpate Evagrius' influence. Climacus has clearly absorbed much of his teaching on the evil thoughts which he reproduces and develops. Most significantly, Evagrius' teaching had a formative influence on the greatest of Orthodox teachers on prayer, Maximus the Confessor (580–682), who, at one point, was believed to be the author of the *Praktikos*. It is chiefly through Maximus that Evagrius' teaching on the passions continues to be central to Orthodox spiritual theology. Eventually the *Praktikos* found its way into the *Philokalia*, the eighteenth-century collection of spiritual writings which continue to be treasured in the Orthodox world. So the influence of Evagrius lingers on in Orthodoxy – he is like Lewis Carroll's Cheshire Cat; a characteristic expression remains in Orthodox theology which can be traced to Evagrius, even though the face has disappeared.

Modern Orthodox scholars have continued to treat Evagrius with a mixture of suspicion and a reluctant recognition of his essential contribution to mystical theology. The suspicion tends to overwhelm the acknowledgement; his name is rarely raised without a health warning. John Meyendorff simply repeats the old charges when he writes: 'He [Evagrius] considered Christ merely as a mind that had escaped materialisation. According to Evagrius "intellectual prayer" was the means of salvation that restored the mind to its original function. Neither the incarnation nor grace were necessary to that effect.'[37] Orthodox distrust of Evagrius has been much reinforced by Guillaumont's interpretation of the *Gnostic Chapters*, which Meyendorff cites earlier in his work.[38]

As scholars discover more of Evagrius' writings it is becoming clear that a much greater proportion of his work was devoted to scriptural commentary than had previously been apparent. Luke Dysinger has suggested that his *Scholia* on the Psalms may be his longest work. Evagrius' reflections on the psalms contain echoes of some of his potentially controversial teachings, but they are also profoundly christological. They certainly provide evidence against those who claim that Evagrius had no place for the incarnate Christ in his teaching on prayer. They also show us that, for all his emphasis on formless and imageless prayer, Evagrius did not spend his time in endless formless contemplation. We should rather remember that Evagrius was part of a monastic culture steeped in the recitation or chanting of the psalms. Dysinger rather intriguingly suggests that we should think of Evagrius the solitary praying the psalms as he had done in community. Psalms were useful both for quieting the passions and for the practice of *theoria physike*, natural contemplation. The language and imagery of the psalms brought the monk to a recognition and appreciation of the 'richly diverse wisdom of Christ who created and sustains the universe'.[39] At the end of the psalm there would be a prayer and, Dysinger suggests, it was in the pauses between the psalms or between the psalm and the prayer that there was an opportunity for the 'formless' prayer Evagrius commends. If this is right then it tells us that Evagrius expected Christian prayer to be rich in emotion and imagery even as it moved towards formlessness. There is an implied rhythm to prayer being outlined here. The psalms enable the one who prays them to encounter Christ in the diversity of the world, in its beauty and its challenges. Yet there are spaces between the psalms in which the differentiations of the universe are suspended in the monk's mind: 'The kingdom of heaven is *apatheia* of the soul along with true knowledge of existing things.'[40] *Apatheia*, for Evagrius, gives birth to love, and so perhaps we could interpret his understanding of prayer as an oscillating movement from expression to silence. The monk's prayer begins with an emotional and physical response to Christ's wisdom in creation and culminates in a moment when the monk holds creation in unpossessive love. That is the moment when the monk is grasped by an existential knowledge of the Holy Trinity.[41]

So there is a rhythm of prayer from images to formlessness, from activity to passivity. This would certainly seem to be implied by the following passage:

> Sometimes the mind moves from one mental representation to another, sometimes from one contemplative consideration to another, and in turn from a contemplative consideration to a mental representation. And there are also times when the mind moves from the imageless state to mental representations or contemplative considerations, and from these it returns again to the imageless state. This happens to the mind during the time of prayer.[42]

It is true that Evagrius regarded formless prayer as 'true prayer', the highest kind of prayer and the goal of the spiritual life. But he did not seem to regard this as a state which could be achieved permanently, nor that experiencing this kind of prayer undermined the value of other kinds of prayer.

Sympathetic readings of Evagrius such as those offered by scholars like Luke Dysinger and Augustine Casiday help us to see that Evagrius might indeed have been what he claimed to be, an orthodox Christian striving to live in response to God's will. They suggest that we should see him primarily as a spiritual practitioner and teacher rather than as a speculative theologian. Advanced theories of the spiritual life were an interest which he was well qualified to pursue, but it was not necessarily at the heart of his concern. Reading what we now have of Evagrius' works reveals him to be a poet and craftsman of prayer, with a discerning mind and an engaging sense of humour. He is a 'technician' of the spiritual life, and his writing reflects that.

He chooses to write in proverbs, maxims, 'chapters' as the ancient world called this style of expression. His short, intriguing sentences are memorable and invite reflection and repetition. They are 'spiritual exercises', intended to help attentiveness and provoke a gradual transformation of consciousness. If at times Evagrius invites us to take flight into metaphysics, it is because he wants to inspire awe at the miracle of creation and to encourage tenacity in pursuing the life of prayer. He knows we can be inspired beyond our limits and he encourages us to stretch ourselves intellectually as well as in terms of practice. This is not a cold intellectualism but a matter of training the heart to attain stability, to be re-formed on the basis of those moments of pure contemplation which take place when the passions are subdued. The practical and contemplative are always interwoven. What modern scholars have sometimes overlooked is that Evagrius was not merely a solitary, intellectualist monk who said some interesting things about the spiritual life. His theology was generated out of his practice and in community with others. He was a pastor, who had himself been pastored at times of great emotional need and spiritual distress. Melania and Rufinus stood by him at his worst moments. He retained his respect and affection for Gregory of Nazianzus. He honoured his two monastic mentors, Macarius the Great and Macarius of Egypt. His aim was to help himself and others to attain the vision of God by the development of virtue. Or, to return to his own teaching, 'If you are a theologian, you will pray truly; and if you pray truly, you will be a theologian.' So how did the practice of training the self in virtue and the theology of the spiritual life come together in his mind?

4

The spiritual teaching of Evagrius

I write of the reasoning nature that fights beneath heaven:
first what it battles against;
second; what assists it in the battle;
and finally, what the fighter keeping valiant watch must confront.
Those who fight are human beings;
those assisting them are the angels of God;
and those opposing them are the evil demons.[1]

Evagrius' spiritual theory

It is important to recover Evagrius' thinking from the negative judgement to which it was consigned in 533. He has things to say to our time, which have been partially retained in Orthodox Christianity, but almost entirely lost in the West. But to do this we need to have a grasp of his spiritual theory because his work on the evil thoughts arose out of his beliefs about the nature of the world and the fall. Evagrius believed, as Origen and many others did in the early Christian world, that human beings were created to inhabit a spiritual paradise in which they were freely able to enjoy the divine Trinity. This was their original state and it is what God intended and still intends for them. But now, as a result of free will human beings find themselves in a fallen world. Where he seems to have differed from Origen is that he does not see the fall of humanity and their present plight as necessarily being part of a historical sequence of events. The point is that it is in present experience that the unity that God created has fallen apart, we experience disharmony and inequality throughout creation. Material existence is a place of frustration for human beings. Yet the material world is not an evil place. In fact it is the creation of God's good providence, designed to keep human minds in existence by ensuring that they are attached to souls and rooted in a material body. The world, then, is a place not only of impermanence and vulnerability, but also of hope and redemption. Our bodies are like seeds sown for the resurrection life, and the whole world is 'a seed of the world that is to come after it'.[2] The material world may be infected by demons, but it is also visited by angels and, supremely, by Christ the incarnate Logos. The demons prey on human weakness, tempting human beings through their physical appetites, fears and desires. The task of humanity on earth is to restore the creation to the beauty it has in the mind of God, in other words to spiritualize matter, beginning with the body. By retraining the senses and the appetites and by opening up the latent capacities of the soul humans can recover their original integrity.

Controlling the appetites and desires, the *passions*, is the first stage of the spiritual life. It is characterized by active asceticism which is given the Platonic label *praktike*: practice. It is in this context that Evagrius describes the struggle with the *logismoi*, the spontaneous thoughts which indicate our lack of inner peace and make us vulnerable to demonic attack. The struggle with the passions is intended to heal the body and restore the integrity of the will. It also takes place in constant reference to Christ. The monk is to refer his struggles in prayer to Christ and ask for the meaning of his thoughts, however disturbing they may be.

> If one of the monks should wish to acquire experience with the cruel demons and become familiar with their skill, let him observe the thoughts (*logismoi*) and let him note their intensity and their relaxation, their interrelationship, their occasions, which of the demons do this or that particular thing, what sort of demon follows on another, and let him seek from Christ the reason for these things.[3]

Evagrius insists that spiritual progress depends on a close observation of the thoughts as they arise in the mind. We see from this how he saw the thoughts as *symptoms* rather than as sins. Just as a doctor would take a case history and note the outward signs of an illness, so the monk was carefully to note the pattern of his thoughts and how one followed after another. But he was not to come to a judgement about his inner state on his own. All must be referred to the true Physician, Jesus Christ. We can also see in this passage the subtlety of the relationship between thoughts and demons. Evagrius believed the demons were everywhere and nowhere. They are like an infestation that seizes on a wound. They buzz around the aspirant monk looking for 'cracks in the heart', that is, points of weakness or vulnerability which can be opened up and exploited. Self-defence takes the form of overcoming the passions. Once some progress in the control of the passions has been achieved the second stage of the spiritual life becomes possible.

Human beings must now learn to overcome ignorance, to understand their true place in the world, not as controlling, nor as subordinate but as those who participate in nature and take tranquil and non-possessive delight in its diversity. This enables them to grasp the world as the creation of the *Logos*, designed to lead beyond itself to pure contemplation. This is perhaps best called natural contemplation, *theoria physike*. Thirdly, they must begin to apprehend spiritual beings, again without the desire to possess or control. In this part of the process they begin to perceive the reason for their own existence: they are created, and yet, at the highest level of being, they are beyond material existence. 'The mind is the immaterial icon of the immaterial God.'[4] Finally they are ready to ascend beyond material and spiritual forms to contemplate the Trinity. This is the goal of the spiritual life, the Kingdom, pure prayer. The process is understood as both active and contemplative: *praktike* and *gnostike*.

In a beautiful passage which recalls the Last Supper and the sacrament of the Eucharist, Evagrius describes the progress from *praktike* to *theoria* and lastly to intimate and abiding *gnostike*, knowledge of God.

Flesh of Christ: virtues of *praktikē*;
he who eats it, passionless shall he be.

Blood of Christ: contemplation of created things;
he who drinks it, by it becomes wise.

Breast of the Lord: knowledge of God;
he who rests against it, a theologian shall he be.

A knower and one accomplished in *praktikē* met each other;
between the two of them there stands the Lord.[5]

This last stanza may refer to the relationship between monk and spiritual father. This is more than a relationship of master to apprentice, 'between the two of them there stands the Lord'. Evagrius never thought that human beings could reach the knowledge of God on their own. The spiritual process was always undertaken in relationship, a journey which involved an ever deepening participation in the mystery of Christ and a dependence on his grace. At the beginning of the *Praktikos* he refers to the words used when the young monks were clothed in their habits:

The fear of God strengthens faith, my child, and abstinence in turn strengthens fear of God, and perseverance and hope render abstinence unwavering, and from these is born impassibility (*apatheia*) of which love is the offspring; love is the door to natural knowledge, which is followed by theology and ultimate blessedness.[6]

The use of the word *apatheia* in this context should make it clear that Evagrius was understanding the term in a biblical and Christian sense. *Apatheia* is the fruit of obedience to God, an untroubled tranquillity in doing God's will. It is simply not true that Evagrius taught *apatheia* as the suppression of emotion as Jerome claimed, insisting (rightly) that this was both impossible and undesirable.[7] *Apatheia* may indeed have meant emotional repression in classical philosophy; a calm indifference to circumstance was the hallmark of the Stoic sage. But the term also has a venerable Christian lineage. It was used by Ignatius of Antioch (*c.* 35–107) with particular reference to the sufferings of Christ. It was also employed by Clement of Alexandria (*c.* 150–215), Origen's predecessor at the catechetical school in that city. For Clement, *apatheia* was a kind of loving calmness which was not characterized by indifference so much as by freedom from aggressive or self-centred emotions. For him, it mirrored the serenity and freedom of God himself. As he would have seen it, passions and impulses were merely human qualities and had no part in the divine life. For human beings to grow into their full potential in the image of God they must find the route to imitating God's divine freedom and joy. Other Christian thinkers followed Clement's lead. Gregory of Nyssa, like Evagrius, regarded *apatheia* as necessary for contemplation.[8] Yet thanks to Jerome the word has aroused suspicion in the West and has produced a climate of hostility to apophatic thought in general. A state which is described as being like 'either a stone or a god' foreshadows a persistent Western fear of oriental thought, whether Christian

or otherwise, in that it involves passivity, indifference and a kind of emptiness which suggests the annihilation of the soul rather than its fulfilment.
Evagrius' understanding of *apatheia* was far from this, and much more obviously Christian. Divine love, *agape*, is in fact the 'child' of *apatheia*. What he
is getting at here is the perfectly Christian insight that God's love is selfless.
The love that frees us is similarly selfless love, purged, at least to some extent,
of our own neediness and anxiety. *Apatheia*, then, is the unpossessive love
which allows all things to be what they truly are without imposing our own
agendas or power games. The apparent negativity of a*patheia* is an expression of real freedom and simplicity, a profound liberation from the im-
prisoning knots of unresolved memory and desire. Only when we are free
from these can we love as God loves.

Evagrius' spiritual theory was not intended merely for individuals. Those
drawn to the ascetic life had a task to do not only for themselves, but for
the whole created order, and in particular for other human beings. Through
the struggle for contemplation the whole created universe is being purified
and restored to its original splendour. The kind of process involved is set
out in a prayer for the Church which is part of the eighth-century Gelasian
Sacramentary:

> O God of unchanging power and eternal light,
> look favourably upon thy whole Church,
> that wonderful and sacred mystery;
> and by the tranquil operation of thy perpetual providence
> carry out the work of man's salvation,
> and let the whole world feel and see
> that things which were cast down are being raised up,
> and things which had grown old are being made new,
> and that all things are returning to perfection
> through him from whom they took their origin,
> even Jesus Christ our Lord.[9]

How Cassian changed Evagrius' teaching

And now we come to the heart of the matter. If Evagrius' teaching has
remained at least partially available in Orthodox Christianity it has had a
rather different fate in the West. The aspects that were passed on were progressively transformed with the result that we have inherited an approach
to the problem of human vulnerability which is in conflict with much that
we now value in our attitude to pastoral care and to the healing of the self
and wider society. The initial figure in this negative transformation was
Evagrius' disciple, John Cassian.

Cassian must have listened to Evagrius' exposition of the spiritual life
at Kellia and perhaps discussed his own spiritual struggles with him. He
had sympathy with Evagrius' theological presuppositions. He would have
accepted the intellectual tradition of Origen, if not the extreme doctrines
which the more virulent anti-Origenists thought Origen had held. Yet,
scarred by his experience of the Origenist controversy, Cassian was sensitive

to the strength of opinion against any spiritual teaching 'tainted' by Origenism. Although there is little evidence that any criticisms of Evagrius were linked to Origenism at the stage when Cassian was writing *The Monastic Institutes* (after 415), it may have contributed to Cassian's decision to airbrush out the name of Evagrius from his *Institutes* and never to acknowledge his influence.

The Pelagian controversy was even more important in Cassian's suppression of the name of Evagrius. Jerome associated *apatheia* with Pelagianism. He was aware of the term's pagan roots. He had a tendency to construe Greek spirituality as an attempt of arrogant individuals to become like God by their own proud efforts. So in his translation of Evagrius' ideas Cassian tried to move away from using terms which might suggest an overdependence on Greek thought.

To do this Cassian changed *apatheia* to the more positive sounding *purity of heart*. This phrase has the advantage of being biblical and so removes any suspicion of latent pagan or Pelagian influence: 'Blessed are the pure in heart, for they shall see God.' But there is a drawback. In our very different context the transition from the negative *apatheia* to the positive *puritas cordis* might suggest that there is a task to be achieved, a war to cleanse the self of selfishness and self-centredness. Pelagianism returns in a typically Western form of a hyperactive consciousness. Evagrius would have expected *apatheia* to be about peacefulness, a relaxed but attentive attitude of mind rather than the busy critical and self-critical guardedness which has sometimes been to the forefront in the Western spiritual tradition.

Cassian's more fundamental change, though, was to the vocabulary used of the *logismoi*. Where Evagrius had written of the eight thoughts, Cassian wrote of eight principal vices. This may seem like a small change, given that the thoughts are never neutral for Evagrius – they always have the sense of being *evil* thoughts. But to describe the evil thoughts as 'faults' or 'vices', as Cassian did, is to take a significant step towards the over-moralizing of human vulnerability which is now embedded in the Western tradition. To *have* evil thoughts certainly suggests a lack of control over our inner spiritual world, in which temptations come and go. Vices, on the other hand, are more embedded and have to be extirpated by moral effort. They are the responsibility of the individual, who can rightly be blamed for having them.

Connected to this is the way in which Cassian treats the demons. In the *First Conference of Abbot Serenus* there is a lengthy discourse on the demons and their relationship to the vices which plague humanity.[10] But in the same Conference there is a discussion of what appears to be a widely held agreement that 'the devils have not now the same power as they had formerly during the early years of the anchorites, when yet there were only a few monks living in the desert'.[11] This former time referred to is probably not the time of Evagrius but the period in the late third and early fourth centuries following the withdrawal of the pioneering hermit Antony. There are two reasons given for the diminishment in the powers of the demons.

The first is that the power of the cross drove them away even in the desert; the second is that the monks of later time were so lacking in zeal that the demons had relaxed their efforts.

Evagrius' belief in the demons were an expression of his belief that the fall extends beyond merely human nature. Human beings are only partially responsible for sin; there is a dimension of evil which lies outside the human will. As he saw it, the aim of the demons is to prevent the spiritualization of matter and to maintain disunity and disharmony throughout creation. Evagrius' demons seem to have no principle of unity other than their hostility to human beings. They express the fragmentation brought about by the fall. For strategic purposes they act both independently and together, but their scope for joint action is limited as their aims and approaches sometimes conflict. They can terrify, but they can also appear as urbane, concerned with mundane and ordinary temptations long before they seduce the individual into the grosser forms of self-deception. Whatever we make of this, Evagrius' diabolism does enable him to distinguish subtleties in human behaviour which a more moralistic and individualistic account tends to neglect.

Like Evagrius Cassian assumes that the demons hover around the monks. They cannot see directly into the human heart but they are extremely skilled at observing our outer behaviour and deducing our changing moods, thoughts and fantasies from our appearance and actions. Cassian suggests that the demons have a mechanism for discovering the thoughts of the heart by randomly sprinkling various evil suggestions and then observing us closely to see whether we respond. Then, 'When they see some bodily affection arise corresponding to their character, they recognise as if by a sort of tinkling sound proceeding from the inmost recesses, what it is that is stored up in the secret chamber of the inner man.'[12]

Cassian goes further than Evagrius in suggesting that the demons are directly responsible for implanting the dangerous passions in human beings.[13] He therefore goes a step towards Augustine's position of suggesting that sin is basic to our human nature. In this way he makes his own contribution to the diminishment of the importance of the demons. The human self is firmly in the centre of the problem of sin. Cassian refers to the fall of Lucifer, but apart from in the two *Conferences of Abbot Serenus* he does not show much interest in the demonic host. The demons fade into the background, leaving the devil to take centre stage. This sets the scene for the Western development of the character of the devil as the personification of evil itself, a worthy rival to God.

Cassian is a figure who straddles East and West, the Greek Church and the Latin Church. He was well acquainted with theological controversy and tried to produce a harmony which preserved the essence of what Egyptian spirituality had to offer while translating it for a different context. It is perhaps worth making a few further points about the way the controversies of this formative period in the development of Christian spirituality still have an impact on our lives.

Contemporary echoes: apophatic Christianity

In both Western and Orthodox Christianity there is definite strand of polemic against the part played by Greek philosophy in the development of Christian thought. There is a suspicion of any understanding of God as one who transcends human words and images. There is anxiety about techniques of prayer that encourage a movement towards wordless contemplation. These aspects of apophatic spirituality raise fears among some of those nurtured in the more activist and word-based Christian West. We have seen the part this has played in the reluctance to give a positive account of the work of Evagrius. Von Balthasar's criticism that his theology is more Buddhist than Christian reflects a general anxiety that apophatic spirituality represents some alien, oriental, pantheistic element which is inimical to Christian orthodoxy, reducing the distance and difference between the divine and the human. Fears of apophaticism surfaced at the time of the appointment of Rowan Williams as Archbishop of Canterbury as some of his writings were taken to suggest that he had a particular sympathy for this strand of the spiritual tradition. There are of course traditions of Christian spirituality in the West which are apophatic in emphasis; and though generally accepted, they have often been suspected of transmitting vaguely heretical ideas. Parallel fears can be found in contemporary Orthodoxy. There is a strong disavowal of 'Platonism' in the writings of such Orthodox theologians as Vladimir Lossky and John Meyendorff.

So what is behind this fear? Those who are critical of the apophatic dimension suspect that it comes with a tendency to reduce the living God to an impersonal abstraction, that a God who is beyond thoughts and words simply cannot be the God revealed in scripture and in the human reality of Jesus Christ. The old monk who wept for the loss of a God he could adore echoed the lament of Mary Magdalene when she came to the empty tomb of Christ: 'They have taken away my Lord, and I do not know where they have laid him' (John 20.13). The old monk,[14] like Mary before Christ revealed himself, was also weeping for his whole life of commitment and trust in God. If he could not know who God was how could he know who he was himself? His whole spiritual life suddenly seemed to have betrayed him. Faced with the sophisticated arguments of the bishop's envoy, he felt he had lost all that he had lived for. Yet those who defend apophatic theology and spirituality remind us that perhaps the deepest of the temptations in the spiritual life is the temptation to idolatry, and the more we strive to make God fit into our images and concepts the more likely we are to end up worshipping ourselves. The person drawn to apophatic spirituality feels claustrophobic where the otherness and strangeness of God is not recognized.

The conflict between the two positions cannot be resolved and if we are to live with them positively we must take them as offering a corrective to one another. One reason why I am personally drawn to Evagrius is that his unashamed apophaticism seems fresh and clear compared with the heavy and sometimes agonized literalism of the Western spirituality I have grown up with. But I am still a Western Christian, deeply imbued with guilt!

Contemporary echoes: the conflict with demons

At the 1998 Lambeth Conference a Nigerian bishop attempted on camera to exorcise the Director of the Lesbian and Gay Christian Movement of the demon of homosexual passion. Richard Kirker, the subject of this intervention, understanding all too well how this would play on television, became silent and let him get on with it, rightly judging that the bishop would be seen by the television audience as dangerously deranged.

It would be interesting to imagine Evagrius' response to this little cameo. He would have recognized the reference to a demon of lust, but might have been baffled by a specific demon of homosexuality. He might also have criticized both parties for giving in to the demons of anger, for allowing themselves to be in conflict with one another, and vainglory, for wanting to display their conflict on television!

Belief in demons today is widespread in some parts of the contemporary Church, but it tends to be in those parts of the Church which are least interested in the restoration of creation. The demons encountered through contemporary charismatic movements are very concerned with rather domestic sins, 'blasphemy', 'swearing', 'lust'. Yet there is not much theological awareness of how the oppression of individuals might be part of a wider oppression within society. Those who conduct the ministry of exorcism today are usually quick to point out that cases of apparent possession by demons are often to be explained in terms of mental illness; true possession is rare. Outside the Church and in popular culture belief in real demons is regarded as strange and deluded. We are more likely to speak of demons as unresolved aspects of the individual self. To 'encounter your demons' is to face inner conflicts of memory or habit or desire.

Evagrius on the other hand lived in a world where it was taken for granted that human beings are influenced by unseen forces of good and evil. For Evagrius demons are not visitors from some supernatural realm, they are as much a part of the material universe as biting gnats and howling winds. The battle going on in the monk's heart was part of a much wider battle taking place in the air, on the ground, in communities and households and palaces. The monk was a target for demonic activity because his prayer subverted the demons' destructive influence. Against the fragmentation wrought by the demons Evagrius believed that the monk's task was to bring creation back to God by holding it in unity in his own heart. This was the meaning of his spiritual practice: first to clear his heart from evil – *praktike* – then to engage in natural contemplation – *theoria physike*. In the literature about the lives of the desert monks demons are described as possessing great ferocity, including the capacity to roar and swear and produce physical injuries. The ascetic movement was, in a sense, a protest movement and a liberation movement. Like the early Christian martyrs the monks' ascetic task was to stand up for Christ against an idolatrous empire. The fact that the empire now proclaimed itself Christian did not mean that it embodied the restored creation; it was still a place of conflict, injustice, inequality and oppression.

What all this shows is that our sense of self is rather different from that taken for granted by Evagrius. We tend to think of the self as a unity; mental illness is a fragmentation of self, 'demons' are usually seen as aspects of the self. Real possession (as contemporary exorcists remind us) is not common. So we are left with no language to express spiritual fragmentation beyond the individual self, or to address those aspects which are reflected in human society and the wider creation. These are either seen as moral and political issues or as technical problems to be corrected, if at all, through research, campaigns to bring the issues into public awareness, and political action. Whatever the difficulties we may have with the notion of demons, they do help us to grasp the fact that evil is not limited to the self. It is, at least in part, located *outside* the human person.

Evagrius' demons are perhaps most accurately seen as cosmic expressions of the deadly aspects of a society and culture organized against God and in enmity to the human soul. How 'real' they were to him and could be to us is a modern question which we cannot really answer. They were certainly real in his experience and he understood them as being part of a cosmos which was both material and spiritual. Evagrius' insights challenge us to consider whether we might need to develop a vocabulary in which to speak of the demonic dimension of evil in our own time. Without such a vocabulary of the demonic we are simply caught between a crude fundamentalist belief in supernatural agents of evil and the reductionist view that evil is merely a human problem.

However sceptical we may be about the independent existence of demons, if we are to understand Evagrius we need to be sceptical about our own scepticism. Disbelief in demons is very much a product of our own cultural environment. We are still to a large extent children of the eighteenth-century Enlightenment, with its radical attack on superstition, miracles and supernatural explanations of phenomena which could be accounted for rationally. The question must be asked whether in our disbelief in demons we have simply become insensitive to a whole realm of human experience which still questions and disturbs us, though we are no longer able to name it.

In this sense, if we were to ask where *our* demons operate, we might find answers in those attitudes, assumptions and influences which play excessively on our anxieties, fears and desires in ways which could enslave us. And here we need both honesty and wisdom. The demon of gluttony may operate in supermarket aisles offering a *truly tempting* choice of 14 types of baked beans. What is it about our society that makes us feel good about excess and distracts us by continual choices? A more subtle manifestation of gluttony could occur when we respond to an excessive pressure to control very precisely what we eat and drink in a bid to live longer, whatever the cost to our sociability or availability to others. Gluttony in these examples oppresses our thoughts and controls our behaviour, and it operates both within and outside ourselves. As Evagrius himself puts it:

> The demons strive against men of the world chiefly through their deeds, but in the case of monks for the most part through their thoughts,

since the desert deprives them of such affairs. Just as it is easier to sin by thought than by deed, so also is the war fought in the field of thought more severe than that which is conducted in the area of things and events. For the mind is easily moved indeed, and hard to control in the presence of sinful fantasies.[15]

Evagrius can even use the language of the law court, but in a characteristic way. So he urges the aspiring monk to 'Judge the thoughts in the tribunal of your heart so that, when the thieves are done away with, the chief thief may take fright; for one who is a rigorous examiner of his thoughts will also be truly a lover of the commandments.'[16]

The eight thoughts as vulnerabilities

Evagrius thinks of the *logismoi*, the evil thoughts, not as sins but as symptoms of the vulnerability that arises from material existence. He does not suggest that having evil thoughts is culpable in itself. The thoughts are troubling and distressing, a sign both of the proximity of demons and a signal to the demons that we may be open to the temptations they bring. Evagrius would have said that to suffer such disturbances is an inevitable part of our material existence. To use a contemporary medical analogy we might say that evil thoughts signify a compromised spiritual immune system. Yet weakness is not illness and evil thoughts are not sins. Nor are the evil thoughts the same as temptations. Temptations, for Evagrius, characteristically come from without, from the demonic realm. Evagrius sometimes uses the terms 'demon' and 'thought' as though they were interchangeable, but he more usually distinguishes between them. Evagrius is clear that the thoughts are not themselves sins. They only become sin when they are surrendered to. There is a contrast here with the later Western tradition, which, having inherited the more depressed Augustinian view of the fall, is not always very clear about the distinction between temptation and sin. It is as though to have a wicked thought is to have a wicked heart: the evil idea does not come from without but is already lodged within. Growth in understanding is then curtailed because there is no encouragement to the careful analysis and self-observation which Evagrius commends. (If my thoughts are wicked it is better not to think, rather than to risk bringing the whole slimy lot into consciousness.) Yet for Evagrius dispassionate observation of evil thoughts is a crucial part of that process of detachment by which the self reaches serenity:

> Let him [the monk] observe their intensity, their periods of decline, and follow them as they rise and fall. Let him note well the complexity of his thoughts, their periodicity, the demons which cause them, with the order of their succession and the nature of their associations. Then let him ask from Christ the explanations of these data which he has observed.[17]

The point is that Evagrius expects *logismoi* to occur, but because he puts their origin outside the self he enables his followers to resist them without necessarily identifying with them or indulging them. Simply observing the thoughts as they arise helps defuse the temptation they represent. The point of reference for the struggling ascetic is Christ, who has real knowledge of the monk's heart and has already overcome all evil and demonic assault. It is a profoundly optimistic vision and yet it begins with very simple practicalities.

The next eight chapters will consider Evagrius' analysis of the *logismoi*, beginning with the summary of each one in the *Praktikos*. I will go on to show the scriptural sources of the *logismoi* he identifies. A consideration of the part each thought may have played in Evagrius' own life will lead on to a consideration of some of the ways in which his teaching in the *Praktikos* summary is amplified in his other writings. I will then attempt to trace the development of each thought in the Western spiritual tradition. Finally, I will make some suggestions as to how Evagrius' insights might speak to us.

Part 2

THE DIAGNOSTIC
TOOL KIT

5

The thought of gluttony

Lord Jesus, think on me,
and purge away my sin;
from earthbound passions set me free,
and make me pure within.[1]

The thought of gluttony suggests to the monk that he ought to give up his ascetic discipline at once. It brings to mind the state of his stomach, his liver and his spleen, the diagnosis of a long illness, the lack of life's necessities, and finally the horror of his body, its tissues bloated with fluid, and no doctors near by to offer relief. These things are depicted vividly before his eyes. The thought reminds him of particular brothers who have suffered from such things. It frequently brings him to recall certain ones among the brethren who have fallen prey to such complaints. And at the same time the thought occurs to those who do suffer from such illnesses to pay a visit and to catalogue their various ailments and describe how these are the consequences of their attempt at an ascetic life-style.[2]

Comment

Gluttony is the first of the evil thoughts to be named by Evagrius. Evagrius uses the Greek word *gastromargia*, which means literally 'madness of the stomach'. Gluttony appears in all subsequent lists of deadly sins and vices and is usually first to be mentioned. We might tend to think of gluttony as it was traditionally depicted in the medieval period, as the most grotesque of the deadly sins. The glutton is a figure of excess; hugely fat, greedy, drooling, out of control, all mouth and stomach, with the body distorted by its indulgence. There is no sense that gluttony is pleasurable in these descriptions. They give a deeply unattractive picture, a warning to all about the perils of giving too much attention to this most basic of appetites.

Yet Evagrius does not start with this caricature, nor does he identify gluttony simply with overindulgence in food and drink. This would have been difficult to achieve in the desert! It would be more accurate to say that gluttony presents itself as a temptation to give up any attempt at a God-centred life, through fear of the consequences to one's health. The thought of gluttony makes the aspirant monk think endlessly about his digestive system and worry about how it is coping with the desert regime. He then finds himself wondering what it would be like to endure a chronic digestive disorder and how it would be exacerbated by the lack of regular food supplies. He thinks of his body as it might become, bloated and malnourished, and of the fact that by going out into the desert he has put himself beyond the reach of medical care. He then remembers that some of his fellow monks have, in fact, damaged their digestions by the desert regime. If he lets himself become really anxious he will even find himself being visited by sick monks who are all too ready to tell him how their chronic illness was caused by too much fasting and abstinence.

This anxiety about nourishment is the first of the evil thoughts to assail the monk because it relates to the first and most practical necessity everyone faces, which is sheer physical survival. The hostile environment of the desert inevitably exacerbated this anxiety. To stay committed required a foundation of trust. Evagrius tells us, that when a new monk was beginning his ascetic life and was clothed with the distinctive habit, these words would be said, 'The fear of God strengthens faith, my child, and continence in turn strengthens this fear.'[3] The whole venture of Christian life turns on faith, a willingness to experiment with trusting in God alone.

In the isolation of the desert, facing long, empty hours and trying to learn to pray, fantasies about food would be difficult to avoid. Perhaps this is why modern retreat houses are usually well supplied with chocolate bars and biscuits!

Gluttony in the Bible

The Bible normally assumes that eating and drinking is to be enjoyed with thankfulness. The children of Israel depended on God for nourishment on their desert journey out of slavery in Egypt. They grumbled though at the rather monotonous diet of 'manna' in the wilderness that God provided and indulged in foodie nostalgia for the delicacies they had enjoyed in Egypt. The result of this was that God produced quails to satisfy their appetites, but this was not an altogether happy experience as God sent a deadly plague to punish the people for provoking him with their craving (Numbers 11.31–34). The lesson of this unfortunate experience would seem to be that God is to be trusted to provide for his people, but the menu is not always very appetising. The essential point, though, is that God provides not only for the human creation but for the animals: 'All look to you to give them their food in due season' (Psalm 104.27).

The ideal life in ancient Israel was one of modest prosperity, for everyone to live under their own vine and fig tree. Oil, bread, wine, milk and honey were the normal staples. Wine, strong drink and abundant meat were enjoyed at festivals. But the tradition of the desert was strong, and various parts of the Old Testament strongly suggest that restricting particular foods and fasting have a part to play in approaching God. In ancient Israel there were those like the hero Samson who took vows not to drink alcohol and to grow his hair long (Judges 13.4; Numbers 6.1–5). Daniel is said to have adopted a teetotal and vegetarian diet when he was at the court of King Nebuchadnezzar. His healthy appearance while on this diet was noted by his captors. Greed for food is not a major theme in the Bible though it makes the odd appearance. Esau, starving after hunting, sold his privilege as the eldest son to his brother Jacob in exchange for a plate of red stew.

Isaac's longing for savoury meat leads him into the deception by which he mistakenly blessed his second-born son Jacob instead of his first-born. Food and the craving for food was the bait in each case.

The theme of trusting in God to provide food is developed in the New Testament. The prayer for 'daily bread' is part of the Lord's Prayer. Jesus encourages commitment in his disciples with his teaching:

> Do not worry about your life, what you will eat or what you will drink, or about your body, what you will wear. Is not life more than food, and the body more than clothing? Look at the birds of the air; they neither sow nor reap nor gather into barns, and yet your heavenly Father feeds them. (Matthew 6.25–26)

Jesus often likened the coming Kingdom to a great feast, and he provided meals in the wilderness for his followers; miraculous banquets of bread and fish. Eating and drinking in company with others was an expression of the abundance, hospitality and generosity of God.

St Paul is really the first biblical writer to name gluttony as an evil, writing of those whose 'god is their belly' and whose end is destruction (Philippians 3.19). Paul was a cosmopolitan Jew, and he may well have been following a view widely held in the ancient world, that people were less than human if they were unable to subordinate the pleasures of the senses to reason. Control of the appetites expressed the ancient virtue of temperance: not too much and not too little.

It is interesting to note that gluttony is not among the inner evils which Jesus lists as coming from the human heart. Indeed, this list (Mark 7.20–23) suggests that no kind of food can in itself defile the human person. But the biblical records insist that Jesus used the discipline of fasting in his period in the wilderness, and encountered the temptation to use divine power to create bread out of stones. He urged his followers to be prepared for God's imminent judgement, and not to be 'weighed down with dissipation and drunkenness and the worries of this life' (Luke 21.34). Jesus assumed that fasting was a necessary discipline, an *ascesis* for the confrontation with temptation and that resistance would lead to victory. The fathers and mothers of the desert sought the same experience and the same victory.

Gluttony in the life of Evagrius

Evagrius had probably enjoyed an intense social life while he was in Constantinople, and, while he is described as taking care to keep himself in trim, there is no reason to suppose he did not enjoy the ordinary pleasures of good food and drink. Perhaps he came to associate dinner parties with sex, because he often made a connection between the thoughts of gluttony and lust. But when he accepted the monastic habit from Melania, and took himself to Egypt to live in community in the Nitrian desert, he simply accepted the disciplines of fasting and abstinence as part of what it meant to take on a life of prayer. The practical discipline had plenty of biblical precedents and fasting was a well-established practice in the early Church. But the theory which went with it derived from views about the nature of the human soul going back to the time of the philosopher Plato. Plato taught that the soul is divided into three parts: the *rational* part (the noblest and highest part of the soul), the *irascible* part (driven by strong feeling), and the *concupiscible* part (driven by bodily appetite). The second and third divisions of the soul are together called the *passionate* part of the soul, and they comprise all the aspects of the soul which are attached to the body. The work of the monk was to establish order in all three parts of the soul. This work began with learning to manage the drives, compulsions, appetites and hungers that derive from the needs and memories of the five senses. The most basic drive is the appetite for food and drink, and so it is here that the monk's struggle begins.

When Evagrius began living the monastic life he would have heard amazing tales of monks so gripped by prayer that they forgot to eat, or so self-controlled that they refused to. Such tales are recorded in the *Lives of the Fathers* which, in Latin, comprises the earliest surviving record of the lives of the desert pioneers. One story tells of a monk who, longing to eat a cucumber, hung one up in his cell and gazed at it until his craving ceased.[4] Another, invited to feast, threw down a cup of wine which he was offered saying, 'Take this death away from me.'[5] Yet there are also stories which show an attitude to food which is, at least from our point of view, less fearful and neurotic. 'When Arsenius heard that all the apples were ripe, he said, "Bring them to me." He took one small bite of each kind, giving thanks to God.'[6]

If we accept for a moment that the point of such extreme fasting was to gain power over the drives of the lower part of the soul we can see how it was believed that the control of appetite was essential for prayer. It is in that spirit that Hyperichius is reported to have said, 'When the monk's body is dried up with fasting, this lifts his soul from the depths. Fasting dries up the channels down which worldly pleasures flow.'[7] By having control of the body the monks believed they were in a stronger position to resist other forms of evil: 'If a man is sincere about fasting and is hungry, the enemies that trouble his soul will grow weak.'[8]

Evagrius would have been deeply influenced by these teachings. He also accepted the commonplace theories about the kinds of food appropriate for curtailing passion and those which inflamed it. These theories were based on the ancient belief that all material reality is composed of combinations of the four elements: earth, air, fire and water. Clement of Alexandria (*c.* 150–215), whose teachings are reflected in Evagrius' own, had taught that Christians should cut down on the variety of their diet: 'Let our diet be light and digestible, and suitable for keeping awake, unmixed with diverse varieties.'[9] Clement suggests that Christians should prefer drier foods, and in particular that they should abstain from sauces. It became accepted among serious Christians with ascetical aspirations that a spiritually healthy diet should be mostly composed of dry foods which, it would have been presumed, were made mostly of fire and air rather than water and bile. Their composition would have an effect on the body and hence on the soul; a drier diet protected against the temptation to dissipation. Evagrius himself is quoted as saying, 'Some of our predecessors used to say that a dry and regular diet combined with love will soon bring a monk to the harbour where the storms of passion do not enter.'[10]

Evagrius, like other desert ascetics, believed that spiritual transformation depended on limiting the body's intake of food. Their programme was ambitious; it was no less than the complete transformation of the human person. Control of the body was an essential first step; the body was the medium through which transformation happened. So it is not surprising that Evagrius relates gluttony not to greed but to anxiety, and in particular to the anxiety for his or her health which anyone might have on starting to live the life of radical Christian commitment.

According to his biographer Palladius,[11] Evagrius ate and drank extremely sparingly. After his initiation into the ascetic life he spent fourteen years in the Egyptian desert where he apparently lived on a pound of bread a day with a pint of oil which lasted for three months. It is not itself a wholly unpleasant diet. The bread would probably have been flavoured with a little salt and the oil would moisten it and give it some richness. Even today good bread with oil and garlic or seasoning plays a basic part in the diet of the southern Mediterranean. Palladius also tells us that Evagrius boasted that he did not touch any vegetable greens or fruit or grapes from the time that he went to live in the desert. (He was even more proud of the fact that he did not have a bath.) However, in a work of instruction for new monks, Evagrius insists that the choice of foods for an ascetic must remain a free one. Nothing is forbidden in scripture. God gave green plants which may be eaten without distinction. All he insisted on was that monks should restrict themselves to one meal a day, though even this rule should be suspended in times of sickness or when it was necessary to provide hospitality.[12] Hospitality should not be excessive, though. Bread, salt and water was quite sufficient.[13] Evagrius makes the point about hospitality because it was a rule of the desert life. (It still is among the Bedouin who still inhabit the Egyptian desert.) If a visitor turned up he or she must not be turned away hungry, even if the solitary were fasting. And if a monk were invited to eat he should consider doing so, for the sake of charity.

> Once Sylvanus and his disciple Zacharias arrived at a monastery. The monks made them eat a little before they went on their way. When they left, the disciple saw a pool by the wayside and wanted to drink. Sylvanus said, 'Zacharias, today is a fast.' Zacharias said, 'But surely we have already eaten today, abba?' The hermit said to him, 'We ate their meal out of love for them, but when we are on our own let us keep our fast, my son.'[14]

Evagrius was also aware that fasting itself could become an obsession. In advice for more advanced monks he explains that when the demon who tempts people to gluttony realizes that he has not been successful he disturbs the mind by producing a passionate longing for an even more extreme asceticism, quoting scripture to support the temptation and reminding the person he is tempting of hermits who have taken fasting to extremes. No one, Evagrius suggests, should attempt to abstain from the basics of bread, oil and water.[15]

But in spite of trying to strike a moderate posture over fasting the years of austerity did not do Evagrius much good. Evagrius' belief in a dry diet involved abstaining not only from moist foods, but even from water as much as possible: 'Limiting one's intake of water helps a good deal to obtain temperance.'[16] The desert monks believed that springs and wells were places where demons liked to congregate, and that they should be avoided. A dry diet and limited water, combined with the dehydration that may have arisen anyway in a desert climate, must have contributed to the illness that Evagrius suffered from in his later years. A Coptic version of Palladius' *Life of Evagrius* (though not the better-known Greek one) declares that 'Evagrius suffered intense physical pain from the stone'.[17] Luke Dysinger, commenting on this observation, suggests that Evagrius may well have suffered from bladder or kidney stones, a consequence of dehydration, the pain from which is often agonizing. Palladius reports that he eventually weakened his digestion to the point where he later needed the comfort of cooked food. In the end he had to stop eating bread altogether and lived on various forms of herb-flavoured porridge. At the age of 55 he felt that death was near. His last recorded act was at the beginning of 399 when he asked to be taken to church so that he could receive Holy Communion for the Feast of Epiphany.

As Evagrius saw it, the thought of gluttony is an obstacle to the ascetic life because it haunts the monk with fears about whether his or her body is strong enough to cope with abstaining from a former pattern of consumption. He was perfectly aware that his chosen diet would harm his body; the horrors he conjures up in his description of the temptation to gluttony were real horrors, and he would have known monks who had wrecked their health by their practices. He was not under the anorexic's illusion that abstinence from food would produce the perfect body. But then, he was not interested in acquiring a perfect body!

For Evagrius gluttony is a kind of timidity, a thought which limits the spiritual imagination by a nagging hypochondria. Out in the desert, miles from any help, supposing I faint and no one comes to help me? What will I do without the pills or potions that have always been readily available to me? How will my body cope in the long term without the mixed and varied diet that I am used to?

Looking at Evagrius' own experience it seems that he was quite right in his analysis. His own diet in the desert was dreadful by any standards, and we are not surprised by the agonies that he suffered in his later years. But the interesting thing about his analysis is that he sees gluttony as an evil thought that plays on fear. Gluttony comes from an over-concern for the health of the body. It arises from the anxiety that there might not be enough, or the right kind of food, and that the body, without proper nourishment, will inevitably deteriorate. From our point of view the urge for variety in the diet is reasonable enough and could be interpreted as a prompting from the body for the range of nutrients that it needs. But for Evagrius this physical craving was a sign of dangerous passions asserting themselves.

His chief aim was for the serenity which comes when the mind is focused on God, not distracted by the needs and compulsions of the body. With his intellectual background in the philosophy that derived from Plato, Evagrius would always tend to think that the mind should control the body. He would also tend to identify the core of the human personality with the rational part of the soul, and see the intellect as being the part of the human person which most truly reflects the image of God. So it was natural for him to believe that true calm of mind was attainable by overcoming needs and desires which to us are natural and necessary.

Gluttony in the spiritual tradition

There was a biblical case for seeing gluttony as the primal sin. Adam and Eve fell from Paradise through eating the forbidden fruit, and some of the early Christian commentators on the Genesis story described their sin in those terms, and even when the consensus had been agreed that the chief sin involved was pride, it was obvious to many that gluttony must have been involved.[18]

John Cassian developed the teaching of Evagrius on the eight thoughts and made it the foundation for the ascetic life in Western Europe, and in particular in what is now the south of France. Twenty-five years or so after the death of Evagrius he wrote *The Monastic Institutes*, which included teaching on what he called the eight principal faults. His other ascetical work, the *Conferences*, which were written at about the same time (425–430), also included teachings on the principal faults. Gluttony was the first of these. Cassian taught that 'the belly generates the seeds of vice'.[19] The mind would not be able to make virtuous choices if the body was 'weighed down' by excessive food and drink. Cassian also developed Evagrius' critique of excessive fasting. He taught that it was pointless, that it could actually cause gluttony. He seems to have recognized something like the dieting and bingeing cycle that is so familiar in contemporary life. He describes three ways in which over-concern with food and drink can ruin the life of prayer.[20] The first is that monks start to anticipate the next meal. The second is by gorging and stuffing. The third is by indulging in expensive and exotic delicacies rather than ordinary food. Cassian's solution is that monks should keep regular mealtimes, avoid gobbling their food too fast, and make do with what is cheap and readily available.[21] He also moderated the ban on variety in the diet, suggesting that those who abstain totally from rich food are more likely to break their rule than those who allowed themselves a little bit of what they fancied.[22] He also recognized that in a monastic community there would need to be considerable flexibility. What was enough food for one individual would not necessarily sustain another.

However, he abandoned Evagrius' careful analysis of gluttony as a kind of hypochondria. He presents it in more familiar terms as a lack of self-control in eating and drinking, an addiction to excess, which weighs down the soul and makes other temptations more likely. One reason for this change is likely to have been that food and drink were more available in southern

France than they were in the desert! In either context, fasting is the cure for gluttony, and the struggle against gluttony is like an athletic contest, the competitor must keep his or her eyes on the target, which is to attain enough control of the body to enter the true contest against spiritual foes.[23]

Cassian inherited the desert tradition that the obligation to hospitality took priority over personal rules of fasting. This no doubt helped keep Christian monasticism within the bounds of sanity. It also ensured that the meaning of eating and drinking together, which is so important in the teaching and life of Jesus, was not lost from Christian ascetical practice. Even monks are social beings. Eating and drinking together builds community and increases the bonds of affection and good will.

Cassian's rules for monastic life had a great influence on Benedict of Nursia (480–550), who composed the most famous and long-lasting of the monastic rules. Benedict followed Cassian in teaching that monastic discipline in eating and drinking should be moderate: 'Don't drink to excess or overeat.'[24] He allowed for two cooked dishes on each table of the monastery and a pound of bread per person per day, which was considerably more than Evagrius had allowed himself. Fruit and vegetables were to be added when they were available. Monks were to abstain from red meat except when they were sick.[25] They were also allowed a half measure of wine, though Benedict granted this as something of a concession and encouraged those who preferred to abstain to do so.[26]

Benedict aimed at a temperate lifestyle in which there was enough to eat, but not so much as to encourage excess. Private austerities were not encouraged. Those who might wish to deny themselves some regular food or drink in Lent were obliged to submit their plans to the superior for approval.[27] It is impossible to read the Rule of St Benedict without being impressed by its moderation and sanity. But at the same time we should be aware of what had been lost. Evagrius was concerned with the negative impact of random fantasies arising from the senses on the integrity of the self. Excessive food or drink impressed the self in such a way as to wound it and harm its freedom. Restricting the diet to starvation levels was an extreme (and from our point of view mistaken) way to deal with this, but it was an attempt to deal with the depth of the problem as Evagrius saw it. Cassian and Benedict, rightly, drew back from the solution Evagrius offered, but in doing so they lost sight of Evagrius's diagnostic insight.

Pope Gregory the Great (540–604), who reformed and consolidated the Western Church in the years following Benedict's death, absorbed the teaching both of Cassian and Benedict and their commitment to monastic life. He seems to have had no awareness that the originator of their teaching, Evagrius, had seen what they called sins as disturbing thoughts rather than faults. This is hardly surprising as Evagrius' teaching had been condemned as heretical in 533 and access to his writings was no longer possible. Building on Cassian and his greater contemporary, Augustine of Hippo, Gregory simply took for granted that human beings were basically flawed as a result of the fall. He took the principal faults that Cassian had described, and made gluttony the sixth of seven sins and pride the first.

Gregory is a key figure in the development of the deadly sin tradition. The codification of the seven deadly sins in the form that have come down to us is almost invariably ascribed to him. He wrote about them in his *Moralia*, a lengthy commentary on the book of Job, used as the basis of reflection on moral themes. Gluttony is a principal sin because it has the power to generate other sins. These Gregory lists as false jollity, dirty jokes, slobbishness, talking too much and dulling of the intellect.[28] Gluttony, then, was a gateway for other well-known human failings. This is an expression of Gregory's belief that our bodily existence is fraught with anguish as a result of the fall. Adam's disobedience in taking the fruit had the result that God gave him what he desired, and human beings have ever since been unable to control their bodily appetites. The basic needs of the body make people constantly vulnerable to the temptations of excess, of the pursuit of pleasure for its own sake. All pleasure, especially bodily pleasure, is deeply problematic for Gregory. It is a sign of self-preoccupation, a turning away from the Creator to the self, and the pursuit of pleasure follows logically from the fall into pride by which Adam and Eve declared themselves independent of God. In the fall God abandons humanity to the consequences of their actions. Men and women are left to cope with an embodied state over which they no longer have control. Gregory found the human body repulsive, particularly when its natural appetites are out of control. Where Evagrius saw the swollen, fluid-logged body as an image of fear in the mind of those who were tempted to give up their monastic fast, Gregory saw it as the inevitable fate of those who ate and drank too much: 'When the belly is extended to satiety, the prickings of lust are aroused.'[29] The 'satiety' of the stomach suggests the prevalence of 'moistness', a dangerous imbalance of the four humours of which the body is composed. Other vices associated with excess moisture are named by Gregory as too much talking and humour, careless speech and 'windiness of spirit'!

The cure for Gregory is obvious. The excess humours which might produce a tendency to gluttony can be dried up by fasting and discipline. Gregory thinks naturally in terms of opposites and contradictions, and for every bodily sin of excess there is a physical remedy. The body is where such sins begin and the body is where they must be cured. But first, the diagnosis of gluttony must be accurate. Following on Cassian's three manifestations of gluttony, Gregory discerned five forms in which the sin shows itself.[30] A glutton is one who anticipates the next meal by eating something in advance, or who eats rich food, or over-elaborate food, or who eats too much, or too eagerly. All these are signs of an appetite out of control.

Though Gregory really set the tone of Western thinking on the deadly sin of gluttony, there were important refinements of the teaching, of which the most interesting comes in the work of Thomas Aquinas. We know that Aquinas happened to be a very large man and was described by his contemporaries as 'a great ox'. He saw gluttony, as he saw other deadly sins, as a moral deformity. But unlike Gregory he believed that the appetite for food was not in itself sinful. Human beings need food for life and a moderate appetite is both necessary and good. Gluttony is to consume food and drink in a way which exceeds necessity and is therefore indulged *purely* for the pleasure of the experience of eating and drinking. His analysis is very close to that of Cassian and less bleak than that of Gregory. Nevertheless, he quotes what he takes as a distillation of Gregory's teaching in what had become a well-known Latin verse suggesting that you are a glutton if you eat 'Hastily, sumptuously, daintily, too much, or greedily'.[31] In other words, you fall into the gluttonous category if you indulge in food before you are really hungry, spend too much on food, eat more than you need, eat too greedily (like an addict), or you are too careful about what you are pre- pared to eat. Gluttony is to have a relationship with food in which the food itself is more important than the well-being of the person it feeds. Such gluttonous habits are irrational. Aquinas had confidence in human reason, and believed that if the dictates of reason are followed we will find our- selves in harmony with divine law. Gluttony is a sin because it is an offence to reason; it infringes the law of God. At the same time, for Aquinas, glut- tony is a sin against the self. It signifies a disorder of appetite. What is inter- esting about Aquinas is that by the sheer power of analysis he works his way back towards Evagrius' original insight. He sees that more is going on in the temptation to gluttony than appears. Yet Aquinas' subtlety is under- mined by the caricatures of medieval art, where gluttony is presented in terms which are clearly intended to arouse amusement and disgust. Here, gluttony is often personified as a hugely fat figure surrounded by vast amounts of food and drink. Some depictions have gluttony vomiting into a bowl, sometimes while being spewed out by some other creature.

Dante condemns the unrepentantly gluttonous to an eternal hell of wallowing in dark slush. The consequence of a life of self-indulgence is to become completely imprisoned in the matter to which one has become addicted, a porridge of half-eaten, vomited, excreted waste. But the repentant in purgatory are trained out of their sinful habits. The remedy for gluttony is fasting, and not any kind of fasting, the gluttonous must starve in a region laden with fruit trees and springs of water. Having to be restrained in the midst of plenty is both punishment and cure. It is a judgement on their per- verted appetites which at the same time purges their appetite for excessive pleasure in food and drink.

It is hardly surprising in the light of the disgust that the medieval world expressed towards gluttony that it also provides examples of saints, mostly female, who were virtually anorexic.[32] They were usually allowed to indulge their revulsion at food; the rules of moderation were not enforced, prob- ably because they were extremely obstinate! Catherine of Siena is said to have lived for years sustained only on the host at Holy Communion. But she also had a tendency to see devils around the kitchen. Taking the tradition in a quite different direction St John of the Cross describes a condition of 'spiritual gluttony' which is an addiction to the 'highs' of devotional practice.[33] It affects those whose spiritual life is dominated by the desire for 'spiritual sweetness', for good feelings, for the sense of being 'filled up' by the presence of God, as though God could be literally touched or tasted.

Evagrius, gluttony and us

The notion of gluttony is very much with us today, and forms the background to the fear and reality of obesity in our society. It is true for us, as it was for our medieval forebears, that the overweight glutton is a figure of fun and dread, whose sin is entirely visible to the eyes of others. In our own context the overweight glutton evokes both pity and contempt, and often feels deep shame because of their addiction to food.

We would all probably tend to aspire to a moderate lifestyle in harmony with the body's natural needs. We are aware that some people are more prone to indulgence in food and drink than others; that different races and cultures are more or less inclined to overindulgence (there is much less drunkenness among Mediterranean peoples than among Northern Europeans), and that different individuals metabolize food at different rates, and need to eat more or less accordingly. We are more aware of food allergies; shellfish and nuts are dangerous to some people, and there is some evidence that these are more common than they used to be. All these make us more conscious of what we eat and drink. Survival is not a pressing issue for most of us in the developed world. We do, though, face the crucial issue of how we are to eat and drink in such a way that glorifies God. How do we learn to trust in a God of providence, who has created the human body in such a way that it is extremely adaptable and can flourish on a variety of different regimes of eating and drinking? Evagrius' diet was appalling by contemporary nutritional standards, but it sustained him for 14 years[34] and enabled him to produce significant insights into the ascetic life and to support others with his prayers and counsel.

Evagrius' insight that gluttony is related to fear strikes a particularly contemporary chord. In this he is more in tune with our experience than those who developed the tradition after his death. People whose lives are overdominated by food and drink often seem to be afraid of hunger. Panic sets in at the first intimations of emptiness or even at the thought of food being unexpectedly unavailable. This panic can be felt vicariously: parents who over-feed their children often do so because they cannot bear it when the child shows any sign of hunger or distress, and come to rely on snacks and treats to prevent the child having to experience, even for a short time, the frustration of his or her appetite. So the child grows up unable to endure its own hunger, and terrified of the sensation of emptiness. Though the manifestation of this fear is physical, the roots of it are often emotional. It is an inner, emotional hunger and emptiness that such people dread. People who eat or drink excessively are often unhappy, not least because they believe their appearance makes them unattractive. The sensation of being 'filled up' is a compensation which hides the craving of the soul, to be poised and at peace in a body which is content. So great is the fear of having to experience the soul's craving that it outweighs the fear of being thought greedy, fat or ugly by others.

But gluttony is not a temptation only for the overindulgent. Evagrius, Cassian and Aquinas all recognized that gluttony could appear as fastidiousness, a manifestation of a different kind of fear. Many of us are fearful of what we eat. We believe, for example, that our daily health depends on eating and drinking exactly the right amount of cereals, fruit and vegetables; we flinch at the very thought of 'fat' or 'sugar' in foods; we consume extra vitamins and minerals because we fear there is not enough in 'ordinary', 'mass-produced' food. Our fears are exacerbated by the knowledge that some people are harmed by particular foods; alongside allergies that can produce severe and even fatal reactions, intolerance to lactose or gluten or other substances in food is not uncommon. There is a widespread fear of 'chemicals' in food, of additives of various kinds which improve the taste or texture of the food we eat. We are so terrified of gluttony that we become gluttons for the perfect diet. The issue is complex for us in a way which it was not for Evagrius, Cassian and Aquinas, for there are economic and ethical issues about the way our food is produced which they did not have to deal with. If we are trying to live and eat in a Christian way should we eat whole-meal bread with added grains and seeds, or the cheapest, white sliced loaf? And does the fact that some of us have no choice but to eat what is cheapest challenge those of us who do have a choice?

Evagrius was perhaps the first to recognize the dangers of excessive fasting and the tradition followed his insights at this point. He recognized that disciplining the appetite could be interiorized in such a way that a person reaches a point of preferring not to satisfy the natural appetite at all. The person at this point has acquired a positive addiction to the sensation of emptiness. Discipline has turned into a kind of masochism, pain into pleasure. The stones of desert hunger are preferred to the bread of moderate satisfaction. It is perhaps because this temptation became widespread in the spiritual life of the desert ascetics that later rules of spiritual discipline insist that fasting itself must be supervised. Moderation is better than excess, even in self-discipline.

The Gospels recall Jesus eating and drinking not only with his disciples and followers, but also with tax-collectors and sinners. The meals that Jesus created in the wilderness were anticipations of the Last Supper, the meal Jesus ate with his closest followers on the night of his betrayal. This is what is recalled every time Christians gather for the Eucharist. Shared bread and common meals are crucial in the forming of spiritual identity. The sharing is important because it takes the emphasis away from the individual. The food goes *round*, round the table, round the circle, from hand to mouth and from person to person. Those who share, who participate in common food, are experiencing a common life, a shared humanity. The people with whom you eat are as important as what you eat, and Jesus showed a willingness to eat with friends, followers, strangers, outsiders and with potential or real enemies. It is worth remembering, and reflecting on the fact, that of all the deadly sins, the only one of which Jesus was regularly accused was the sin of gluttony.

6

The thought of lust

The demon of lust compels one to desire various bodies. It especially targets those who practise sexual abstinence, trying to make them give up in the belief that they are not achieving anything. This demon bends the soul down towards those sexual acts which defile it, making it say certain things and even hear certain words almost as if the reality were visible and present.[1]

Comment

Lust is the second of Evagrius' evil thoughts. Evagrius uses the Greek word *porneia* for lust, a word from which we derive pornography. Evagrius believed that lust, like gluttony, arose from the lowest and most inferior part of the soul, the concupiscible part, which is the seat of bodily desire. Lust would naturally follow on from overindulgence in food and drink. In a treatise for beginners on the foundations of monastic life Evagrius comments on St Paul's teaching that only the unmarried are free enough from the anxieties of the world to be able to concentrate on pleasing the Lord (1 Corinthians 7.32–33). Celibacy, he urges, is an essential part of the call to withdraw from the world. Without embracing singleness no one can hope to practise the stillness in which true prayer develops.[2]

Evagrius' remarks on the demon of lust are brief in the extract from the *Praktikos* quoted above. He has more to say elsewhere. But these initial remarks are important because they show that Evagrius believed that the demon of lust concentrates particularly on those who are attempting to live the celibate life, in the hope that they might be so depressed by their experiences of sexual temptation that they decide to abandon their asceticism as worthless. The demon works through the would-be celibate's own resolution to stand firm. It 'bows the soul down', forcing into the individual's mind the thought of forbidden sexual practices and bringing sexually explicit words and exclamations into consciousness. Elsewhere,[3] Evagrius writes of the demon of lust appearing to the monk in female form to try to persuade the monk to have intercourse in fantasy. Evagrius insists that the monk must resist the temptation to 'bow down' to the mental image that has been produced – the implication is that to do so would be to fall into idolatry.[4] It is the shame of forbidden sex in the mind that disturbs the ascetic, and leaves him weighed down by the sense that he is defiled in spirit and unworthy to live the life of prayer. The enjoyment, even if momentary and involuntary, of sexual feelings makes the ascetic feel cut off from God, and that is exactly what the demon of lust intends. With this in mind Evagrius warns (male) monks against all encounters with women. It is all too easy, he insists, to become overfamiliar with women, who may outwardly appear pious but actually harbour thoughts of seduction.[5] These remarks are particularly harsh, and from our point of view reflect that neurotic conviction which is sometimes encouraged by religious thinking that all women are temptresses, predestined to lead men astray. In fairness, Evagrius also writes movingly to a young woman set on the life of consecrated virginity, and counsels her not to be over-influenced by male teachers who might have designs on her virtue.[6]

Evagrius cites many examples of monks having sexual dreams, or finding themselves tantalized by sexual fantasies. But progress in defeating lust is possible. Evagrius taught that when a monk finds he is able to think of a particular woman of his past without becoming sexually excited he has reached the threshold of genuine chastity. But he advises the monk against spending too much time on conversing 'with the form of a woman in the intellect'[7] because such thoughts easily kindle desire. He also expands on the different strategies employed by the demon of lust in attempting to seduce those who are well established in the spiritual life and those who have let themselves become lax. (The former may still be surprised by a sudden attack in the form of an image or sexual thought; the latter can be overcome more gradually.)

The antidote to lust is to step up the regime of fasting; exerting a stronger control over the appetite helps to wither away unwanted desire. The monk is also recommended to pray through the night, 'hold a vigil of tears that you may receive help for the warfare at hand',[8] and to use intense, angry prayer to drive away this troubling demon: 'The boiling heat of the irascible part [of the soul] directed against this demon is extremely useful.'[9]

Evagrius seems to assume that sexual temptation will always be orientated towards the opposite sex; the only mention of same-sex relations is a warning not to employ a servant boy[10] as this might be an opportunity for 'the adversary' to provoke a scandal.

Lust and the Bible

The Bible, on the whole, accepts sex as a fact of life. As far as the Old Testament is concerned sex is necessary to the establishment of God's special people. Men and women have a vocation, given in their creation, to be fruitful and multiply. What is condemned in the Hebrew Bible is sexual behaviour which fails to produce children. The sin of Onan, who spilled his seed on the ground (Genesis 38.8–10), has been regarded as a biblical condemnation of masturbation. Onan's actual sin was a social failure rather than a question of sexual perversion. He refused to do what was regarded as his duty, and produce children with the widow of his brother. Male homosexual activity and bestiality are both condemned in the Old Testament. There is an evident double standard in what was expected of men in comparison with women. Virginity before marriage was expected only of women. Sexual activity on the part of an unmarried woman was regarded as prostitution. This could be tolerated in exceptional circumstances; the story of Rahab the harlot (Joshua 2) indicates that at least one such woman was honoured in ancient Israel. More usually, however, prostitution was punished. Adultery referred to sexual activity by a married woman outside marriage and was universally condemned. Men, on the other hand, were not judged so harshly. The patriarch Jacob had two wives and two concubines. King David and his son and successor Solomon were famous for their wives and concubines. The sexual ordering of Israelite and Jewish society left plenty of scope for bad behaviour and, not surprisingly, the Old Testament has its share of stories of intemperate sexual desire. King David lusts after Bathsheba and his lust is punished in the death of his oldest son Amnon at the hand of his half-brother Absalom, who later mounts a rebellion against his father. The book of Proverbs and the book of Ecclesiasticus are full of warnings against loose women and the dangers they pose to men. The good wife, in contrast, is praised as a paragon of wisdom and prudence.

The world reflected in the Old Testament is not unlike some societies today where the right ordering of society is thought to depend on women's lives being prescribed and controlled by their fathers and husbands. Women are regularly blamed, as they still are in many faiths and cultures, for inflaming the passions of men, and are required to prove their modesty and virtue in ways which are not generally required of men.

The Old Testament often uses sexual sin as a metaphor for unfaithfulness to God. Israel is constantly tempted to disobedience, and, in particular, to falling into the sin of idolatry. Hosea, Ezekiel and other prophets compare faithless Israel to a prostitute or an unfaithful spouse who needs to be controlled, punished and wooed back by God, her lover.

The glorious exception to the gender inequality of the Old Testament is the Song of Songs, a series of erotic dialogues depicting the love of man and woman. It is a passionate, poetic text in which there is no hint of female subjugation; both partners are equal in their desire for one another. There is no reference to God in the text, but it came to be part of the scriptural canon after a rabbinic judgement that it 'defiled the hands', which meant that it possessed a holiness which was contagious. Both Jewish and Christian commentators later tended to spiritualize the text and see its primary value as conveying mystical truth about God's relationship with humanity.

From the earliest years there were Christians for whom total sexual abstinence was a powerful sign of the priority of God's rule. Jesus himself was celibate as far as any records tell. St Paul, as we have seen, urged both men and women to take the challenge of sexual abstinence seriously, though he conceded that for those who could not restrain their urges, it was not a sin to marry. But his admiration for the single state was certainly one of the factors which led to the belief that celibacy was far superior to marriage, a prerequisite of the ascetical life.

The most commonly used word for lust in the New Testament is the word *porneia*. This means fornication, which is not only prostitution, but any kind of illegitimate sexual activity. Jesus does not preach purity at women in particular but lists both fornication and licentiousness as among the inner evils which come from every human heart (Mark 7.20–23). *Porneia* was one of the three great sins which Gentile converts to the Church were instructed to avoid, according to the decree of the Council of Jerusalem (Acts 15.28–29).

St Paul describes 'fornication, impurity and licentiousness' as 'works of the flesh' (Galatians 5.19). He often ends a letter with a list of contrasted vices and virtues in which sexual vice is prominent. Though Jesus says less about sexual sin than about avarice, anger and envy, he is unequivocal in condemning adultery, and does so in ways which condemn not only the act but the very *thought*, which he suggests is as serious as the deed itself: 'Everyone who looks at a woman with lust has already committed adultery with her in his heart' (Matthew 5.28).

The force of this teaching is in the shock of the exaggeration – which man has not looked at particular women and fantasized about them? And though male desire is usually more urgent, women too have their fantasies about men. The sharp point of Jesus' teaching is to state what is obvious, but not always admitted, which is that lust originates as an image in the mind, an image which produces the anticipation of pleasure. Lust, then, is a thought before it is a deed, a fantasy before it is any kind of relationship. Sexual fantasy, in other words, is not neutral. This is the background to what the Christian spiritual tradition teaches about sex and desire, and it runs against those tendencies in contemporary society which assume that sexual feeling and expression is harmless unless it involves betrayal.

Lust in the life of Evagrius

Evagrius was a Christian formed not only by the Bible and his Christian upbringing but by what he absorbed, consciously and unconsciously, from the philosophy and lifestyle of the ancient world. He assumed, as many of his contemporaries did, that when it came to sexual activity the mind should rule the body. The physical and mental excitement of sexual attraction and desire would have been for him a sign of the kind of disturbance which many in the ancient world found vaguely disagreeable, a reminder of animal passion and lack of control.

When Evagrius writes about lust he is chiefly concerned with its effect on the mind. Lustful thoughts, feelings and fantasies make their impression on the individual; they mould the soul and wound it, distorting its true shape and inhibiting its ability to mirror the divine. Sexual thoughts were not so much wrong in themselves as disturbances which should be avoided by those committed to the life of prayer.

Evagrius was well aware that sexual thoughts are often triggered by memory. This was probably true for him. It was his illicit affair in Constantinople which eventually caused him to flee the city for the refuge of Melania's monastery, and thence to the desert. This affair brought him considerable spiritual conflict. He was, according to his biographer Palladius,[11] 'ensnared in the contemplation of desire for a woman', who, Palladius goes on to tell

us, 'loved him in return'. The phrase 'ensnared in contemplation' is interesting because it suggests that Evagrius was infatuated by an *image* of the
person. Mental images play an important part in vulnerability to lust, as
Evagrius was only too quick to recognize. Unfortunately the woman, who
was 'of the highest social class', was already married. (The Syrian version of
Palladius' biography suggests that the affair had not been consummated,[12]
but the Greek text does not include this detail.) Evagrius' response was to
turn to prayer. He could see disaster beckoning, though it is somewhat
disturbing to modern sensibilities to read that what really worried him was
the prospect of his own social disgrace and of the delight his religious
opponents would take in his downfall. His prayer was that God would put
'some impediment in his path'. Meanwhile his paramour, no doubt sensing
his ambivalence, was becoming more demanding and hysterical, and he
found he was unable to make the break.

His prayers were answered by a dream or vision, brought to him, apparently, by an angel. He saw himself arrested, chained and imprisoned, without anyone offering any explanation as to why this had happened. The angel
then appeared and asked him, referring, significantly, to his ecclesiastical
order, 'Why is his deaconship detained here?' (One might speculate that in
his unconscious mind Evagrius' pride in his status as a deacon was still
intact!) Evagrius then, in his dream, claimed ignorance of the charge against
him, suggesting that the governor had been 'smitten by some silly jealousy'
and that 'the judge himself will be bribed with money and may punish me'.
The response, even in a dream, suggests denial – Evagrius presents himself
as the wronged victim of a trumped-up charge. The angel, however, presents himself as a friend and offers friendly advice to leave the town as it
is no longer safe for him. Evagrius still hesitated: 'May God free me from
this predicament, and if you still see me in Constantinople, know that I
would undergo this punishment without complaint.' At this point in the
narrative, Evagrius shows that he still has some integrity. He is prepared in
his dream to pay the price for his dangerous relationship. But the vision is
not yet complete, and now the angel speaks as the friend of his soul and
his true vocation: 'I will bring the Gospel; you will swear on it that you
will leave this town and will have concern for your soul, and I will free
you from this strait.' So in the vision the gospel was brought and Evagrius
swore. Perhaps there is still a moment of hesitancy, because he refuses to
leave immediately – he wants a day to pack. But as he finished making his
oath he comes out of the dream. Even though the oath was made in a dream
state, Evagrius accepted it as binding, and took ship for the Holy Land.

This was not the end of the story of Evagrius and lust. 'The spirit of
fornication' was a trial to him for many years, so much so that he was
driven to standing in a frozen well all night in an attempt to quench the
flames of passion. (Another would-be hermit, the young Benedict, threw
himself into 'some dense bushes with nettles and brambles' when stricken
by the fires of lust.[13]) Shortly before his death, Evagrius confessed that it
was only for the last three years that he had been free of carnal lusts.
And it was only after he had been freed from lust that he felt able to make

public the reason for his original departure from Constantinople. Temptation lingered on in his life. The demon of lust had a number of strategies. One was to make the victim depressed; another was to produce fantasies of conversations with friends, banquets, 'whole choruses of women' and other stimulating images designed to produce delight.[14] He may be drawing on his own experience when he suggests that the monk who desires to be chaste will take care to avoid being out in public places, and even on feast days will prefer to pray at home rather than risk the enticements of mixed company, which might result from attending a non-monastic church.[15] His nasty description of women as temptresses is deeply distasteful,[16] but it is fairly typical of the way some early Christian male ascetics tried to deal with their sexual desires.

It seems unnecessary from our perspective that this eminently intelligent radical Christian, who struggled to live a life of prayer and to develop an understanding of the dynamics of the spiritual life, was tormented by sexual desires which he was unable to accept as a natural God-given part of his nature. His demon of impurity remains one of the swiftest to attack, 'swifter than the speed of thought', as he puts it.[17] On the other hand it is important to notice that Evagrius does not reject the sexual body as such. There is nothing of the hatred, shame and disgust which has sometimes been invoked against the body by ascetics both within and outside the Christian tradition, from the Neoplatonist philosopher Plotinus who was 'ashamed of being in a body'[18] to the only recently abandoned practice of some contemplative nuns of never being naked even in the bath.

To illustrate the point that Evagrius did not hate the body as such, it is interesting that when pondering the phenomenon of nocturnal emissions Evagrius does not express any fear or disgust but simply concludes that if these occur 'in sleep without accompanying images of a stimulating nature' they might indicate that the soul is relatively healthy. However, if the sleeping monk sees distinct images (presumably of a sexual nature) this is to be taken as a clear indication of sickness, a sign of 'wounds that are still fresh'. Memory is also involved here. It is not unreasonable to speculate that Evagrius would have dreamed about his mistress for years in the desert. He came to believe that the more ill-defined the face in his dream the more it was likely to be a manifestation of a love that was over and past. An indistinct image would indicate that the soul was still marked by the impressions of an earlier emotional experience.[19]

One of the works of Evagrius that was most valued was his *Antirrhetikos*, a compilation of biblical incantations against various temptations. These are remarkable for their precision and realism. For those male monks who might be tempted to develop over-intimate relationships with those they are supposed to be giving spiritual advice to he suggests Proverbs 5.20, 'Why should you be intoxicated, my son, by another woman and embrace the bosom of an adulteress?', and comments that this text should be helpful 'against thoughts of spending hours in the company of a married woman, making frequent visits for intimate conversation, as though she were gaining spiritual assistance from our efforts'.[20]

One can't help wondering whether the 'long periods of time, with frequent visits at close quarters' was an echo of his youthful affair. But it is perhaps reassuring to know that Evagrius also recognized the attraction of the perfectly legitimate choice of marriage and family life: 'Against the demons who press upon my mind the idea that I should marry a woman and become a father of sons instead of staying here starving and fighting filthy thoughts.'[21] He did not despise sexuality for its own sake, and knew the cost of his own particular vocation.

Lust and the spiritual tradition

The word Evagrius used for lust, *porneia*, did not, at least until the Christian era, carry any great moral overtone for the majority of people. In the ruins of Pompeii in southern Italy you can still see the shape of the phallus etched in stone on the street, pointing the way to the city brothel. In the Roman world a 'prick and balls' were regarded as an everyday symbol of good luck, like a rabbit's foot or a four-leafed clover. Yet in spite of an easy acceptance of casual and commercial sex, moderation was prized in sexual life. The female ascetic Syncletica, whose sometimes caustic comments are preserved in the *Lives of the Fathers*, commented that 'Even among men of the world chastity is highly regarded.' She goes on to say, though, 'But in the world they are also stupid about it. For they peep indecently and laugh immoderately.'[22]

Married women were certainly expected to be faithful to their husbands, and men, at least those trying to pursue a virtuous life, would have believed that the appetites should be kept under rational control. Like gluttony, a 'habit' of overindulgence in sexual activity showed a lack of the virtue of temperance.

The Christian monastic tradition built on this, urging the would-be monk to seek integrity, unity within the self, rather than the fragmentation of the self which, it was believed, would be the result of sexual relationships. As the state of virginity began to acquire spiritual value, there was a growing tendency for the Christian spiritual tradition to be embarrassed by sex. There are stories from the desert era which reveal the inadequacy of some spiritual guides to cope with the sexual issues that were brought to them. One example is of a young and eager monk who was troubled by lustful thoughts. He confided in a hermit who was deeply shocked at what he told him and responded that his thoughts were a sign of his wickedness and unsuitability for the ascetic life. This threw the younger monk into despair and he concluded that he would have to return to the world. Fortunately, on his way, he met a wiser brother who encouraged him to persevere and not be overanxious. He also assured him that he, too, was troubled by thoughts of this kind.[23] This story illustrates Evagrius' concern that a monk experiencing sexual temptation might be so 'bowed down' by shame that he could easily conclude that he was unfit for the life of prayer.

Another tendency revealed by the stories was to be judgemental about others, and to assume that sexual sin has taken place where there is no evidence:

A brother, being tempted by a demon, went to a hermit and said, 'Those two monks over there who live together live sinfully.' But the hermit knew that a demon was deceiving him. So he called the brothers to him. In the evening he put out a mat for them, and covered them with a single blanket, and said, 'They are sons of God, and holy persons.' But he said to his disciple, 'Shut this slandering brother up in a cell by himself; he is suffering from the passion of which he accuses them.'[24]

Such occasional stories show that the desert fathers were aware that it was possible to be over-concerned about sex to the point of prurience. Their approach to sexuality can be criticized from another angle – they tended to see sex from an almost exclusively male point of view. *Porneia* is virtu- ally equated with women; any contact with a woman is spiritually danger- ous. They encouraged an exaggerated fear of women as the embodiment of sexual temptation, which is more pronounced than anything in the Old or New Testaments. Evagrius was not the only ascetic to be tormented by images of naked women and prostitutes. He never married, but others were saddened by thoughts of a loved wife they had abandoned in their spiritual quest. Sometimes the advice they received for dealing with sexual tempta- tion was extreme and cruel. Aunts and even mothers were seen as dangerous conveyers of temptation. One dreadful story tells of an ascetic who was travelling with his elderly mother. When they came to a river they found that the only way she could get across was if her son carried her. So he did so, but not before wrapping his cloak round his hands so that he avoided direct contact with her. 'His mother said to him, "Why did you wrap up your hands like that, my son?" He said, "Because a woman's body is fire. Simply because I was touching you, the memory of other women might come into my mind." '[25] This is an extreme example, more extreme than anything found in Evagrius' writings.

We would say today that such anxiety about the danger of sexual thoughts leads to a fear of women that is unholy and inhuman. There are many examples of such behaviour and attitudes in Evagrius' desert world, though they do not go without criticism. One monk who turned off the road to avoid meeting some travelling nuns was roundly rebuked by their abbess: 'If you had been a perfect monk, you would not have looked at us, and you would not have known that we *were* women.'[26]

The life of the desert also attracted women, and among them many with strong sexual desires. There is a particular genre of desert literature which refers to these women, many of whom are depicted as converted prostitutes. Mary of Egypt is an archetype of such ascetic women, and the legends which grew up around her are later applied to Mary Magdalene – there are elaborate stories of the years she spent in solitude and penitence after the resurrection.

What is missing in the early period of the Church's life is any real cele- bration of the spiritual value of marriage and family life. Marriage was almost always seen as a third best way of life after virginity and widow- hood (though of course one has to be have been married to acquire the status of being a widow!). Evagrius' contemporary, Jerome, was convinced that marriage could not be undertaken without sin. Others, including Augustine, while allowing for marriage, thought that the pleasure involved in sexual activity could not be enjoyed without sin. These attitudes have been formative for the Christian spiritual tradition and still persist to some extent to this day, however much they are deplored. One only has to look at the calendar of saints to see how few married people make it into the top ranks of holiness.

Evagrius' condemnation of *porneia* was taken up by John Cassian who wrote at length of the battle against the 'spirit of fornication'.[27] For Cassian this battle was an epic one, beginning at puberty and only ending when all other vices have been conquered. Like Evagrius, he saw the struggle as having both physical and spiritual dimensions. Abstinence from sex is doubtless part of the monastic vocation, but it needs to be reinforced by an inner chastity. Mere avoidance of sex is not enough. True chastity involves an active desire for purity.[28] To reinforce this desire Cassian recommends that monks should discipline themselves as athletes might for a contest, abstaining from the sort of food and drink that might tempt them to relax their efforts, shunning unhelpful company or worrying about worldly issues. Cassian tells us that it was a practice of men engaged in athletic competitions to cover their lower bodies with lead plates to prevent erections at night which might dissipate their strength.[29] He does not actually recommend that monks follow this example, but, like Evagrius, Cassian urges them to shun mental images of women and to avoid, as far as possible, actual contact with the opposite sex. He also pondered about nocturnal emissions and came to the conclusion that a monk was not doing too badly if these occurred only once every two months.

Although the basic elements of Evagrius' teaching on lust is simply passed on by Cassian, there are important differences. Where Evagrius sees the monk's struggle with sexual temptation primarily in terms of avoidance, Cassian requires more than abstinence from sexual acts and a refusal to entertain sexual fantasies; there must be a positive attempt to establish chastity in the heart. Sexual temptation can never be overcome without humility: 'It is necessary for us to endure the attacks of this vice until we acknowledge that we are fighting a war beyond our strength.'[30] Cassian implies – rather more than Evagrius – that human beings are simply helpless in the face of sexual temptation.

Cassian had good reason to take a rather different approach to sexual temptation from that of Evagrius. One of the questions which had arisen in the communities of monks that Cassian had founded in Aquitaine was what they were to make of the good qualities of the pre-Christian philosophers, many of whom advocated Christian virtues, such as chastity and frugality. Cassian's instinct was to commend such philosophers, but he was embroiled in the controversy that followed Augustine's sustained campaign against the teaching of Pelagius. With Augustine's condemnation of Pelagius in mind, Cassian wrote in the thirteenth of his *Conferences* that though it could rightly be said that such philosophers practised *continence*, they did not practise true *chastity*, which could only be received as a gift of God. Nowhere, Cassian says, is the role of free will more apparent than in the struggle to attain and preserve chastity.[31] God's grace is effective both in evoking a free response from human beings, and in encouraging and strengthening the genuine desire for God which arises spontaneously in the human heart. In going some way to compromise with Augustine's teaching, Cassian raised the stakes a little, expressing a rather deeper pessimism about human sexuality than earlier generations had assumed, even though his larger aim was to preserve the more optimistic and universal insights he had encountered in his time in the Egyptian desert. What he found most objectionable about Augustine's teaching was that grace should be limited to a few. He feared that such teaching would be deeply discouraging to those struggling to hold on to an ascetical lifestyle. If God had decided in advance who would be saved and who would be damned, what was the point of the monks' sacrificial lifestyle? In making a small concession to Augustine's thought it could be said that he brought the end he dreaded a little nearer, for Augustine had come to the infamous view that sexual intercourse was the mechanism by which all human beings were infected with original sin.

To summarize: the first pioneers of desert spirituality saw the human body as a kind of medium which could be modified by will and practice to serve the needs of the spiritual life. Fasting, scant sleep and mental dis-cipline would transform the body into a site well guarded against demonic attack and ever more transparent to the activity of the Spirit. Evagrius inherited this tradition. For him sexual temptation was a serious issue, and lust indulged in thought or deed was a barrier to prayer. Yet there is little in Evagrius' writings which suggests a suspicion and hatred of the sexual body itself. Sexual temptation is almost a *technical* issue for Evagrius, a fact of life which the demons exploit and which has to be dealt with by tak-ing appropriate precautions. Jerome, on the other hand, who distrusted Evagrius, seems to have been much troubled by sexual temptation, as was Augustine. Cassian was by instinct closer to the spirit of Evagrius than to his Latin-thinking contemporaries, but he was also a pragmatist and a politician and he knew how to shape the tradition he had received to meet new sensitivities.

However, it was Augustine's teaching that came to permeate the life of the Latin-thinking Church. Augustine accepted the biblical account of cre-ation with its clear teaching that God wished the human race to propagate itself. Unable to accept the irrationality of the sexual impulse he suggested that in the Garden of Eden intercourse would have taken place without sexual arousal or pleasure; the organs of generation would have been under the control of the will.[32] The result of the fall has been that human beings no longer have control over their own bodies.[33] The shame of lust is where human beings reveal most clearly their alienation from God. Sexual sin then becomes an almost archetypal sin; the sin of disobedience is intensified and concentrated in sexual pleasure.

Augustine's teaching had a deep effect on Gregory the Great. For Gregory the fundamental human problem is our addiction to pleasure. This is a consequence of our embodied state. The real needs of the body make us constantly vulnerable to desire. Since we lost the capacity for obedience to God in the fall, God has given us over to our self-sufficiency and we experience a compulsion to seek the pleasurable satisfaction of our bodily impulses. Of all the impulses of the body the craving for sex is the hardest to cope with, the most obviously unruly, in that the male organ responds to sexual stimuli automatically and obviously. So the shame of lust is its own punishment, a peculiarly intense example of what is involved in original sin. Gregory uses the Latin word *luxuria* for lust, a word which originates in the idea of something out of place, or out of joint, and comes to have the meaning of debauchery. There is always a sense of surfeit and excess involved, hence our word luxury, which does not always have a sexual meaning, but does suggest a decadent immersion in comfort or pleasure.

For Gregory lust was a significant branch on the deadly tree of sin. Because Gregory sees sin as inextricably linked to our bodily nature he intensifies the tendency for Christian spirituality to involve a hatred and distrust of the body, and especially of the sexual body. Also, through his acceptance of the theory of the humours, he would see the female body as being particularly dangerous. The hard, muscular male body might be thought to express a well-disciplined and defended Christian self; the softer female form is much more of a problem. As one of the principal sins, lust gives rise to lesser sins, which Gregory lists as blindness of mind, lack of consideration, inconstancy, rashness, self-love, hatred of God, an obsession with the present moment and despair about the future.[34]

Gregory sets the tone for what the Western spiritual tradition has to say about lust. But it is important to notice that Benedict of Nursia, the ascetic teacher whom Gregory most admired, had remarkably little to say about it. What he does say can be briefly summarized. In discussing the first steps towards humility he speaks of the importance of recognizing that our sensual desires are not hidden from God. We should therefore be on guard against evil desires.[35] Benedict does not dwell on this point, and even suggests that God may give a little leeway during this life, though he also warns that God's patience does not last for ever. Persistent failure to control sexual desire will eventually be punished. He also dictates the sleeping arrangements in his monasteries. The young are not to be put together, but dispersed among the older monks, and the monks are to sleep clothed.[36] So Benedict on this subject, as often, is cautious and realistic. He does not threaten or exaggerate, but expects his monks to act responsibly, neither concealing from themselves, or God, the desires which they find troubling, but taking steps to ensure they do not encourage temptation.

In spite of the more negative strands in the Church's teaching the human race continued after Gregory and, of course, the majority of Christians did not adopt religious life, but married and were given in marriage, and had children who did the same, even though they were encouraged to believe that monastic life was a higher calling. During the early Middle Ages the Church presumed a high degree of control over people's sex lives. Intercourse was banned on all fasts and some feasts and on certain days of the

week and seasons. There were punishments and penances of graded severity to deal with infringements of the Church's sexual code. But in all this
excessive concern it is possible to find a more moderate response to the
complexities of sexual desire and temptation.

In his *Summa Theologiae*, Thomas Aquinas considers the views of Augustine
and Gregory on lust, and in the light of their teaching reflects on whether
the sex act can ever be without sin. Thankfully he concludes that sex has
to be seen in the light of the purpose of life, in which the continuance of
the human race is a good thing. Although it is true that the pleasure involved
in the sex act might 'cast the soul down from its peak' it is wrong to say
that it deflects the soul from virtue. If this were true of sex, it would also
be true of sleep. Aquinas concludes that 'The abundance of pleasure in a
well-ordered sex act is not inimical to right reason.'[37] What Aquinas then
goes on to do is to determine what a well-ordered sex act might be, and thus
to separate out what he sees as legitimate sexual activity from that which
does not serve the purpose of creation.

Aquinas also and interestingly raises the question of what might be called
the opposite of lust, which he characterizes as 'unfeelingness'. He says that
this is not often encountered because most people are drawn to pleasure.
But he regards this level of coldness as a vice, and criticizes it in those men
who 'so dislike intimacy with women that they are unfair to their wives'.[38]

This is a very different voice from that of the earlier tradition, a voice
that is beginning to work its way towards a theology of intimacy that might
measure up to the kind of hopes and aspirations of modern and post-
modern times. Aquinas' cool discussion takes some of the steam out of the
Church's debate about lust and it leaves the way open for more positive
developments. The problem is that his insistence on the morality of others'
acts being judged by their ends, which he takes from the philosophy of
Aristotle, leaves the Church without any theological reason for seeing sexual
pleasure as a good in itself, or even as a legitimate means to build up affection and stable love. This is why the Catholic Church continues to teach
that the only legitimate sexual acts are within heterosexual marriage, and
must be open to the possibility of conception.

Dante is relatively kind to at least some of the lustful. He recognizes that
properly ordered sexual activity is good and within the will of God for
humanity. Lust is a sin that usually implies relationship, and therefore a
striving for the good. Desire is not sinful for Dante, it is a dim reflection
of the call of God within us drawing us to himself. Desire, even when perverted, still bears a relationship to our longing to love and be loved. Our
human problem is how to deal with sexual desire within the laws of God.
In his *Inferno*, those whose lust has led them into relationships are condemned to the upper circles of hell just above limbo where the unbaptized
and virtuous pagans are suspended in an indeterminate state. The lustful are
condemned to drift for ever in a black wind of helpless desire; they experience in eternity the consequence of being 'carried away' by their passions.
Dante's generosity is not extended to those whose sexual sins were thought
unnatural. Sodomites are classed among the violent against nature and

occupy a lower level of hell where their punishment is to have to run for ever without purpose or goal.

In purgatory, where sin is finally healed, the lustful are purged by fire and then work out their penance on the terrace nearest to the summit. In Dante's vision the lustful are not the greatest of sinners, but their position in purgatory puts them nearest to the remission of sins. Their therapy is curious – those repentant of natural lust and those repentant of unnatural lust are to run in opposite directions round the terrace, circling the mountain, and greeting each other as they pass with chaste kisses!

Evagrius, lust and us

Returning to Evagrius it is clear that his chief concern was not with deeds so much as with thoughts. He was more a psychologist than a moralist; he tried to describe and analyse the vulnerabilities and disturbances about sexuality which go on in the mind of someone trying to live a chaste and holy life. This raises questions for us today because it is not entirely clear what constitutes a chaste and holy life. The current general rule, which is in line with the broad sweep of Christian tradition, is that sexual expression takes place properly only within marriage, though some would want to extend this to other committed and exclusive relationships.

But it is dishonest not to acknowledge that Christianity has perpetuated some dreadful sexual hang-ups. It is not beyond living memory that Catholic schoolgirls were told to emulate the practice of nuns and never to look at their naked bodies, or that extraordinary attempts were made to conceal menstruation. The early Christians absorbed some of the negative attitudes to sex and the body which were prevalent in the ancient world, and in some respects intensified them by seeing the body as the gateway to sin. This ran counter to the more general tolerance which we find in Greek and Roman culture. Both the negativity and the tolerance were expressions of sexual pessimism. Most people in the ancient world regarded sexual activity as inevitable, even necessary, but they did not really see it as a way to personal fulfilment as many believe it is today. Perhaps we are wrong, and we expect too much of sexual relationships. But the Song of Songs reminds us that at least some men and women have always dreamed of the possibility of deep personal fulfilment through sexual intimacy. The rabbis accepted it as a holy book because it simply celebrates the erotic instinct in a way that even the ascetically minded have been unable to ignore. It also indicates why lust might be a particular problem for those drawn to a life of prayer. People who feel attracted, drawn to or even driven to seek intimacy with God are perhaps also likely to long for intimacy with others. The loneliness of religious life sharpens both desires, and it is perhaps not surprising that many committed to a life of prayer have found themselves constantly distracted by sexual thoughts and fantasies.

So what are we to make of this? Our society is two-faced about sex and sexuality. We like to believe that we are adult and tolerant and have a healthy attitude to sex and relationships. But in practice there is an unrestrained appetite for sexual titillation which has nothing to do with actual relationships. As part of this the word 'lust' is often used with an edge of humour and approval as though it were something to boast of. We do not speak much of 'impurity' or 'uncleanness', though there is the prurient use of the word 'filth' to describe sexual behaviour or innuendo which goes beyond the boundaries of acceptability. But there is very little clarity about what the boundaries of acceptability are. It has been rather shocking to a generation which took sexual liberation for granted to find that minority communities – Muslims, Hindus and some old-fashioned Christians – claim to have much stricter codes of personal sexual morality. To the liberalized majority it is only the rather old-fashioned word 'lechery' which suggests something rather distasteful, the gloating, predatory appetite of unattractive older men for younger women. The word 'fornication' has almost fallen out of use. At the same time there is in our society an enormous concern for the young, that they should not be corrupted or damaged by being exposed to the sexual interests of adults. This is contradicted by the constant exposure of young people to adult sexuality through media and advertising.

We might well be wrong simply to assume that our contemporary attitudes to sexuality are much more healthy than those assumed by Evagrius, Cassian, Augustine and Gregory. There have been some real advances – it is less publicly plausible these days for men to blame their desires on women, though some still do. (Disturbingly, this occurs quite often in communities where religion is most important as a marker of identity.) It is an advance to be able to accept that we really are sexual beings, and that God created us with sexual desires and appetites. In theory we understand that we need to teach our children how to express their sexuality appropriately. But many parents are over-afraid of giving them hang-ups, and do not always commend the virtues of self-restraint and discrimination. The lonely and the anxious are too easily pressured into sexual relationships that they do not really want and are not ready for. We are sometimes dishonest about the way in which obsessiveness, secrecy and shame often accompany sexual passion, particularly where it is regarded as illicit. The sense of being 'bowed down' by sexual desire is still common, especially among those of high moral and spiritual ideals. In a strange way that Evagrius recognized, those who are strictest in their practice of continence seem most likely to be haunted by temptation. There is a fascination with filth, a conflict between attraction and revulsion to obscene language and gestures which hover in the recesses even of upright Christian souls. The Roman Catholic Church demands the highest standards of sexual continence from its clergy, and yet it is precisely among the clergy of the Catholic Church that a really damaging form of sexual abuse against children has become alarmingly widespread.

Though much has changed it remains true that sexuality and prayer still do not go together easily. Perhaps they cannot. Prayer is a preparation for heaven; the Christian view of sex is that it is for this life only. Marriage is guarded by vows which are to last 'until death us do part': 'When they rise from the dead they neither marry nor are given in marriage' (Mark 12.26). Christians believe in a God who created sexuality; but God is not sexual in anything like the way that we are. God created the universe by the speaking of the Word, not by any kind of divine intercourse. The love and mutuality within the persons of the Trinity transcend both the intimacy and the happiness of human sexual relations; though these perhaps give us some inkling of what the life of the Trinity might be like. All this is to say that there is a real tension between the ultimate goal of Christian life, that is, the vision of God, and the relationships of love and passion which give us so much anguish and joy on earth. In some ways, it was simpler for Evagrius and his like because they did not even *attempt* to integrate sexual love with spiritual love. What we need to remember is that at this stage Evagrius was not interested in sexual morality as such. And by not being so he provides us with another insight which is useful. Whatever we think about the attitudes to sex that the desert fathers and mothers manifest, they are right up to a point in their analysis of sexual fantasy. Sexual fantasy can become obsessive to the point of idolatry. We might also reflect that it is self-defeating not only because it hinders prayer, but because it proscribes genuine relationships. A genuine relationship is negotiated and discovered, not imposed by one partner upon the other.

Evagrius' embarrassment about sex invites us to ask some searching questions because he, and the other desert monks, faced in an extreme way the temptation which belongs to all of us. Our imaginations are constantly being stimulated by suggestive sexual imagery. Our culture encourages sexual fantasy as a permanent background wallpaper to daily life. We are all tempted to impose our own sexual imaginings and fantasies on those to whom we are attracted, and then to blame them when they fail to fulfil these; or indeed even when they succeed in fulfilling these. Sexuality, for all its promise, and for all the hopes of happiness that it brings, is still a powerful and potentially fragmenting force. I remember being chastened when a young man who worked for me told me of what happened when he consulted a Christian counsellor about his strong sexual feelings, only to be told that they were natural and healthy, and that he should simply befriend his desires. Yet, as he told me, his problem was not how to befriend his desires but how to prevent them from ruining his life. In the desire to be tolerant and free from hang-ups the well-meaning counsellor had not listened to what was being said.

The attempt to integrate spiritual and sexual love is a lifelong task, because we are designed to love and desire. The problem of sexual temptation has much to do with anxiety. Anxiety can feel like guilt; it weighs on the spirit in a very similar way, and hinders prayer because it produces similar feelings of unworthiness. Evagrius is aware of this. The person under sexual temptation feels that the commitment they have undertaken is beyond their power to fulfil. Shame enters the recesses of the soul and hinders the sense of freedom before God.

Evagrius believed that the control of the passions was the beginning of true prayer, which for him was contemplation. What he meant was that the soul, once freed from its inner turbulence, would begin to see things as they really are, as they are held and sustained by God. He is telling us that we can only really see the landscape ahead of us if we remove from our field of vision the shadows cast by our own desires and excitements. Love and lust, for Evagrius, were in the end incompatible. It is only being free of desire or possession that the soul comes to real knowledge, the kingdom of God and the vision of the Trinity.

What he could not see was that this freedom might be attainable by those whose lust is tamed and ordered by becoming an expression of faithful and fruitful love of one person for another. Many can testify to the fact that when lust is accompanied by, or becomes, genuine love, we feel that we are seeing the person that we love not simply as the object of our own desires but in some extraordinary and unexpected way as they truly are. This insight is sometimes miraculously given at the beginning of a loving relationship, when the miracle for the lover is simply that the other person *is*; their very being is a gift. It is as though we have been let into a divine secret. But though this is true, sexual desire does not last for ever. Evagrius is right in seeing that love transcends lust; when desire fails, love endures. Millions of human relationships down the ages bear witness to that fact.

7

The thought of avarice

Love of money (avarice) suggests a long old age, and the inevitable inability to earn one's keep with one's hands. On top of that, there will be famines, illnesses will visit us and the bitterness of poverty, and with all that the terrible shame of having to accept the necessities of life from others.[1]

Comment

Love of money is the third thought which makes people vulnerable to demonic attack. The word Evagrius uses is *philarguria*, which literally means love of silver. He identifies avarice as a 'passion of the soul', which means it is not located in the higher rational soul but in the lower parts, which are subject to the disturbances of strong feeling and bodily desire. Avarice comes just 'above' lust and gluttony, which are passions of the body. The passions of body and soul are not easily healed; Evagrius observed that they hold out until death.[2] In his consideration of avarice Evagrius is clearly reflecting the teaching of Jesus in the Gospels about the danger of accumulating possessions. Again, Evagrius' summary in the *Praktikos* is short and leaves out a good deal that he says elsewhere and that plays an important part in the developed tradition. Love of money is usually personified in terms of the miser, the hoarder, the person who preys on the fortunes of others and is obsessed by gold. This figure was well known in the classical world and is satirized in Greek and Roman comedy. The hoarder is thin and unkempt; his chief concern is not for what money can buy but for the accumulation of it, the sheer pleasure of possession. Greed, for the hoarder, is an end in itself.

Yet, as we saw with the way Evagrius treated gluttony, he does not simply accept the caricature of avarice, but links it to anxieties and dreads which are both common and ordinary. In this, though it may not at first be obvious, he is also following close to the gospel teaching which commends trust in God as an antidote to anxiety about material needs such as food and clothing. Old age, infirmity, loss of income through retirement, disability or, in our time, inadequate pension provision – these anxieties provide the soil in which avarice grows. Fears may spring up about wider issues, shortages, illnesses, chronic poverty, and, worst of all, being dependent on others. These ordinary human issues are not really addressed by later spiritual writers who simply condemn avarice as a vice without understanding its emotional roots and how these provoke all too familiar anxieties.

It is not entirely clear whether Evagrius thought that avarice was one of the compulsions that came from the concupiscible part of the lower soul or from the irascible part, which he thought was located in the heart. Love of money is certainly aroused by strong desire; and for Evagrius this was primarily the desire for comfort and security. Evagrius saw avarice as a hindrance to the freedom offered by monastic life, which required the embracing of insecurity as its condition. Even after the initial withdrawal into solitude the monk would be tempted by avarice, sometimes in subtle forms, to keep aside a little more than was strictly needed in order to have resources available for others, for example. Yet for Evagrius possessions weigh down the soul and indicate enslavement to the material world and its values, its approval of wealth and the status given to the wealthy. To embrace the monastic habit meant giving up all this for something far more satisfying and lasting: the wealth of the knowledge of God.

Avarice and the Bible

Avarice as love of money is most clearly condemned in the Bible in the First Letter to Timothy:

> Those who want to be rich fall into temptation and are trapped by many senseless and harmful desires that plunge people into ruin and destruction. For the love of money is a root of all kinds of evil, and in their eagerness to be rich some have wandered away from the faith and pierced themselves with many pains. (1 Timothy 6.9–10)

The phrase 'the love of money is the root of all evil' is memorable both in the original and in translation and it has stuck, becoming something of a proof text of the dangers of accumulating wealth.

The Old Testament does not condemn riches as such. Solomon was gifted with great riches. Job had his fortune restored after his trials. Prosperity when it is allied to virtue is a sign of blessing, and the point of Solomon's wealth is that he did not pray to be wealthy, but to be wise. It was a requirement of the law of Israel that God's people should offer a proportion of the produce of the land and of any earnings, usually one tenth, to God.[3] It is acceptable in the Old Testament to pray for prosperity. But prosperity brings dangers and wealth is not always allied to virtue. The prophetic books are fierce in their condemnation of those who defraud the poor, or use their economic muscle to deprive the poor of their wages, rights or property. The wickedness here is not the fascination with wealth in itself but covetousness; the greedy desire for what rightly belongs to someone else.

Covetousness, in fact, is the last of the Ten Commandments. It is clearly designed to censure theft and promote social harmony. 'You shall not covet your neighbour's house, you shall not covet your neighbour's wife, or male or female slave, or ox, or donkey, or anything that belongs to your neighbour' (Exodus 20.17).

The most obvious story of covetousness in the Old Testament is of King Ahab's greedy desire to acquire the vineyard which belonged to his neighbour Naboth (1 Kings 21). Ahab wanted to make it a vegetable garden, but Naboth refused to give it up. Ahab was consumed by his covetousness – he sulked and took himself to bed. The result was the plot of Jezebel which led to Naboth's murder. Covetousness also appears in the story of David's desire for Bathsheba; covetousness in this case is allied to lust and also ends in the murder of Bathsheba's innocent husband (2 Samuel 11).

Avarice is not quite the same as covetousness, but the same emotions are involved. There is the greedy brooding for what one does not have, and the plotting and planning of how to acquire it. The most pointed story of avarice in the Old Testament is about the servant of Elisha, Gehazi, who tries to extort money from Naaman, the Syrian general whom Elisha has healed from leprosy (2 Kings 5.15–27). When he realized that he had been healed, Naaman begs Elisha to accept a gift, but Elisha refuses. Gehazi notices this and his desire for gain is aroused; he feels that Elisha let the Syrian off too lightly. The prophet's contempt for payment gives Gehazi an opportunity to get something for himself. So he pursues Naaman with a false message from Elisha to the effect that he has unexpected visitors and would, after all, like some silver and some clothing in return for his services. Naaman gladly and innocently hands over what Gehazi asks for, and more. But when he returns, the prophet has guessed at his deceitfulness. Punishment quickly follows. The leprosy of Naaman falls on Gehazi and his descendants for ever.

The New Testament is much more radical in its condemnation of those who accumulate wealth, where it is frequently seen as a positive hindrance to salvation. Jesus was adamant that those who followed him should be prepared to give up their possessions. The rich are in fact condemned outright in Luke's version of the Beatitudes (Luke 6.24), and the rich young man, who cannot bear to part with his possessions, disqualifies himself from following Jesus and goes sadly away (Matthew 19.20–22). Jesus insists that it will be hard, if not impossible, for the rich to enter the Kingdom of heaven (Matthew 19.23–24). The parable of the sower describes the seed which was choked by the thorns growing around it. This is interpreted as the fate of those who hear the word of God, 'but the cares of the world and the lure of wealth choke the word, and it yields nothing' (Matthew 13.22). The parable of the rich fool (Luke 12.13–21) suggests the folly of trusting to accumulated wealth as it can do nothing to save us from death and judgement.

The essential point of the gospel teaching is that material treasures have such a powerful pull on human life that it is impossible to serve God and involve oneself with them. Breaking the link is hard, but the counter-attraction is the Kingdom of God, which Jesus shrewdly compares to treasure hidden in a field (Matthew 13.44) and a priceless pearl (Matthew 13.45). In this he is following the Old Testament Wisdom tradition in which the knowledge of wisdom and her instruction is considered better than gold and silver (Proverbs 8.18). But Jesus goes much further than this. Everything material that can be possessed is corruptible; moth, rust and theft eventually reduce accumulated wealth to nothing. The only treasures genuinely worth storing are treasures in heaven, 'for where your treasure is, there your heart will be also' (Matthew 6.19–21). Avarice is a matter of the heart, of what attracts the heart and what the heart is focused on. Though Jesus urges his disciples to give their wealth and possessions to the poor, there is no clear 'social justice agenda'. This is not about the redistribution of wealth, but freeing the disciple's heart from bondage to money: 'You cannot serve God and money' (Matthew 6.24, GNB).

St Paul instructs members of the church in Corinth to set aside a proportion of their income for the needs of the church in Jerusalem. He has given similar instructions to the Galatian church (1 Corinthians 16.1–2). Giving must be a free act, for 'God loves a cheerful giver' (2 Corinthians 9.7). The Pastoral Epistles set out the ethical requirements of Christian life in a pagan world, often drawing on classical notions of vice and virtue. The key text from the First Letter to Timothy urges the virtue of contentment: 'We brought nothing into the world, so that we can take nothing out of it; but if we have food and clothing, we will be content with these' (1 Timothy 6.7–8). The first half of this quotation is often read as one of the funeral sentences, a reminder of the ultimate folly of the accumulation of riches, frequently summed up in the phrase, 'You can't take it with you.'

On a rather different note, the Letter of James mocks the rich who face divine judgement for their fraud and affluent lifestyle. They are regarded as having crucified Christ (James 5.1–5). In similar vein the book of Revelation gloats over the judgement of Babylon – here a symbolic name for Rome – and the downfall of all those who have accumulated wealth under the rule of the empire or profited from its commerce (Revelation 18.9–19). A condemnation of all who are involved in trade is also found in the apocryphal *Gospel of Thomas*, but there is no equivalent of this in the biblical Gospels. In fact Jesus took for granted a world of buying and selling, and even draws a parallel between achieving a good profit on investments and the obedience which leads to fruitfulness (Luke 19.11–24). This story, the parable of the talents, particularly in Luke's version, does not condemn the two servants who took risks with their master's money. It was the cautious, anxious servant, afraid of his master's judgement, who wrapped the money in a cloth and buried it in the ground who was condemned. If this is avarice, the spiritual error is to treat money with the reverence that is owed to the dead. It should be used, circulated and not held on to.

Avarice in the life of Evagrius

Avarice, in Evagrius' analysis, is not simply wickedness, selfishness or a desire to cheat the poor. It may include those things of course, and may result in them, but its starting place is usually the vulnerability of feeling insecure. It is often assumed that the desert ascetics dropped out of society simply because they were disillusioned, and that extreme poverty was something they gladly and easily embraced. But this was not the case, as stories about monks secretly hoarding treasures or holding on to property they should have disposed of bear witness. Evagrius had been 'delicately reared in a refined and fastidious manner of life',[4] and, if he had continued his ecclesiastical career in Constantinople, he would have had no reason to fear an impoverished old age. As it was, when he withdrew to the desert, he made a small income from his ability to write. His biographer tells us that he had very beautiful handwriting, and it is likely that, as well as producing his own compositions, he occupied himself in copying manuscripts.

But he did not do this for profit. He took care not to take on more work than was required for his immediate needs: 'He wrote during the year only the price of as much as he ate.' This suggests that Evagrius resisted the impulse to put a little aside for a rainy day, because he clearly thought that it was spiritually dangerous to make such provision. In his *Ad Monachos*, his advice for monks, he says:

> He who loves money will not see knowledge
> and he who amasses it will become dark in himself.[5]

The knowledge referred to here is the contemplative knowledge of God, which, for Evagrius, is the whole purpose and end of prayer. Being concerned to make a little extra money would have obliterated the freedom he needed to reach contemplation. This may have been because it would have meant spending more time on earning his keep than strictly necessary, and therefore limiting the time he was able to spend in prayer. Maybe he feared creating a demand for his work which he then would have felt obliged to satisfy. Or perhaps he was worried that the habit of saving would feed anxiety about the future, and having started to save money he would find that he needed more and more in order to feel secure. Evagrius had no quarrel with the aim of self-sufficiency. Monks were to use their skills to earn their keep. But he believed that the exchange of money was never innocent.[6] He advised those beginning religious life to deliberately aim at making a small loss on any financial transactions, to avoid an over-concern with exact fairness that might lead to greed. He also recommended entrusting any necessary buying and selling to another person.

Evagrius sees anxiety about clothes or food as forbidden by the gospel. Christians should be more trusting than their pagan counterparts and realize that they are looked after by the angels.[7] They should be content to live in old and shabby clothes, because anything newer or more fashionable could lead to vainglory.[8]

Anxiety about material well-being is a hindrance to the mind, and the monk must constantly struggle to throw it off, and try to fix the mind to the true treasure. The antidote to anxiety is to be proactive in giving money away, and trusting that in the counter-cultural economy of the gospel, almsgiving is a better insurance than holding on to what he might earn.

> The monk who gives no alms will himself be in need,
> but the one who feeds the poor will inherit treasures.[9]

Evagrius also helps us to understand that there are treasures of creation given freely, in which we may legitimately rejoice. In a collection of reflections on the evil thoughts Evagrius suggests that thoughts about the treasures of the earth – gold, for example – should not be simply rejected. If they come into the mind innocently they can lead to contemplation of the wonder and beauty of creation. Evagrius tells us that thoughts such as these come to us from angels whose intention is to encourage us to 'seek to discover the nature of things and their spiritual meaning'.[10] The thought of gold can lead to a fruitful reflection on why it exists, and why it is so rare and valuable. Such reflections can lead to thoughts about the use of gold in making objects used in worship and the spiritual treasures these might symbolize. To think along these lines is, says Evagrius, to imitate Cleopas, whose heart burns with the mysteries of God (Luke 24.32). The demonic thought of gold, though, has no understanding of this kind of contemplation and produces the thought of gold only to suggest it as an object of acquisition. In other words the demon of avarice tempts us to see the resources of our earth only in terms of their monetary value; the contemplative seeks to see them as integral and beautiful parts of creation.

Avarice in the spiritual tradition

Early Christianity spread among the mostly uneducated urban lower class; migrants, slaves and women were particularly attracted to it. Luke suggests that the early Jerusalem church held all things in common, but this is likely to be an idealization. However, the example he gives of an attempt to disguise personal wealth reflects an attitude that probably was widespread in the early Church. The story of Ananias and Sapphira (Acts 5.1–5), who withheld part of their profits from a property sale, was often quoted as a proof text against the rich, the ungenerous and those who seemed half-hearted in their commitment. With this was a robust criticism of wealth and affluence, which shows not only the influence of the Bible but of the old Stoic virtues of the Roman Republic which were hostile to any form of ostentatious lifestyle. There was a class of wandering preachers in the ancient world who scorned wealth and material possessions. Many of them were influenced by the teachings of Diogenes (400–323 BC) whose behaviour earned him the title 'Cynic', which means dog. The Cynic philosophers lived in extreme simplicity and encouraged others to sit lightly to the seductions of money, status and materialism. Early Christian ascetics were sometimes mistaken for such wandering philosophers, and the radical teaching and alternative lifestyle of the Cynic preachers may well have influenced the early Christian movement.

It was not until the end of the second century that there were enough affluent Christians for wealth to have become a theological and moral issue. Clement of Alexandria was the first to suggest that the problem of wealth lies in the attitude the wealthy person has to it. He taught that it was indeed possible for a Christian to be rich, as long as wealth was matched with perfect detachment and generosity of heart. But his teaching was not universally accepted. Tirades against wealth are common in the writings of the Church fathers, as they are in certain parts of the New Testament. Evagrius' contemporary John Chrysostom, the brilliant, austere Patriarch of Constantinople (347–407), argued that not to share with the poor was a form of theft, and that just investment of wealth in those who had need of it was a guarantee of salvation.[11] What everyone agreed about was the sinfulness of taking interest on money that was loaned. Usury was condemned by both Plato and Aristotle. It was believed to be in some way unnatural, a form of theft. Money is not a living thing, and it should not be treated as if it were. Money cannot and should not breed.

By the middle of the third century there were enough middle-class Christians for them to form a significant minority of the imperial civil service. It was about this time that a trickle of individuals began to seek the austere way of life of the desert. Antony of Egypt, who is regarded as the founder of Christian monasticism, abandoned his former village life in order to follow the challenge of Christ to give all away to the poor and follow him. Antony himself was stern about those who thought they could get the benefits of desert life without stripping themselves of wealth. Like Ananias and Sapphira they would find they were self-deceived. 'Those who renounce the world but want to keep their money are attacked . . . by demons and torn in pieces.'[12]

Evagrius himself is quoted in the Sayings of the Fathers as telling of a brother who owned nothing except a book of the Gospels, which he sold to provide money to feed the poor. His memorable response to his own action was to say, quite truthfully, 'I have sold even the word that commands me to sell all and give to the poor.'[13]

The monks were fierce about the importance of poverty. To them, the poverty of Jesus was an obvious model, and his teaching on trusting God to supply one's basic needs, coupled with a willingness to give and share with others, needed no further justification. Any attempt by an aspiring monk to hang on to personal possessions such as a hood, a few coins or a handful of books provoked angry criticism from others. One story tells of an ascetic who was a working gardener, generous in giving alms, who fell into the typical trap that Evagrius warns about, of trying to keep a little extra for when he was old. He began to store his spare coins in a pot. After a while he developed gangrene in his foot. Facing the possibility of having to have his foot amputated he recognized that the real gangrene was in his pot of coins. Before the surgeon came to operate he repented and was instantly healed by an angel.[14]

For the desert fathers and mothers the accumulation of more than is necessary is a symptom of a spiritual sickness, a basic failure in trust. The sharpness of this insight was somewhat softened when John Cassian interpreted Evagrius' teaching as the basis for monastic life in the West. Cassian taught that avarice is not a fault which arises from our natural needs, but one that has to be learnt. The sins of our appetites, lust and gluttony, arise from the nature of the body, and their origins can be discerned even in children, though they are innocent of the sins they might lead to.[15] But avarice has no preceding cause in nature, it is a fault that has to be acquired. For this reason, avaricious desires should in theory be easily repelled, but 'if they gain a hold over the mind they make it miserable'.[16] Cassian follows Evagrius in showing how the roots of avarice lie in anxiety, fastening on a monk who is, perhaps, a bit sluggish and lazy and worrying about whether the monastery he belongs to can really provide enough for his particular needs.[17] He begins to accumulate small amounts and then greater ones, and then he has to worry about how to invest it and what to do with it, until he is overwhelmed and 'prefers to love and contemplate gold stamped with the image of man, rather than God'.[18] Such a monk inevitably becomes discontented with religious life and seeks opportunities to leave. Cassian's point is that the giving up of one's possessions is fundamental to the ascetic life. There are monks who never manage to comply with this command, keeping some property in their possession just in case. This failure of initial commitment will always lead to failure in religious life. Even among those who do make the commitment to poverty, the spirit of avarice lingers on, in some, who, after a period of obedience, want to claim back what they first gave up, as though it were still theirs.

For Cassian avarice is a matter of the heart and needs to be rooted out. Discontent spreads in community, and if one member has secret possessions or aspirations it breeds discontent in others. He uses scripture to demonstrate the dangers of this fault, quoting in particular the story of Elisha's servant Gehazi and of Ananias and Sapphira. At root, avarice is a question of justice, as the biblical stories show. The privilege of one is the deprivation of another. The conquest of avarice requires patience and punctiliousness, and it helps to remember that, in the end, no amount of possessions can protect against the uncertainties of life. It would be a tragedy for the day of the Lord to come without warning, and 'to find your souls stained even by a half-penny'.[19]

Benedictine monasticism depends on a strict sense of justice and equality within the community. Benedict insists in his Rule that all possessions, including tools and clothes, should be held in common.[20] He instructed that a careful inventory be drawn up of what particular tools or equipment has been allocated to each person according to the responsibilities each one bears. This enables anyone succeeding to the same responsibilities to know exactly what he is entitled to use. Benedict also bans all personal gifts or presents, unless the superior gives permission for them to be received. Benedict's reason for this strict ban on private property is grounded in the argument St Paul makes in favour of sexual chastity. The monks' bodies are temples of the Holy Spirit; they do not belong to their apparent owner, but are consecrated to God. Benedict skews the text to assert that this consecration implies that no one in community should claim anything personal for themselves. In return they are to expect the community to supply everything that they need.

The story reveals the major problem of avarice in the eyes of the Church, which is its social consequences. The belief that avarice was a form of theft was deep rooted, and was held in various ways in Greek and Roman thought, Judaism and Islam as well as Christianity, manifesting itself in restrictions on money-lending. To take advantage of another's need by charging interest was regarded as fundamentally immoral in the early Church. In a letter to the bishops of southern Italy, Pope Leo I took the unusual step of condemning lay people for lending money at interest.[21] He reinforced his point in another letter in which he suggested that it is difficult to avoid sin in the course of buying or selling. Once the point had been made it was repeated and became the established outlook of the Church, supported by moral theology and canon law. It explains the suspicion of commerce in general and of capitalism in particular that is still found in the Catholic Church, though less so in the Churches of the Reformation.

Gregory the Great puts avarice fourth on his list of principal vices. In his *Dialogues* he tells a terrible story from his monastic past to illustrate the dire consequences of this sin. While he was abbot of his monastery there was a certain monk, Justus, who had medical skills and had nursed Gregory through a variety of illnesses (Gregory suffered from poor health for most of his adult life). Justus himself became ill and when he was near death he confided to his brother that he had secretly stored up three gold coins. These were quickly discovered. Gregory felt he could not overlook the matter and instructed that the dying man was to be left alone, untended. At his dying hour his brethren were to visit him only to tell him that they detested him for his crime. He was then to be buried on a dunghill with the money. These instructions were carried out as Gregory commanded. From his point of view the cruel attitude achieved two aims. It brought about Justus' repentance – after thirty special masses Justus' soul was relieved from torment. It also terrified the other monks and acted as a deterrent against any avaricious tendencies they might have been harbouring.[22] Avarice being a principal sin, it generates others: treachery, fraud, lying, perjury, restlessness, violence and callous indifference to the destitute.[23]

Gregory also adds a principal vice which is not previously listed by either Cassian or Evagrius. This is the vice of envy, which Gregory puts second on his list after vainglory. Evagrius does not deal with envy as a separate thought, though he recognizes that envious people are a danger to those attempting to live a spiritual life.[24] He suggests that monks should protect themselves against the envy of others by not drawing attention to any praise or success that comes their way. Jealous people need to be treated with generosity – they are victims of Satan. The proper response to a jealous person is to praise him and soften his envy by inviting him to a meal.

But envy is a more serious issue for Gregory. It is the cause of both public and private strife, generating hatred, gossip, scorn, rejoicing in a neighbour's bad fortune and being upset when a neighbour succeeds.

In spite of Gregory's warnings about the dangers of avarice, there was plenty of what might be called institutionalized 'avarice' in the medieval Church. The Church was often in need of money and managed to find ingenious ways round the ban on money-lending and borrowing at interest. Tithes, sales, savings and investments enabled the Church to build up treasures on earth. Think of the legacies and endowments which have funded and supported cathedrals, monasteries, even universities. There are many historical examples where communal or personal wealth has accumulated alongside the practice of personal thrift. The Benedictine abbeys of the Middle Ages became fabulously wealthy on the simple lifestyle recommended by St Benedict, so much so that a whole succession of monastic reformers were needed to try to bring simplicity and austerity back to the religious life.

Thomas Aquinas, with his usual balanced perspective, taught that the desire for material goods is not in itself sinful. Human beings need material goods in order to survive and it is reasonable to seek to accumulate the necessities of life. For him, the problem comes when the desire is excessive to the point that a person exceeds the limits of necessity. For Aquinas, this is not only a sign of spiritual and moral disturbance, it is also a sin against justice. His judgement on this has been extremely influential: 'It is impossible for one man to enjoy extreme wealth without someone else suffering extreme want, since the resources of the world cannot be possessed by many at one time.'[25]

Aquinas is assuming here, of course, that the resources of the world are, in fact, limited. On the basis of this assumption he argues against material inequality in strikingly bold terms which still resonate today. Avarice is simply wrong because it is a sin against the neighbour and particularly against the poor. Catholic social teaching has consistently followed Aquinas on this point, and it still forms the bedrock of the Catholic Church's teaching on economic justice. Aquinas also saw avarice as sin against God, a deliberate turning away from eternal values in favour of earthly prosperity.

Dante condemns the avaricious to the fourth circle of hell, which they share with those who have spent money too freely. Both groups are quite near the entrance to which they can never hope to return. The mutual antagonism between those who have hoarded wealth and those who have squandered it leads to punishment in the form of endless conflict. The two groups run at each other with huge rocks as weapons, shouting abuse at each other for their opposing errors. The fight can never be resolved, and so those who have misused wealth are condemned to the strife it generates. (Dante reserves worse regions of hell for those whose financial misdeeds include fraud and corruption.)

The third layer of purgatory, the lowest region of its upper terraces, is where the covetous do penance. This takes the form of being bound to the earth with fetters. As their interests were attached to earthly wealth, so they are now themselves attached to the earth, captured by what captivated them on earth. Here they learn the ultimate worthlessness of wealth.

Avarice was a particularly loathed sin in the medieval mind. It was seen as a form of greed, a sin closely related to gluttony. It was manifest not only in the rich, but in those who practised fraud, or cheated in the marketplace by giving short measure when selling bread or ale. Portraits of avarice personified in wall paintings are sometimes based on such figures of daily life. At St Ethelbert's, Hessett, avarice is female. She wears the kind of apron that a baker might wear and grips a bag of money tightly in her left hand.

Aquinas' assumption that the earth's resources are limited, and that the accumulation of wealth is therefore inherently unjust has been challenged. John Calvin, though deeply concerned for social justice, brought into Reformation Christianity an understanding that the material world could be 'worked' to increase its bounty. Part of the purpose of humanity under the sovereignty of God was to work for God's glory; the world was a 'theatre' of the glory of God, and good stewardship of material goods might involve the seeking of material profits. Calvin was the first theologian to experiment (cautiously) with the idea that money-lending and borrowing might be permitted to Christians. This new theology of wealth marked an important turning point in the development of the Western spiritual tradition, and was an encouragement, particularly to Protestants, to seek wealth alongside a sober, simple, thrifty lifestyle. Calvin and others were well aware of the temptations of wealth. The pursuit of gain was permissible. But on a spiritual level the heart must be guarded from the seduction of riches. In the post-Reformation world the thrift and self-discipline of the Quakers produced huge profits in their commercial ventures, which were often turned to philanthropic purposes.

There is still a divide in the Christian world today about whether the pursuit or accumulation of wealth is morally permissible. There is an ascetical streak in Catholic Christianity, a sense that an interest in money 'taints' those who entertain it, and that it is a basic Christian duty to live within limits; giving away any excess income both as a matter of justice and to prevent the inevitable corruption of soul that follows from the accumulation of wealth. Those more influenced by some aspects of the Protestant tradition might tend to see money more pragmatically, as a way of making the world 'work' harder and produce more. From one side of this divide it is simply obvious that the world has 'enough for everyone's need but not for everyone's greed'; on the other side it is part of the human vocation to transform the world by human activity, and the liberation of the poor is a fruit of the opportunities afforded by economic freedom and expansion. These are huge issues that embrace ethics and politics as well as spirituality.

Evagrius, avarice and us

What can we draw from Evagrius' insights? Evagrius knew that avarice works by stealth. He also recognized that it held a particular fascination for those who adopted a marginal lifestyle. They had put themselves at risk, but were not immune from anxiety. The great temptation for them was to agonize about the future. How would they cope when their resources ran out and they had neither friends nor family around to help?

Odd though it may seem, the individualism of Western society puts us more in tune with the desert ascetics than we might imagine. The desert ascetics chose to be alone; many in the West feel alone and vulnerable. In an affluent society, there is a degree of competitiveness which makes everyone feel marginal and at risk of losing out. Most of us regard money as a private matter. We rarely discuss our personal finances; our bank balances are often more private than our sex lives. Temptations to avarice often spring from insecurity, which increases with old age. Cassian is right when he recognizes avarice as a tendency which is *acquired* rather than innate. The demon of avarice tempts the monk, as it tempts us, by conjuring up a picture of what it would be like to have no control over one's destiny, to be unable to work, caught up in food shortages, sick, poor and (worst of all) dependent on others. The thought of avarice is that money is the answer to all this; plenty in the bank, stashed away, accumulated and growing. Evagrius recognized that the thought of avarice plays into our tendency to become control freaks, compelled to protect ourselves against the unexpected. While all this is true in our individual lives we are at the same time very ready to condemn avarice when we see it around us.

Avarice is personified in contemporary media in terms of greed. We are all familiar with figures such as the exploitative landlord, who charges more than his property is worth and fails to keep it safe or in good order; the corporate fat cats who hold down their workers' wages while accepting hefty pay rises for themselves; the corrupt dictators whose peoples starve while millions are hoarded away in Swiss bank accounts. These figures evoke scorn and cynicism, and perhaps a faint trace of envy from those who have not been so successful in the quest for material wealth. In times of economic prosperity we are all caught up in the temptation to avarice, because the quest to have more of everything becomes an overwhelming compulsion. Lending, borrowing and spending stimulate the economy; more leads to more, until the inevitable bubble bursts, and we realize we have been living and buying and spending on no more than air and promises that cannot be fulfilled. Avarice is the sin of those who have and want more, envy is the sin of the have-nots. The justification of greed is often made in the rhetoric of capitalism; the legitimacy of envy is part of the rhetoric of socialism. As Evagrius and Cassian recognized, the passion of avarice burns slowly. It is a desire that has to be learnt. But the split between avarice as a personal sickness, a weighing down of the self, and avarice as a more social problem, leaves us with some difficulties. We are all perhaps familiar with champagne socialists, who preach the redistribution of wealth while enjoying an affluent lifestyle. (There are also of course austere capitalists, who spend little on themselves, but whose commercial strategies, if unchecked, can impoverish others.)

More subtle and more challenging for most of us is the way in which even a modest accumulation of capital is regarded as a virtue rather than a vice. Saving, investment, taking responsibility for oneself, putting money aside against an uncertain future – our entire financial system is caught up in these attempts to make ourselves more secure. What Evagrius defined as avarice we might consider to be simple prudence, forward planning and common sense.

So what is wrong with this? Most of us are not living the radical commitments of the desert fathers and mothers. We are caught up in a system which requires us to be financially literate. It is not clear to us that it is a virtue to throw caution to the wind when it comes to money. What is more, there are strands of Christianity which appeal to our insecurities much as life-assurance companies do, and preach a gospel that includes the promise of wealth alongside salvation. The assumption is that God rewards faith by taking special care of those who put their trust in him. Those who hold this view point out that to pray for wealth is not unbiblical. A few years ago a book by Bruce H. Wilkinson called *The Prayer of Jabez*[26] encouraged Christians to emulate a minor biblical character who prayed to God for prosperity: ' "O that you would bless me and enlarge my border, and that your hand might be with me, and that you would keep me from hurt and harm!" And God granted him that which he requested' (1 Chronicles 4.10). Wilkinson's book is said to have sold four million copies. This is, no doubt, because it gives spiritual support to those whose true prayer is, 'Please, Lord, make me really rich'! In a world where there is so much emphasis on material well-being such prayers are understandable. The 'prosperity gospel' has spread from the USA to Africa and Asia and is producing forms of Christianity where riches are a sign of God's blessing and poverty a sign of God's disapproval. This is a return to a perspective which is found more in the Old Testament than the New, and which does not sit easily with the teaching of Jesus on wealth and poverty. But it is perhaps an understandable point of view in a world where some are in a position to accumulate riches and the vast majority are not. The Bible promises that God will raise the poor and put down the rich and mighty, and it is hardly surprising if the poor take God at his word and ask God to make them rich. Contentment, being satisfied with one's lot, is only possible for those who have something, not for those who have nothing at all. Even Evagrius had his pint of oil and loaf of bread, a cell or cave to sleep in and the writing equipment with which he committed his spiritual teachings to paper and made copies of other works.

We need to bear in mind what for Evagrius was the object of the Christian life: constant prayer and dependence on God. The real problem of avarice is that it is an attempt to control the future, to write the script of life in advance so that one comes out materially and emotionally secure. But the challenge to our prayers is to live with God in the present and to be genuinely open about what the future holds. In his *Chapters on Prayer* Evagrius writes, 'Trust in God for the needs of the body and then it will be clear that you are also relying on him for the needs of your spirit.'[27]

Avarice makes us discontent with what we have and this is spiritually debilitating. Contentment is a rare virtue in our competitive society. We are all driven to seek to improve our material lot, and if not our own, then our children's. Everyone cares about their children's material welfare, but it is curious how over-concerned affluent parents can become, driving them through competitive hoops and stirring them to exhausting anxiety about the future.

But then at the heart of the contemporary tendency to avarice is a lack of trust in there being anything beyond material existence. Avarice feeds and is fed by the assumption that only this present earthly life is important. It is often moving to see how an elderly person prepares for death by tidying up their material affairs, writing a will, and often disposing of a good deal of their possessions and property. This is exactly what we should be doing in old age, and it is not just a matter of prudential self-management. The way we leave this life is a spiritual issue: 'We brought nothing into the world . . . we can take nothing out of it' (1 Timothy 6.7). Evagrius believed that the life of prayer is a preparation for death and heaven beyond death, and he was not interested in the mere perpetuation of earthly existence. In holding to this and seeing avarice as a spiritual danger for all he was simply spelling out what Jesus meant when he told us not to store up for ourselves treasures on earth, for 'where your treasure is there will your heart be also' (Matthew 6.19–21).

Gluttony, lust and avarice are all ancient temptations. They are considered serious faults in classical philosophy; they are identified and condemned in various ways in scripture. The spiritual traditions of the East and the West urge us to be restrained in our bodily appetites and in our desire for material security. How far we have moved from this universal recognition of what is bad for us can be seen any night on television as celebrity cooks compete with mouth-watering recipes, sex is used to sell cars, and banks and building societies offer their own 'mouth-watering' deals. We are hungry all the time for pleasure and satisfaction and vulnerable to those who would persuade us to buy them. Any training in spirituality should begin by helping individuals to resist being led astray by these strong and compelling desires.

8

The thought of sadness

Sadness tends to come up at times because of the deprivation of one's desires. On other occasions it accompanies anger. When it arises from the deprivation of desires it takes place in the following manner. Certain thoughts first drive the soul to the memory of house and parents, or else to that of one's former life. Now when these thoughts find that the soul offers no resistance but rather follows after them and pours itself out in pleasures that are still only mental in nature, they then seize her and drench her in sadness, with the result that those ideas she was just indulging no longer remain. In fact, they cannot be had in reality either, because of her present way of life. So the miserable soul is now shrivelled up in her humiliation to the degree that she poured herself out upon these thoughts of hers.[1]

Comment

Sadness seems a rather unexpected item on Evagrius' list of evil thoughts. Unlike lust and gluttony it does not arise from a desire for bodily satisfaction, nor, like avarice, from a longing for the security of material goods. In fact sadness does not arise out of any kind of desire at all. It is unique among the evil thoughts in that it only arises when desire is frustrated. Sadness comes from the irascible part of the soul, and it is linked to anger, though its symptoms are, as we might expect, quite different.

Evagrius' inclusion of sadness may at first glance seem to be unreasonable. Everyone is sad at some time or another. We would think a person abnormal who never felt sadness. It is a natural reaction to loss. The Greek word Evagrius uses is *lupe*, grief. Grieving is a necessary part of what it is to live a human life. Evagrius himself frequently commends weeping for one's sins, which implies you are meant to be sad in some way about them, though he is careful to insist that this must not become self-indulgent. For Evagrius the sadness that leads to sin is a reaction to loss, which, in the stillness and isolation of desert life, has got out of perspective and become all-consuming, so that memories for a lost past begin to constitute the ascetic's identity. To get some sense of what Evagrius means by sadness we should think perhaps of nostalgia or bitter regret. It is a temptation fuelled by memories of the past. These, if we allow them to, will flood into the mind in the form of images. These images may or may not be accurate, but whether they are or not they are still only images, no more than mental representations. And this is the problem. Because the reality they represent is no longer available, a further wave of sadness follows. This double grief is enervating and exhausting. It diminishes the soul, leaving as a final sting the memory of how deeply the individual soul has 'poured herself out upon these thoughts of hers'. This has a specific meaning in the austere life of the desert, but it also has a relevance to us. We, like the desert ascetics, can be spiritually harmed if we overindulge in nostalgia for a past that is no more. The end of all this is pure misery; the soul is diminished, shrivelled and humiliated by its loving but unwise recollection of the past.

Sadness and the Bible

It is hard to find much sense that sadness is a deadly temptation from the Old Testament. There is certainly plenty of grief in the Old Testament, but this is not condemned, it is accepted as a natural response to loss. Children weep over dead parents and friends and lovers over lost loved ones. The prophets mourn over the sins of Israel and Judah and the terrible loss of Jerusalem and the subsequent exile. The psalms take up these themes in haunting, bitter lament. All this assumes that sadness in the sense of mourning is part of the experience of life. It is therefore part of prayer, both of the nation and of individuals, who bring their pain and loss into the presence of God. It is important to acknowledge past sinfulness and to mourn the dead. Recovery from sadness is triggered by memory. Remembering God's deeds of justice and deliverance in the past creates the expectation that he will act in this way again. There is hope. 'Remember . . .' is often a cue for renewed trust and joy in God.

The Old Testament values human memory. But not all memories are good ones. Now and then we get a sense of that empty, frustrated memory of which Evagrius speaks. One example would be the sadness of the Israelites in the wilderness as they contemplated their former lives in Egypt. They had longed for freedom from oppression; but with freedom came hunger, danger and insecurity. Their memories of their time in Egypt became distorted. It was not the hardship, the injustice or the oppression that they called to mind, but the food: 'If only we had meat to eat! We remember the fish we used to eat in Egypt for nothing, the cucumbers, the melons, the leeks, the onions, and the garlic; but now our strength is dried up, and there is nothing at all but this manna to look at' (Numbers 11.5). I mentioned this passage earlier in connection with gluttony, but it also illustrates the problem of distorted memory which lies at the root of Evagrius' thought of sadness. Memory here traps the people of Israel in an idealized past. What God provides as bread in the wilderness is not nearly as interesting as the memory of free fish, fruit and veg in Egypt!

The Israelites' lament triggers a curious reaction from God. He takes the complaint as a challenge to his own powers and promises that he will indeed produce meat, enough quails to last not for a day or a week but a month. But at the same time he sees Israel's nostalgia for the diet of slavery as a rejection of him and threatens to give them so much that they become sick of it, 'until it comes out of your nostrils and becomes loathsome to you'. In the event God provides the quails and simultaneously brings a plague which kills off those who have complained (Numbers 11.4–9, 16–35; Psalm 78.18–31; 106.13–15).

We should not read this as a literal description of God's emotional reaction to human discontent. What is interesting about it is that it is an example of how memory becomes coloured by nostalgia. The Israelites' memories of the food they enjoyed in Egypt is controlling their thoughts at a time when such rations are no longer available. The sickness, the loathing that ensues from having so much meat that they vomit it out of their nostrils is simply disgusting. The implication is that indulging in this kind of nostalgia, based on half-memories recalled and indulged, leads to a kind of absorption in the past which brings disgust and destruction.

The New Testament is written from a very different perspective. The Gospels and Epistles assume that the entire world has changed, with implications for both the past and the future. The coming of Jesus and his death and resurrection have transformed the world. There is good news for everyone, and in particular for the poor, the sad and the grieving. Joy is the appropriate response, grief and sadness belong to the old world. As Jesus himself says, 'The wedding guests cannot mourn as long as the bridegroom is with them' (Matthew 9.15). Joy is the authentic response to the gospel, a fruit of the Spirit and a sign of God's life and blessing. There are passages in the Gospels which even suggest that sadness is a kind of spiritual ingratitude, a failure to grasp what God has given in the person of Jesus Christ. The Easter story of the travellers on the road to Emmaus is illuminating here (Luke 24.13–32). The two travellers meet Jesus in the guise of a stranger on the road. When Jesus asks them what they were discussing, 'they stood still looking sad'. Then they recount to him the story of the crucifixion of Jesus and the rumours of his resurrection, declaring, as they do so, their disappointment that the final liberation of Israel from its enemies has not taken place. In responding to them Jesus accuses them of foolishness and lack of faith. They have heard the message of his resurrection and yet they have not received its true significance. So he tells them all over again, pointing to the meaning of his life and death 'in all the scriptures'. It is later, when he has revealed himself to them in the meal at the inn, that they are able to say, 'Were not our hearts burning within us while he was talking to us on the road?'

But joy is not the whole story. The New Testament has plenty to say about the importance of contrition; the grief that comes with the recognition of one's own failure or weakness. The denial of Jesus by Peter is the most significant example of this, and his subsequent restoration is movingly told at the end of John's Gospel. In sharp contrast is the remorse of the betrayer Judas, who has given the Lord up to his enemies for thirty pieces of silver. Judas repented of his treachery when he saw Jesus condemned and tried to return the money in a vain attempt to undo what he had done. But it was too late. All he could do was throw down the silver pieces in the Temple, leave the scene and hang himself. The stories of Peter's betrayal and Judas' betrayal are told together in Matthew's Gospel, and the contrast between the reactions of Peter and Judas is often taken to spell out the difference between contrition and remorse. Peter wept bitterly, recognizing what he had done. There was obviously sadness, regret and desolation. Judas did not weep, but tried to put things right himself by attempting to get rid of the evidence of his betrayal. This did not bring him either release or hope and he did away with himself in despair. The point is that the sadness of contrition leads to forgiveness and opens the way to a new future, whereas the sadness of remorse cannot begin to imagine a new beginning and ends in self-destruction.

Christian discipleship is not an easy option; it challenges all family and personal priorities in ways which go to the root of our loyalties. The extreme example of this in the Gospels is the disturbing, even offensive, remark Jesus made to one would-be disciple who asked for a little time to arrange his father's burial. (It would have been a very little time, too, a matter of hours rather than days.) Yet Jesus brushed his perfectly reasonable request to one side with the chilling remark, 'let the dead bury their own dead' (Matthew 8.22), summoning up a morbid picture of corpses and skeletons processing to the graveside with the recently dead person. This is hardly a pastoral or even a humane response, and perhaps can only be understood in the light of the urgency of the gospel and the shocking way in which Jesus confounds conventional expectations. Jesus is not rejecting human grief. He is himself often identified in Christian reflection with the figure of Isaiah, 'a man of sorrows' (Isaiah 53.3). He weeps over the death of Lazarus (John 11.35) and Mary Magdalene weeps when she comes to his tomb (John 20.11). It is not that death and loss are unimportant and should not be mourned. It is more that the perspective of all our grieving must be the new life of the resurrection which Jesus has brought into the world. We are to live with the confidence that there is a new creation in Christ (2 Corinthians 5.17). Death itself will be destroyed as the last enemy of humankind (1 Corinthians 15.26).

The vision at the end of the Bible is of the new creation brought to fulfilment:

> 'See, the home of God is among mortals.
> He will dwell with them;
> they will be his peoples,
> and God himself will be with them;
> he will wipe every tear from their eyes.
> Death will be no more;
> mourning and crying and pain will be no more,
> for the first things have passed away.'
> And the one who was seated on the throne said, 'See, I am making all things new.'　　　　　　　　　　　　　　　　　　　　　　　　(Revelation 21.3–5)

Sadness in the life of Evagrius

Palladius does not give us examples of any particular sadness in Evagrius' life, though his reluctance to take on the monastic habit under Melania's instruction suggests he might well have had times of aching nostalgia, not only for the glamorous life he had once lived in Constantinople, but for the opportunities lost to him. The fact that he gave up so much means

Evagrius was probably very alert to the dangers of sadness. He could have been a magnificent theologian, even a bishop. He could have enjoyed high status and the respect of others. He could have married and known the blessings of family life. Knowing how much he gave up gives a poignancy to his observation that 'Sadness tends to come up at times because of the deprivation of one's desires'.

When Evagrius entered the solitary life he deliberately embraced a state of permanent loss. Loss of possessions, of family, of the prospects of marriage and worldly advancement. No doubt there were flashes of memory, thoughts of his past life which seemed innocent enough. Why should he not smile as he remembers good times enjoyed in the past? But then he comes to see that such reveries do not bring peace but anxiety and discontent. The more he mentally enjoys the sights, sounds and smells of his former life, the harder it is when present reality crashes in. So there is a double sorrow. A sorrow for what is lost, and a sorrow for having drowned in sorrow! Evagrius' teaching on the evil thoughts comes out of his practice as a spiritual guide. We know how much he was valued for his discretion, his ability to analyse temptation and to suggest practical remedies. He must have listened to younger monks moaning about their losses and pondered how to help them live positively with the choices they had made.

Sadness is unique among the temptations because it has no desire or appetite to go with it. There is no real pleasure in sadness and the demon of sadness has no pleasure to offer. Evagrius compares it to a viper, claiming that the viper's poison is effective against the poison of other animals, but if taken in excess itself destroys.[2] This suggests that Evagrius was also aware that sadness takes two forms. It can be 'godly sadness',[3] which 'calls the soul back with tears', bringing about repentance and genuine detachment from the world and the passions. Or it can drown the soul in bitter reverie. Sadness is either the contrition of Peter or the remorse of Judas. When it is the latter it tends to feed on other frustrated desires. All the other passions are *for* something. As Evagrius sees it, avarice, for example, makes a person vulnerable to the sense of loss, and when this happens sadness is the inevitable result.[4] Sadness 'is begotten of opposing forces',[5] it is the spiritual paralysis of frustrated desire. Vainglory involves a craving for the esteem of others, and anger a strong desire for revenge. When these cravings and desires meet frustration, the ensuing dejection suggests the presence of the demon of sadness. The only way of finally defeating sadness, then, is by defeating all the other passions.[6] Finally, sadness is enervating because it cuts off natural and innocent pleasures, such as the enjoyment of the sunrise,[7] and is thus a bar to deeper contemplation.

Evagrius does not spell this out in his writings, but it seems as though one of the reasons he finds this kind of sadness a dangerous temptation is his accurate recognition that our memories, and the hopes and desires they give rise to, are never wholly innocent. We 'work on' our memories, constructing narratives about our lives with the aim of explaining ourselves to ourselves. The images which lie at the base of these narratives are coloured, at least in part, by fantasy. If we are always looking to our past lives as a source of pleasure, if our past lives seem always to be richer and more fulfilled than our present lives, it may well be that we have become enslaved to memories which have themselves become inaccurate, 'rose-tinted' as we say. We assume there was a time when we were not made angry, or when our anger was assuaged, or when our craving for the admiration of others was satisfied. But nostalgia, as we have seen, can be a nostalgia for what has never been. And whether our memories are accurate or not, the reality is that family and home have moved on, the old pattern no longer exists and, anyway, the commitment to the desert life means that a return to anything like the former life is out of the question.

Evagrius does not have a great deal to say about the cure for sadness, apart from conquering the passions through resistance and prayer. But in a note which is found in only one manuscript of his reflections on the eight thoughts (which means it may have been added by someone else), we find, 'He who loves the Lord will be free of sadness since the fullness of love drives out sadness.'[8] This could almost be a reflection on the contrition of Peter at the end of John's Gospel where Christ asks him three times if he loves him and in answering him three times finds his mission, purpose and hope restored to him in the experience of forgiveness.

Sadness and the spiritual tradition

I have already observed that the Bible, and in particular the Old Testament, rarely condemns sadness. But the Stoic tradition of Greek philosophy regarded *lupe*, grief, as a less than rational response to circumstances. Stoics valued detachment, not only from material things, but from the passions and drives which upset our equilibrium. We cannot change the circumstances of our life, but, the Stoics thought, we can exercise discipline over our response to them. In strict Stoicism it is a kind of self-indulgence to allow feelings of sadness or grief to have a place in our lives. The desert ascetics absorbed this attitude from Stoic philosophy, at least when they contemplated change and loss in their own lives.

The desert ascetics fled to the desert to save their own souls, to live out the life of true discipleship as they saw it. The urgency of the gospel call to repentance and faith is echoed in their teaching. In their zealous commitment they stressed the importance of penitence, fasting and tears. Yet there is also a note of carefree joyfulness in some, at least, of the teaching that has come down to us; a refusal to be sad even at natural times of grief. Yet when we look at the way this refusal to be sad was expressed, it seems to owe at least as much to the Stoic attempt to reach emotional indifference as it does to the good news of the New Testament. This is both disturbing to us and deeply challenging. The last thing Palladius tells us about Evagrius is his response to his father's death: 'The death of his father was announced to a certain monk. He turned to the messenger who had brought him the news and replied, "Stop your blasphemies. My father is immortal."' This story of Evagrius is also told anonymously by Evagrius himself, and it appears in the Sayings of the Fathers.[9] The twist of the story is in the meaning of 'father'. Is Evagrius talking about his father having reached immortality, or is the story meant to shock us into insight by the substitution of 'Father', meaning the fatherhood of God? The brutality of the response is akin to Jesus' response about letting the dead bury their dead. Both are shocking to us, but perhaps in a world where death was a much more common and public occurrence the Christian faith introduced an alternative view of the world which, for all its 'unnatural' bravado in the face of death, was found by many to be attractive and compelling. There is certainly evidence that one of the things that impressed people about early Christianity was the courage of the martyrs who died for their faith in the full expectation of their heavenly reward.

Evagrius recommended that his monks spent time remembering the inescapability of death, thinking about their own deaths and noticing that they were getting older.[10] Such meditation turned their attention from the past to the future. They were to meditate on the slow deterioration of their own bodies and to consider both the fate of the souls condemned to hell and on the blessings of heaven. They were to weep for sinners and pray not to share their fate. By such mental discipline the demon of sadness was driven away and the monk was liberated to experience interior stillness.

John Cassian puts *tristitia*, sadness, after anger, changing Evagrius' order in the *Praktikos*, though Evagrius is not strict about which comes first in his other writings. Cassian also follows Evagrius in seeing a link between the two temptations. For Cassian sadness is an insidious tendency that eats away at the heart of a monk, like a moth eating holes in clothing. He does not link it to memory and nostalgia in the way that Evagrius did, but sees it more as a kind of depression, to be cured by meditation. Cassian also tells a story which illustrates very accurately how nostalgia is related to sadness. The story[11] is about a monk who had been in solitude for 15 years when a large packet of letters from his mother and father and friends was brought to him. Instead of opening them, he hesitated, suddenly worried about the effect reading the letters would have on his spiritual life. Either he would be moved to senseless joy or to useless sadness; either way the content of the letters would distract him from contemplation. He would find himself recalling the words and looks of each individual writer and longing to see them and hear them again. Although he would remain apart from them in the body, his heart would be drawn back to them. As he saw it, the memories evoked by the letters would undo years of struggle in the life of prayer. So he decided to burn the letters without reading them.

To us, this inevitably seems harsh. And yet we can see what a difficult challenge it is to live genuinely in the present moment, when much of our identity is built out of memories of the past. Even today, those embarking on an enclosed life of prayer are usually required to limit their contacts with friends and families, especially in the early years of their religious profession, when they are absorbing the rhythms of the monastic life.

Sadness is one of the sins listed by Gregory the Great. Like Cassian he lists sadness after anger, and clearly sees a link between the two. Sadness gives rise to other sins, and he lists aggression, rancour, cowardice, desperation, lack of self-care, restless thoughts and what he describes as 'other illicit things'. Gregory does not have sloth in his list of principal vices but includes restlessness and lack of self-care, which might be thought to belong to sloth as much as sadness. The spiritual tradition from Gregory onwards tends to run the two together. Gregory was sensitive to the differences of human temperament and was aware that some people tend to be frequently sad, or to have what we might call a depressive personality. In his *Pastoral Rule* he suggests that such people should be treated gently, and encouraged by the hope of reward rather than the fear of punishment.[12] Combining sadness and sloth, Gregory claims that the consequences of sadness include torpor, restlessness and a search for distraction.

Thomas Aquinas follows Gregory in combining sadness with sloth, but he lists the consequences under sloth, not sadness. He sees sloth as spiritual apathy, a particular kind of sadness. He is clearly very aware of the history of the deadly sins, and makes frequent mention of what Cassian has to say about sadness in his treatment of sloth. Sadness as a distinct temptation dropped out of later lists. This was probably because it had never been wholly satisfactory. We have seen how Evagrius himself commended some kinds of sadness as it led to repentance and joy.

Evagrius, sadness and us

When Evagrius writes of the temptation to sadness he is not talking directly here about the sadness we associate with bereavement, nor with the accidental losses and traumas of life. What he is talking about is the rosy image of the past which can bleed the life out of the present. Indulging in an idealized view of past life undermines the original decision to live differently and for that reason can become spiritually dangerous.

A Roman Catholic religious sister once told me that 'all religious have idealized childhoods'. I thought at the time that this was an interesting comment, especially as she was speaking of people, like herself, who choose to leave family and home for the sake of the gospel. She was puzzled by the phenomenon but came to see it as an example of the way memory is selective; the religious brothers and sisters she was speaking of were prone to remembering only the positive parts of their former family and life experiences. This selective remembering may have been a way of forgetting the actual reasons why they chose to take on a vowed life. To construct the past in terms of a seamless continuity from a happy and fulfilled childhood to the challenges of religious commitment suggests that fulfilling the will of God was something natural and which did not require struggle and discernment. It might be hard for a present-day monk or nun to trace the seeds of their vocation to, for example, a pious family which put pressure on the children to consider priesthood or religious life, or to a family which, though conventionally religious, lacked warmth and affection. If religious life has been found to be lacking in warmth also, then the childhood story may take on glowing colours that it lacked in reality. Either way, Evagrius sees in nostalgia a temptation which applies to all of us, not only to those trying to live a religious life. It is the refusal to accept the fact that we live in time. 'The past is another country' and we cannot enter it without bringing our present experience to bear on our memories.

He was aware that we human beings construct our life stories out of our memories. These stories become very real to us; they make sense of the mass of impressions and events and experiences which belong to us. But we can never really go back and check our version of events, because the reality they refer to is no longer there. What Evagrius is suggesting is that to let our selective memories determine the way we think about the present is to endanger our spiritual freedom. It makes the past more solid, more real than the present. Nostalgia is a temptation for all who have a memory, old and young alike. Teenagers can be seriously bereaved by the loss of childhood freedoms and the seemingly impossible challenges of adulthood. The recent experience of being cared for and protected by their parents and teachers does not necessarily help them to make the leap into responsibility. They can easily get stuck in a gloomy misery, sometimes exacerbated by raging hormones and acne, in which, instead of expanding as personalities, they feel that they are shrivelling, diminishing into nothingness. The terror of this sense of diminishment can barely be communicated. No one can understand the savage quality of despair that can come to a teenager from the recognition that he or she is now responsible for their own choices. For some, of course, this is exciting and creative, but others will be overwhelmed by a grief, which, if it were discussed with a doctor, might well be diagnosed as anxiety or depression.

People in mid-life can also be tempted by nostalgia to idealize the world in which they grew up. The values they received from their parents and schools carry much more weight for them than the values they find reflected around them in the present. Their parents and teachers remain in their lives as figures of authority whose views should not be challenged. On top of this, because time appears to go faster as we grow older, the lessons of childhood can seem much more solid and real than the lessons we draw from adult experience. Those middle-aged people who indulge in nostalgia can find themselves unable to see any good in present-day values, and cynical about attempts to improve things. In old age, as short-term memory begins to decline, the memories laid down in childhood become more vivid and more reliable than what happened yesterday. At any age we can be tempted to feel that life has conspired against us and that we are washed up on an alien shore struggling to cope with an unfamiliar age whose values we do not share.

Yet the Christian faith requires us to live in the present and with an orientation to the future. We are to imitate the patriarchs in being ready to set out in faith, looking forward to 'the city that has foundations', and living as 'strangers and foreigners on the earth' (Hebrews 11.10, 13b). The Promised Land is always ahead. The gospel requires freedom from the past for us to become what God desires us to be. Though it is important for us to construct a narrative of our lives, to have a working story of who we are and what has formed us, we also need to recognize that in the light of the gospel any such story needs to be open to revision and transformation.

It is difficult to get the balance right, and many people in contemporary society feel that they have been prevented from having contact with their memories, particularly childhood ones. They need to recover their memories and grieve and let go before they can reach wholeness, and this is not accomplished in a moment, but frequently takes years. Even so, the memories recovered can only ever be partial and personal ones – one of the sad discoveries is that there is no 'objective' account of the past.

I remember recognizing this for myself when I was asked by the writer and journalist Monica Furlong to write a piece about my childhood for a collection of essays she was compiling. It was a delightful commission to fulfil and I poured myself into it, letting memories unfold into a story which explained who I had since become. Then I showed it to my mother. Her response was not negative so much as surprised. 'But it wasn't like that,' she said again and again, as I described some incident that had lodged in my mind and come forth in a particular way. She had seen the same incident from a wholly different perspective. I eventually realized that my version of the story, though a legitimate 'take' on a shared past, was far from exhaustive and was limited in its accuracy by my need to give an account of my childhood which was satisfactory to me.

This all sounds very obvious. But it needs to be remembered because there is a great emphasis in society at present on the importance of personal and collective stories as the key to identity. In a complex world where there are many voices all crying for significance, those who are able to construct and articulate a compelling story will always command attention. In a media-saturated world, their needs and their claims are given weight over those who at least appear to be able to live with contentment in the present. It is attractive to be able to identify with a group that has a clear sense of its own story, particularly when that story is based on grievance (the word in English is an obvious cognate of grief, an alternative translation of Evagrius' *lupe*). Where there is a grievance it is all too easy to use highly selective memories against other people to build identities based on opposition and hatred. Nostalgia is at the roots of discontent, which can spread out from personal misery to political fascism and terrorism. Sadness is linked to anger, as Evagrius noted, and a sense of communal grievance can break out in violence against others who are blamed, rightly or wrongly, for having caused the grievance in the first place. To keep the grievance in place communal memory must be selective and carefully trained, so the bitterness is passed down intact, increasing through the generations. Such mechanisms produced years of violence in Northern Ireland. They are employed today to corrupt the children of both sides of the conflict in Israel and Palestine.

Evagrius was right to think that too much emphasis on what memory produced was positively harmful to the spiritual life, and limited our ability to grow closer to God. His sense that the nostalgic soul ends up diminished is important. His take on sadness was never really developed by his successors; it is yet another example of how his insights were lost to history, and yet, rediscovered, speak vividly to us.

9

The thought of anger

The most fierce passion is anger. In fact it is defined as a boiling and stirring up of wrath against one who has given injury – or is thought to have done so. It constantly irritates the soul and above all at the time of prayer it seizes the mind and flashes the picture of the offensive person before one's eyes. Then there comes a time when it persists longer, is transformed into indignation, stirs up alarming experiences by night. This is succeeded by a general debility of the body, malnutrition with its attendant pallor, and the illusion of being attacked by poisonous wild beasts. These four last mentioned consequences following upon indignation may be found to accompany many thoughts.[1]

Comment

Evagrius writes frequently about anger, not only in the *Praktikos* but in his other works as well. The word he uses is *orge*, which has the sense of rage or wrath. Anger, it seems, is often on his mind, perhaps more than the other evil thoughts, because, as he sees it, it is a fundamental barrier to prayer which leaves the soul helplessly vulnerable to being shipwrecked. In the *Praktikos*, Evagrius lists anger after sadness, though in other places he shows that he also thought sadness could be a consequence of frustrated anger. He thought that both sadness and anger were found in a part of the soul that is particularly subject to strong emotion, the irascible part of the soul, which he probably believed, as many did in the ancient world, was located in the region of the heart.

Evagrius' analysis of anger as set out above is worth attending to. He describes a process which is all too familiar. Anger is fierce. It is bound by its very nature to destroy any aspiration towards that harmony of spirit which he describes as *apatheia*. Evagrius pictures anger boiling away like water in a pot, and the metaphor is a vivid one: you can see the churning, the bubbling, the steam, the chaos. This is very far from the condition of the soul as clear and still. In fact there is no clarity or stillness at all. The soul is in turmoil against the offender, and it does not matter at this point whether the offence which has stirred up the anger is real or imagined.

Evagrius demonstrates that the sense of having a grievance against another person or persons affects us like a physical injury. We want to rub the wound, caress it, and turn it over and over in our minds. It intrudes into our thoughts the whole time. We speak of nursing grievances and that is precisely what Evagrius is referring to. Like the grief that is part of the evil thought of sadness, the resentment of anger depends on keeping the memory of injury fresh in the mind. It is not surprising that it disrupts prayer. As soon as the monk attempts to pray, the image of the offender flashes across the mind. Once again it is a mental image that is at the root of the problem, an image based on a lingering memory which may seem to arise spontaneously, but once it has appeared it is difficult to dislodge. In a work of instruction to monks Evagrius writes, 'The one who binds memory of injury to his soul is like one hiding fire in chaff.'[2]

Anger is a habit which can grow until it becomes a fundamental part of our personality. It comes into our dreams. It wakes us up at night. Finally, it leads to a paranoid relationship with the outside world in which everything and everyone is a threat, and the world itself is experienced as persecutory.

Anger in the Bible

There is plenty of anger in the Old Testament. God's love for his people is a passionate love. He is angry with them when they reject his love or take it for granted. In the narratives of ancient time in the book of Genesis, God's anger with human beings reaches such a point that he regrets creating them and resolves to destroy all living beings, and the earth itself. This is the prelude to the story of Noah's ark and the great flood (Genesis 6–9). Though God's people are not equal with God, God treats them as partners who have responsibilities and he expects them to play their part in the relationship he has initiated with them. God is angry at disloyalty. When God's people fall into habits of idolatrous worship they are condemned as though they had been unfaithful in a marriage relationship. This theme is particularly developed in the prophetic books of Hosea, Jeremiah and Ezekiel. But it is not only in matters of worship that God's anger is aroused. God is also angry when injustice and oppression arise in the community. This is a double betrayal, because it is from injustice and oppression that he has delivered them. In the psalms and prophetic writings idolatry and injustice are often seen as two sides of the same coin. A heart that can be led astray to worship false gods is a heart that has turned in on itself and is therefore closed to the cries of the poor. The Bible assumes that there is such a thing as righteous anger, and it is necessary to express it when relationships are threatened. The psalms speak to and of God as one to be both loved and feared. His anger is never far away: 'His wrath is quickly kindled' (Psalm 2.11). The psalms plead with God not to be angry: 'O LORD, do not rebuke me in your anger, or discipline me in your wrath' (Psalm 6.1; 38.1). The anger of God is a potent force against injustice and oppression, and the psalms often call on God to punish and destroy the wicked: 'Rise up, O LORD, lift up your hand; do not forget the oppressed . . . break the arm of the wicked and evildoers . . .' (Psalm 10.12, 15a).

In the Old Testament anger is often linked to hatred and murder and it is these which provoke God's condemnation. Resentment spurs Cain to kill his brother Abel and Saul to try and kill David (1 Samuel 18.10–11). This anger does not come from a basis of equality, but assumes that the person who has given offence cannot be confronted or treated as an equal, either because they are stronger and superior or weaker and inferior.

Hatred against sinners and against enemies is not condemned, but even this must be moderated. Psalm 37 suggests that trust in the Lord is better than anxious fretting over the wicked: 'Refrain from anger and forsake wrath. Do not fret – it leads only to evil' (37.8). A verse of Psalm 4 provoked a good deal of interest in the early Christian era because it raised the question of when human anger might be legitimate: 'When you are angry, do not sin; ponder it on your beds and be silent' (4.4). The words translated 'be angry' here could have a range of other meanings, and modern scholars have offered different translations, such as 'When you are disturbed do not sin' in the New Revised Standard Version. But the apparent distinction between being angry and sinning contributed to a long-running spiritual debate about when and whether anger might be justified. This debate begins in the Letter to the Ephesians where the author quotes Psalm 4.4, 'Be angry but do not sin', and adds to it, 'Do not let the sun go down on your anger, and do not make room for the devil' (Ephesians 4.26–27). Anger may be felt, or even expressed, but not indulged or nursed.

Jesus showed anger against the devil in his temptations in the wilderness, an example which the desert hermits would follow. He displayed anger in his denunciation of injustice, most particularly in his violent attack on those who bought and sold in the Temple. But he also showed angry indignation at illness and at demonic possession, an indignation which is closely linked to compassion. His anger in such circumstances is visceral; the gospel writers describe it using a verb which suggests 'snorting like a horse' (Mark 1.41, *kai splanchnistheis*, translated 'moved with anger', or 'moved with pity'). The anger of Jesus was a frustration at the sickness and oppression which held the world in bondage; a sickness and oppression which had demonic origins, though it was worked out on the human scale in unjust relationships. He was not angry on his own account. When turned away from a Samaritan village he refused to entertain the thought of vengeance (Luke 9.51–56). His anger instead is directed at his disciples James and John, who had suggested that they should call down fire from heaven on the inhospitable villagers. Perhaps most significantly, and poignantly, when Jesus was crucified, he did not call down anger on his enemies but prayed for them to be forgiven because 'they do not know what they are doing' (Luke 23.34).

In Matthew's Gospel Jesus offers a radical analysis of various human behaviours in terms which contrast with the Jewish law. Anger is considered against the background of the sixth commandment, 'You shall not murder.' Murderers put themselves outside the law, and are therefore liable to judgement both from God and from society. But Jesus says that it is not enough to abstain from the ultimate act of violence. His followers must prevent angry feelings getting to the point when they boil over and produce irrevocable consequences: 'But I say to you that if you are angry with a brother or sister, you will be liable to judgement; and if you insult a brother or sister, you will be liable to the council; and if you say, "You fool", you will be liable to the hell of fire' (Matthew 5.22). Jesus suggests that there is a sliding scale of anger, in which the most serious offences receive the most serious punishment. The first 'judgement' here may refer to some local arrangement for settling disturbances. The 'council' could be a reference to the central Jewish court in Jerusalem, the Sanhedrin. The final offence of dismissing a brother as a fool takes the offence out of the human realm all together and renders the offender liable to divine judgement. There is, of course, some hyperbole here, as there is in Jesus' teaching about adultery. But the underlying insight is that murder is an extreme outcome of something which is much more common, the angry feelings and resentments which most people harbour without much self-questioning.

Not only is anger against a brother or sister disciple forbidden by Jesus; the one who has caused offence must be proactive in seeking reconciliation. This takes priority even over the worship of God: 'When you are offering your gift at the altar, if you remember that your brother has something against you, leave your gift at the altar and go; first be reconciled with your brother' (Matthew 5.23). This teaching implies that when a person comes into the presence of God having been violently angry, he comes into God's presence with his identity altered, attached to the object of his hatred and to his own self-righteousness as firmly as to an internal idol. Being reconciled with the one who has caused offence dethrones the idol from the heart and enables the worshipper to offer his gift to the one true God.

St Paul lists 'enmities, strife, jealousy, anger, quarrels, dissensions, factions' (Galatians 5.19–21) among other 'works of the flesh' to be avoided by Christian people. And yet it is undeniable that there is an unattractive, gloating anger in parts of the New Testament directed at those who have opposed the spread of Christian faith, or questioned its divine origin. It is also directed at the rich and the exploitative. The book of Revelation indulges appalling visions of the wrath of God, which seems purely destructive. Much of the imagery in which this anger is expressed is drawn from earlier Jewish writings about the end of the world and the judgement of God. These passages have been interpreted in ways that have justified hatred, war and anger in the name of Christ; and they are still so invoked today. We need to remember the context and focus of these difficult parts of scripture; for the vehemence was a way of expressing to a hostile world the Christian claim to be living in God's future, where enmity between peoples and oppression had been overcome. In this sense biblical expressions of anger can be seen as an attempt to challenge those who are complacent about injustice, or who benefit from it in ways which they are reluctant to acknowledge.

Anger in the life of Evagrius

It is likely from his educated background that Evagrius would have accepted the analysis of human emotions offered by the various strands of philosophy in the ancient world. His analysis of anger goes back to a discussion in Plato's dialogue *Timaeus*, which was widely admired in the early Christian era.[3] It is here that Plato describes the three-part division of the soul and attempts to locate them in different parts of the body. The 'irascible' part of the soul, concerned with emotions and feelings, is positioned in the chest. For Plato this arrangement serves a practical purpose: the chest is 'the guardroom' of the soul.[4] Courage, passion and ambition are called up from the region of the heart to defend the soul against any threat from outside itself. In Plato's physiology this region is influenced primarily by the element of fire. The warmth of this region is generally positive in Plato's thinking, it is the source of high spirits, enthusiasm and drive. Evagrius' description of anger as boiling, seething or frothing destructively is derived in part from this description. It also owes something to Plato's pupil Aristotle, who speaks specifically of anger (*orge*) in terms of boiling heat. However strange the physiological assumptions of these ancient philosophers, their description rings true to our experience. We all know that feeling of energetic warmth in the heart when we are in high spirits, and the fullness and heat in the chest when we are indignant or angry.

Evagrius would also have absorbed the biblical material on anger, particularly in the Psalms and the Gospels. However, he was heir to an approach to the Bible which saw much of what the Old Testament assumes about God in terms of prophecy and symbolism. It would not have occurred to him to take expressions of divine wrath literally. He would have assumed that it was as wrong-headed to conceive of God as having human emotions as it was to think of him as having a body. He, like many of his theologically sophisticated contemporaries, thought of God's nature in terms of absolute unity, simplicity and passionlessness. These divine qualities were what ascetically minded Christians were encouraged to imitate.

There are no obvious episodes of anger in the biographical material about the young Evagrius. However, he was known for his rhetorical skills, and these required him to use the language of anger against those he perceived as heretics. Ridicule, sarcasm, mockery and exaggeration would have been his stock in trade.

Anger seems to have been a real temptation for him, though, especially during the months he spent in community living alongside simple Coptic monks who were no doubt somewhat sceptical about his motives – he was a cultured, sophisticated theologian after all. On an initial visit to Macarius the Great he was rebuked for asking for advice and told not to speak before being asked to do so. Evagrius replied hotly that he had read many books and could not accept such instruction. However, he apprenticed himself to Macarius the Great, indicating that he was willing not to let his anger undermine his determination.[5]

Another example of how he dealt with provocation comes from the *Sayings of the Desert Fathers*. Attending a meeting of hermits in Kellia, Evagrius ventured to make a speech. At this, the priest presiding over the assembly rebuked him, commenting sarcastically that if he had stayed in his own country he would no doubt be a bishop by now, with authority over many others. But here he was no more than a pilgrim. One could hardly think of a less encouraging attitude, but Evagrius, apparently, 'was pierced to the heart at these words' and, without haste, bowed his head and wrote with his finger on the ground. Eventually he spoke, to agree with the rebuke and to quote the book of Job. 'I have spoken once and I will no more answer' (Job 40.5).[6]

Evagrius may well have been full of his own opinions as a fashionable theologian in the imperial city, but he was clearly prepared to give up the right to be heard in the desert. This, no doubt, is a testimony to his willingness to learn from the other monks, but it was also a prudent strategy. There were probably inevitable divisions between the educated Greek-speaking monks who had withdrawn into the desert and the more simple Coptic monks of peasant stock. Evagrius knew that inappropriate anger could be hugely destructive to community life and did not want to contribute to it.

From Evagrius' point of view, solitary withdrawal did not cure anger so much as reveal it for what it was, a disturbance of the spirit, which was easily exploited by demons both to create and exacerbate tensions between people and to wreck the work of prayer. The problem of anger for the desert ascetics was that it disturbed their striving for inner peace. For Evagrius this peace was *apatheia*, the passionless detachment and serenity that was the goal of his life. Others describe peace in terms of a state of *ataraxia*, a state of being untroubled. This is the word Athanasius uses in his biography of the first Christian hermit, Antony of Egypt. The whole mechanism which produced anger, the rising of heat in the region of the heart and the boiling over of passion, so graphically described by Evagrius, threatened the very goal for which he was striving. The heat of the soul needed to be controlled not so much because it was an evil but because it had a crucial place in the war against the demons. 'Anger', he asserts, 'is given to us that we might fight against the demons and strive against every pleasure.'[7] The demons, for their part, try constantly to divert anger away from them and towards other people. Their strategy for doing this is to remind us of our worldly desires, our ambitions and longings for achievement and possession. Once they have got us thinking about these things we are hooked into an envious or competitive relationship with others, and at this point lose spiritual awareness and the desire for virtue. Among his other works, Evagrius wrote a long work of quotations from the Bible which were to be used against various demons; texts to be spat out as weapons in the battle with evil thoughts. This work is called the *Antirrhetikos*, which could be translated 'How to Answer Back'. His strategy is simple, use anger to destroy what is out to get you:

> When you are tempted do not fall immediately to prayer. First utter some angry words against the one who afflicts you. The reason for this is found in the fact that your soul cannot pray purely when it is under the influence of various thoughts. By speaking out in anger against them you confound and bring to nothing the devices of the enemy.[8]

Evagrius also suggests that we are helped in dealing with our anger by good thoughts, which come from angels. These thoughts fill us with the hope of spiritual pleasure and blessing.

Evagrius believed that there were other cures for anger, and that the most important among these was the regular chanting of the psalms. This would have been part of his routine while he was training for the solitary life, and it continued to form the background to his life of prayer during his 14 years as a hermit. Palladius, his biographer, says that Evagrius 'recited one hundred prayers a day',[9] and a recent commentator, Luke Dysinger,[10] has suggested that these prayers may have been modelled on the prayers which were said at the end of each of the psalms as they were sung at dawn and dusk in the monastic communities that Evagrius was familiar with. Dysinger adds that if this is correct, in the course of a normal day Evagrius would have offered a brief prayer approximately every ten minutes. Evagrius saw the psalms not only as worship and praise but as therapy for the troubled soul.[11] Plato commended music as a way of quietening the irascible part of the soul, cooling the heat of its passions, and it is likely that Evagrius saw psalmody in this light. Dysinger refers to a letter of Athanasius, the Archbishop of Alexandria, which describes the psalter as a 'picture in which you see yourself portrayed', 'the Psalms . . . serve him who sings them as a mirror wherein he sees himself and his own soul'.[12] Athanasius sees the psalms as compositions of the Holy Spirit. They reflect the movements of our own souls, and as we say or sing the words we not only come to an understanding of the state we happen to be in but take into ourselves the 'pattern and model for amendment of our lives'.[13]

Anger is an issue in relationships, especially when it comes to rebuking or disciplining other people. Evagrius accepted that there might be occasions when it is appropriate to reprimand an individual, but this has to be done with care. Macarius the Great is quoted as saying, 'If you are stirred to anger when you want to reprove someone, you are gratifying your own passions. Do not lose yourself in order to save another.'[14] This is an insightful turn of phrase, which suggests that correcting another person can all too easily provide an excuse to discharge anger. The rebuke may itself be a conduit for the inner tensions of the one giving the rebuke. From the Christian perspective of the desert, Evagrius warns against expressing anger so powerfully against a brother that he 'becomes a fugitive'. I suppose Evagrius means by this either that he avoids us physically or that he in some way hides or runs away because he cannot trust us not to diminish him by our anger once again. 'For if this should happen your whole life long you will yourself not be able to flee from the demon of sadness. At the time of prayer this will be a constant stumbling block for you.'[15]

Anger and the spiritual tradition

Anger as such was not generally condemned in the ancient world. It was an emotion which interested philosophers who subjected it to various kinds of analysis. As we have seen, both Plato and Aristotle had theories about its origin and purpose. What needed clarification was when and whether anger could be justified. The physical effects of certain kinds of anger were always found to be unappealing. Gregory the Great summarized them thus: 'The heart throbs, the body trembles, the tongue is clogged, the face inflamed, the eyes glare and fail to recognize people, the mouth makes noises but sense knows not what is said.'[16] Aristotle had distinguished between three forms of anger – sudden loss of temper, long-lasting resentment and anger

that seeks vengeance – and these distinctions were well understood throughout the early Christian era. Thomas Aquinas used them in his own analysis
of anger and was aware that they had classical roots.

In general in the ancient world anger was regarded as a proper response
to individuals who failed to show appropriate respect for another person's
opinions and loyalties. Anger was seen as the drive to take righteous
vengeance on any person who has slighted you, and thus attempt to restore
a relationship of respect. Anger, in this sense, could be seen as a noble emotion
which evoked awe and admiration in others,[17] a righteous and necessary
assertion of one's dignity as a person, a 'flaring forth of the whole personality'.[18] This kind of anger is based on a recognition of human dignity. It
closely parallels the way divine anger is treated in the Bible. It treats the
offender as an equal by letting him or her know how they have given
offence and so makes possible restitution and forgiveness.

There was also a kind of anger which was reserved for gods and heroes,
a permanent rage against individuals and communities which could be
neither assuaged nor forgiven. Such was the anger of the hero Achilles, as
described in the *Iliad*, an anger which was both righteous and unrelenting.
There is no obvious parallel for this kind of anger in the Christian spiritual
tradition except perhaps in the place where one might least expect to find
it, in the character ascribed to God in certain parts of the Bible. There is
a tendency, which I have already noted in some passages, for the writer to
gloat over God's righteous wrath against sinners, and to allow to God a
level of wrath against sinners which would not be remotely acceptable in
any of his creatures. These passages presented a difficulty to many of the
early Christians who, reflecting the assumptions of Greek philosophy,
thought that God must be beyond such human emotions. They never
assumed by this that God condoned sin; they were clear that human corruption would meet a righteous judgement. But they tended to veer away
from attributing the emotion of anger to God.

More to our immediate purpose, there is yet another aspect of anger
which was condemned in the ancient world. This was the kind of anger
which is passive and unexpressed, the silent fury which assumes that I am
not the equal of the person who has wronged me and therefore have no
capacity to call them to account. This is anger which cannot achieve a good
outcome, it eats away at the person who suffers from it. It also transforms
in two directions. Towards the person who is the cause of the anger it
becomes hatred, and to the self it becomes depression.

On the whole the early Christians were not unduly troubled by feelings
of anger, especially in the early centuries of persecution. Although there is
plenty of evidence that they took to heart Jesus' emphasis on forgiveness,
they were not above using the rhetorical tools of the day to defend themselves against those who treated their beliefs with ridicule. The writings of
the early Christian apologists are full of scorn for idolatry and unbelief, and
use the devices of heavy irony, sarcasm and threat. In theological controversy no holds were barred, and Christians of different factions regularly
accused each other of overweening vanity, ambition and immorality.

A more general condemnation of all anger in human relationships can be traced to the beginning of the ascetic movement. The sayings that have come down to us from the fathers and mothers of the desert are unanimous in their refusal of anger: 'One of the brothers asked Isidore, the priest of Scetis, "Why are the demons so afraid of you?" He said, "Ever since I became a monk, I have been trying not to let anger rise as far as my mouth." '[19]

Angry words, angry gestures, angry thoughts were experienced as destructive to prayer. They also gave rise to other demonic temptations. In the sayings of the desert ascetics we do not see any obvious distinction between good and bad anger. All anger is a problem for someone trying to pray. The monks may even have assumed that the kind of anger which would have been respected as a virtue in civil society was something they had left behind along with status and possessions. Yet in their experience they found anger was not so easily left behind. There is a telling story from the desert about a restless monk living in community who was often irritated by his fellow monks. He decided to go and live alone, believing that when he was unable to interact with others he would find peace. But he was deluding himself.

> One day he filled his jug with water and put it on the ground. Suddenly it happened to fall over. He filled it again, and again it fell. This happened a third time. In a rage he snatched up the jug and smashed it. Coming to his senses, he knew that the demon of anger had mocked him, and he said, 'Here am I by myself, and he has beaten me. I will return to the community. Wherever you live, you need effort and patience and above all God's help.' So he got up and went back.[20]

John Cassian, following Evagrius, describes anger as a deadly poison which must be rooted out from the inmost corners of our soul. Cassian finds anger disturbing because it makes the soul blind to reality: 'As long as this virus lurks in our hearts and blinds our mind's eye with its evil darkness, we are incapable of acquiring the discretion to decide righteously.'[21] He follows Evagrius, though, in finding a use for anger. Where Evagrius uses anger to rebuke the demons, Cassian believes we should use it only to express indignation against ourselves. This is important, because Cassian has much less to say about the role of the demons in temptation than Evagrius. It is the self which is the central problem, and at this point we see how the self is beginning to take on demonic aspects, which, for Evagrius, remained external to the self. Cassian agrees with Evagrius, though, in teaching that anger against another person is never justified. He even takes issue with scripture on this point. In the version of Matthew's Gospel which he knows, Jesus says to his disciples, 'If you are angry with your brother without cause you will be liable to judgement' (5.22). Cassian insists that 'without cause' is an interpolation, 'made by those who fail to understand that Scripture intends to eradicate the root of anger totally'.[22] He prefers those versions of the text which omit the words, as modern scholars in fact tend to. So for Cassian 'the fruit of patience is not in righteous anger, but in not being angry at all'.

In contrast Augustine had begun to develop a more impassioned language of God's anger against sinners in his increasingly strident assaults on Pelagianism. Augustine's view of the human condition became more pessimistic over time, and as a result of developments in his understanding of the fall, he came to the view that every human being from the moment of conception deserved to be damned for eternity.

The theme of God's righteous wrath was taken up by Gregory the Great. Gregory believed that the power of the devil to tempt and punish human beings is a just power, permitted by God. Gregory's teaching marks an important, if depressing, development in theology and spirituality. The spiritual battle that Evagrius engages in with the demons is based on the assumption that the demons are fundamentally unjust, wicked and mischievous. They represent false conceptions of the world and tempt human beings at points of vulnerability. But Gregory has come to think of the devil as of an instrument of God's justice, one who is in some kind of contractual relationship with God to tempt people and extort punishment as his reward, rightly executing God's wrath.

Gregory lists anger as the third of the deadly sins. He places it after vainglory and envy. The logic of this change of position is that frustrated vanity (not getting the admiration one craves) turns to envy (of those who are admired). Envy then produces anger against the person or persons who possesses the status one most longs for oneself, 'because however much the spirit is wounded by an internal wound of envy so much it loses its accustomed tranquillity'.[23] Gregory introduces envy into the list of deadly sins as a separate category. Gregory understands that the resentful anger which causes so much mayhem in human experience often has its roots in a sense of want and shame. Those who experience this kind of shame tend to feel angry with people who appear to have what they believe they lack. Envy is what fills the gap; the resentment against others who seem to have deprived one of the dignity that one believes is one's due. Anger is, of course, a principal vice and it generates other vices in its turn: scowling, big-headedness, quarrelling, rowdiness, indignation and blasphemy.[24]

Gregory does believe, however, that there is a positive use for anger. This is not directed against the devil as such but at all that is wrong in the world. Anyone with a reasonable sense of right and wrong cannot be complacent in the face of injustice. The anger that is aroused by vice is justified, because it defends the place of reason in human judgement. It is a proper use of anger to rebuke vice robustly.

This point is noted by Thomas Aquinas who begins his consideration of anger with a lengthy discussion of whether or not it might be justified; that is, whether it can constitute a rational and reasonable response to certain conditions. He discusses Aristotle's three-part classification of anger and Gregory's teaching on the appropriateness of rebuking vice. He then considers Jesus' teaching on anger in Matthew 5 and shows how anger can move from a feeling of the heart, to words and then finally to deeds. Anger, he says, is one of the more unstable of the passions, and part of its danger is in the words and actions it gives rise to. Hatred is one of the obvious consequences of anger, and Aquinas adds this to Gregory's list of anger's offspring. Finally Aquinas considers whether a person is guilty of sin when there is a good cause for anger and he or she shrugs it off. Does the tolerance of vice reveal the kind of moral indifference which actively encourages vice? At the end of a finely balanced argument Aquinas concludes that the passion of anger is useful to human beings as it spurs them into right action in accordance with the judgements of reason. If a person lacks 'spirited feeling' when reason is outraged it suggests a failure in judgement which is itself culpable.[25]

Dante condemns the unrepentantly angry in the fifth circle of hell. This is an area of marsh and mud called Styx. In classical mythology the River Styx circled the underworld and ran out into marshland at its centre. Here those who have wrecked their lives through the habit of wrath live out the consequences of their behaviour. There are two classes of wrathful sinners for Dante: those whose anger was violent against others, and those whose resentments and loathing simmered below the surface. On the surface of the marsh the actively violent fight each other endlessly:

> . . . . not with fists alone, but with
> their heads and heels, and with their bodies too,
> and tearing each other piecemeal with their teeth.[26]

The resentful lie beneath the surface of the mud, their groans of regret come to the surface as bubbles. Their sin was sullenness, the refusal to take joy or pleasure in the creation; so choked were they by their own unspoken anger. This category of wrathful sinners has something in common with those who give in to the sin of accidie, or acedie. What they refused was the 'joy of the good'.[27]

Those being cured of the sins of anger in purgatory are purged by having to endure the choking smoke of their own rage. They are made to understand the consequences of violent lives; the lack of judgement, the blindness, the loss of insight into self and others that goes with a lifetime of nursing angry feelings. Just beneath the wrathful on a separate terrace of Mt Purgatory are the envious, who are condemned to wander about with their eyes sealed up so us to be healed of the pain of longing for what belongs to others.

Anger is portrayed visually in various ways. Weapons often play a part. In the fifteenth-century mural of the 'tree' of sin at Hessett, anger is shown as a young male figure in yellow hose holding above his head a whip or a sword, as though ready to strike. In his left hand there is a dagger that seems to be directed at his own right thigh. The point is clear: anger, though often directed against others, wounds the self most of all. It is ultimately self-destructive. This crucial insight has survived from the time of Evagrius and makes an important point which still speaks to us today. We have no business hating ourselves, resenting ourselves or intending harm to ourselves – which is precisely what we do when we hate, resent or harm others.

Evagrius, anger and us

Few would quarrel nowadays with the view that anger is an appropriate response to injustice or insult, and that it often provides the energy that fuels change and reform. Modern Christians read the Bible and see the anger of Jesus against sickness and oppression, and find it difficult to understand the view that anger should be eradicated from the soul. A person without anger might be thought to be indifferent to suffering and injustice, and unable to stand up for or defend his or her own rights. Yet there is a negative side to the expression of anger in our contemporary world. We think of defiant, banner-waving crowds gathered to impress television, angry individuals mouthing their hatreds into the camera, the anger of impatience and what has come to be called 'road-rage', foul words, insults and violent behaviour as a feature of everyday life even in the school playground. There seems to be no evading the extent to which anger has become a feature of our contemporary world. We are often encouraged, on psychological grounds, not to hide or deny angry feelings, but to express them. Yet the anger we face is excessive and destructive. It does not seek the restoration of relationships but a continued diminishment, humiliation and even destruction of those who are thought to have given offence.

The teaching of Evagrius addresses this contemporary problem of anger, with a directness which is not found in the later sources, where anger tends to be analysed in moral rather than psychological terms. Evagrius has acute insights which speak to our time. He reminds us of something that we are inclined to forget, that our sense of having been injured is not always based on fact. We may indeed have been slighted by others, but there is also that in us which can be programmed by our past experiences to expect slight. We can be temperamentally touchy, sensitive and quick to take offence. We may simply assume that others harbour hostile thoughts towards us, or believe without specific reason that they are out to shame us in some way. We always feel touchy where we feel inadequate, as though our nakedness is exposed. It is when we carry this expectation of slight around with us that we are vulnerable to those flashing mental images of people or situations which have, as it were, exposed us and brought us shame.

The problem deepens when we turn the person who (knowingly or unknowingly) offended us into an image. Then they become a *thing*, an object in our heads, on whom we feel justified in pouring out not only feelings of anger but more lasting resentment and hatred. In this way the person who has injured us ceases to be a person who is alive and could be addressed and even confronted. We may even feel anger and resentment when we meet someone who reminds us of the original offender, who shares their accent or mannerisms or skin colour or some other characteristic. We then feel justified in hating everyone or anyone who reminds us of our internal object of hatred.

Evagrius' analysis invites us to consider not whether our anger is justified or not, but what we might be doing to ourselves by turning the offender into a static piece of our own mental furniture in order to justify our own continuing anger against them. To do this, as Evagrius sees it, is to court spiritual disaster because it means our adversary has become a part of our identity; we begin to define ourselves exclusively in relation to the one we hate. At this point, Evagrius believes, the anger begins to affect our unconscious life, bringing disturbances in our dreams and, eventually, paranoia.

This all rings true. Anger produces more anger. Often we know all too bitterly that overvehement language on our part has destroyed any possibility of a free and equal relationship with people we have hurt. They no longer trust us and we no longer trust ourselves in relationship to them. What has been said cannot be unsaid. The result is that we are diminished – the anger we expressed against the other person turns inward and wounds us. The same is true of the desire to seek vengeance on others, an all too understandable desire when we have been slighted or wronged. And yet, Evagrius reminds us, echoing the gospel teaching of Jesus, that we cannot offer ourselves to God in prayer when we are nursing resentments against others. He is also very aware that it is precisely when we are trying to pray that bitter and resentful memories are likely to arise.

The destructive effects of anger have been explored by those who have devised the 12-step programmes which combat various addictions. Often at the root of addictive behaviour there is a sense of deep grievance against those who have frustrated the individual in the past. The addict sees him- or herself as a victim, whose rage against others is justified. Alcoholics, in particular, are often violent and abusive when drunk. The effect of alcohol releases inhibition, and at the moment of rage there is a temporary sense of liberation, the 'flaring forth of the personality'. The point is not whether their anger is just or not; at the stage of addiction it is destroying them and those around them. The temptation to anger in this sense, as Evagrius saw so accurately, is a temptation to see oneself as a perpetual wronged victim, as a person with no power and no agency, who is therefore entitled to flare up against others. Such a view of the self is based on a lie, for no one is without some power or agency. We could perhaps learn something from Evagrius' suggestion that a good cure for anger lies in chanting or reciting the psalms. It takes practice, patience and genuine self-respect to begin to free the heart from its ancient resentments.

10

The thought of sloth

The demon of acedia – also called the noonday demon – is the one that causes the most serious trouble of all. He presses his attack upon the monk about the fourth hour and besieges the soul until the eighth hour. First of all he makes it seem that the sun barely moves, if at all, and that the day is fifty hours long. Then he constrains the monk to look constantly out of the windows, to walk outside the cell, to gaze carefully at the sun to determine how far it stands from the ninth hour, to look now this way and that to see if perhaps . . . Then too he instils in the heart of the monk a hatred for the place, a hatred for his very life itself, a hatred for manual labour. He leads him to reflect that charity has departed from among the brethren, that there is no one to give encouragement. Should there be someone at this period who happens to offend him in some way or other, this too the demon uses to contribute further to his hatred. This demon drives him along to desire other sites where he can more easily procure life's necessities, more readily find work and make a real success of himself. He goes on to suggest that, after all, it is not the place that is the basis of pleasing the Lord. God is to be adored everywhere. He joins to these reflections the memory of his dear ones and of his former way of life. He depicts life stretching out for a long period of time and brings to the mind's eye the toil of the ascetic struggle and, as the saying has it, leaves no leaf unturned to induce the monk to forsake his cell and drop out of the fight. No other demon follows close upon the heels of this one (when he is defeated) but only a sense of deep peace and inexpressible joy arise out of this struggle.[1]

Comment

Evagrius has more to say in summarizing this troubling demon in the *Praktikos* than he has to say about any of the others. This is because the demon of acedia has particular qualities which, if surrendered to, destroy monastic aspirations. Acedia is a Greek word which is not easy to translate. In medieval spirituality it became *accidie*, and this is most commonly rendered as *sloth*. But acedia is more than extreme laziness. Andrew Louth[2] translates it as 'listlessness', but this may not be quite strong enough for what is implied. Acedia is like a thick wet blanket that inhibits all energy and purpose. Evagrius taught that it does not arise in any one part of the soul but affects the soul in its entirety. He identifies the demon of acedia with the 'noonday demon' mentioned in Psalm 91, who launches his attacks as the sun rises to its zenith. For Evagrius the premonition of this troubling malady comes well before noon, at the fourth hour, that is, about ten in the morning. The demon manifests as extreme boredom and a sense that time has slowed down intolerably. Concentration is impossible, the monk longs for distraction. The main meal of the day (usually at the ninth hour, at 3 p.m.)

seems an eternity away. The labour of the day becomes impossible in the monk's mind. He cannot bear to get on with his usual tasks.

Alongside this he finds himself reflecting on how unloving his brother monks are towards him and each other. No one cares for anyone, there is no human warmth or encouragement. Everyone is surly and boring. This is the point at which the monk begins to fantasize about how things could be different. He begins to imagine other places where life would be easier, and along with this comes the pious thought that it is wrong to think of God as being confined to any particular place. Since God is to be adored everywhere, surely it is a matter of indifference where the monk himself should live! At this point memory afflicts the monk – a touch of nostalgia, perhaps, presaging the return of the demon of sadness – and affects the monk as he contemplates the loved ones he has left and his former way of life. Time, meanwhile, stretches out before him, an endless wasteland of effort which leads nowhere but to more of the same. The struggle seems entirely purposeless.

Yet the conquest of this particular demon by overcoming the thoughts that encourage its attacks is a significant victory which leads, as Evagrius puts it, to deep peace and inexpressible joy.

The Bible and sloth

Sloth in the Bible is usually identified with laziness. In the book of Proverbs the slothful person is a 'sluggard' who is advised to consider the example of the ever active ant, 'Go to the ant, thou sluggard' (Proverbs 6.6, King James Version – the New Revised Standard Version translates 'sluggard' as 'lazybones'). The consequence of sloth is a decline into poverty. The slothful person neglects the work that ensures they have shelter and enough to eat. 'A little sleep, a little slumber, a little folding of the hands to rest, and poverty will come upon you like a robber, and want like an armed warrior' (Proverbs 6.10–11). The lazy person is storing up trouble in the future. They are unprepared for calamity; they have no reserves when things go wrong.

The wider sense of acedia can only indirectly be found in the obscure psalm reference which the desert fathers and mothers picked on. Psalm 91 celebrates God's provision and care for those who choose him as their shelter. He is utterly trustworthy. He protects his people from danger and delivers them from every calamity. He is a defence against accidents and violence. The one who trusts in God need have no fear of 'the terror of the night', nor of 'the arrow that flies by day' (v. 5). Then come two dangers which are possibly to be thought of as supernatural, 'the pestilence that stalks in darkness' and 'the destruction that wastes at noonday' (v. 6). One contemporary commentator[3] regards both these as dark angelic forces that prowl around seeking to exploit human weakness and vulnerability. We can see from this how the desert fathers elaborated the notion of a noonday demon. It is precisely at that time of greatest boredom, when nothing appears to be happening at all, that those who trust in God are at greatest danger.

There is another description in the Old Testament which comes close to Evagrius' description of acedia. It is in the book of Deuteronomy in a passage which describes the giving of the law to the people of Israel. The law constitutes the covenant relationship between God and Israel; God promises that Israel will receives protection, blessing and fulfilment on condition that the ethical and ritual obligations of the law are met. The blessings that follow the keeping of the law are listed, followed by the curses that will result from disobedience. The curses are appalling and include a catalogue of disasters, many of which actually occurred in subsequent history. (Deuteronomy was written with the wisdom of hindsight, after most of these disasters had taken place.) At the end of the list there is a description of the pathetic state God's people can expect to find themselves in if they fail to obey the law. Exiled from their own land, scattered among the nations:

> You shall find no ease, no resting-place for the sole of your foot. There the LORD will give you a trembling heart, failing eyes, and a languishing spirit. Your life shall hang in doubt before you; night and day you shall be in dread, with no assurance of your life. In the morning you shall say, 'If only it were evening!' and at evening you shall say, 'If only it were morning!' – because of the dread that your heart shall feel and the sights that your eyes shall see.   (Deuteronomy 28.65–67)

This description of restlessness, of loss of energy and purpose and of time hanging heavy is here seen as a consequence of life turned away from God. Here, of course, it is a punishment, an exile from the sphere of God's blessing, whereas the desert fathers took on a self-chosen exile in hope of finding God's blessing. But the vulnerabilities involved in exile as punishment and exile as choice here sound very much the same.

Sloth as laziness reappears in the New Testament. In his correspondence with the Thessalonians Paul advised his flock to 'keep away from believers who are living in idleness and not according to the tradition that they received from us'. It appears that some Christians had given up work and were making nuisances of themselves by sponging on others. Paul's response was to give such people short shrift: 'We were not idle when we were with you . . . anyone unwilling to work should not eat. For we hear that some of you are living in idleness, mere busybodies, not doing any work' (2 Thessalonians 3.7b, 10b, 11). Paul recommended that such people should calm down, do their work without fuss and earn their keep like everyone else. The gospel was not to be used as an excuse for dropping out of normal life.

The teaching of Jesus starts by following the general line of the teaching of Proverbs. The parable of the talents (Matthew 25.14–30; Luke 19.11–25) suggests that those who follow him should use to the full whatever gifts they have been given; failure to do so leads to condemnation. The fig tree which fails to produce fruit is condemned for wasting the soil in which it grows (Luke 13.6–9), but it is given one more chance to produce figs. (Of course, the fig tree is standing for Israel and so the parable is not just about idleness in general, but the failure to fulfil a vocation.) Those who sit back and let themselves become complacent are in greatest danger of finding themselves without resources. But Jesus alters the focus of the Proverbs teaching in a way that would later be taken up by the desert ascetics and help to form their thinking on sloth. The parable of the rich fool (Luke 12.13–21) develops the theme of the 'sluggard' who ends up in poverty and transposes it to comment on the failure of those with material riches to prepare for their encounter with God beyond this life. The rich fool stores his surplus grain in new barns and prepares for a life of luxury and self-indulgence, but his dream is cut short by sudden death, for which he is totally unprepared. No amount of grain stored up in silos can protect him from the summons of his maker.

Jesus also develops conventional teaching about laziness and poverty in an unexpected direction, going so far as to question any straightforward link between work and prosperity. Anxiety about having enough food or suitable clothing betrays a lack of trust in God (Matthew 6.25–33; Luke 12.22–31); the spiritual attentiveness of Mary is preferred to the busyness of Martha (Luke 10.38–41); the labourers who stand idle in the market-place and work less than the full day in the vineyard are rewarded with a full day's wage (Matthew 20.1–14). These different approaches may reflect the fact that Jesus was more sensitive than the compilers of Proverbs to the anguish of those whose poverty cannot be relieved by hard work; who are born into conditions of debt which cannot be repaid, or whose wages are insufficient to cover the basic necessities of life. Jesus knew that the anxiety which inevitably accompanies acute poverty cripples the spirit. It is not a romantic escape but a practical discipline to rely on the generosity of God who feeds the birds and clothes the lilies of the field (Matthew 6.26–28). The hungry disciples snacked on ears of corn as they went through the fields on the Sabbath and Jesus did not discourage them (Matthew 12.1–8), but quoted scripture to show that there was precedent for breaking Sabbath rules when human well-being was endangered by hunger.

Jesus' teaching on the need to rely on God's generosity could be seen as an encouragement to develop sufficient spiritual confidence to challenge injustice and demand a fairer distribution of the world's resources. The parable of the man who woke his neighbour at midnight to ask for three loaves of bread to feed an unexpected visitor (Luke 11.5) and the widow who kept battering away at a careless judge (Luke 18.1–7) for a verdict in her favour are examples of active trust in God which refuses to sink into despair. The later monastic teaching against sloth reflects Jesus' insistence that his disciples actively oppose the temptation not only to complacency, but to defeatism. Such despair is a kind of complacency, deadly in its spiritual consequences.

Sloth in the life of Evagrius

Evagrius himself does not come across as a particularly slothful person. In his youth he was ambitious and an achiever. He lived for almost two years as part of a community of monks and then withdrew into solitude. Yet he was far from completely alone. He occupied himself with the pastoral care of others, with his theological and spiritual writings and with copying manuscripts in his fine handwriting. Yet perhaps he discerned the roots of sloth in himself during that period of his life in which he vacillated about his true vocation. Evagrius had enjoyed the opportunities of cosmopolitan life, good company, fashion, intellectual argument. Yet it led him into a relationship which he knew was destructive. If he had been a different kind of person he might have been able to live with integrity in the city, but for him the attractions it offered divided and distracted him, eventually leading to the illness he suffered while staying with Melania on the Mount of Olives. Sloth, for him, may have taken the form of a lack of focus, a persistent refusal to shoulder the self-discipline of his true vocation.

If this is true then we can widen the scope of what Evagrius meant by sloth to include the attempts we all make to evade what we really should be doing with our lives. Sloth becomes the pursuit of distraction, the deliberate frittering away of time in the attempt to escape choice and commitment. It means keeping all possibilities endlessly open rather than committing ourselves to a particular task, person or way of life.

Evagrius knew that the monk afflicted by acedia will want very much to leave his cell. Evagrius depicts the troubled monk staring at doors, hoping for a visitor, jumping up at every sound and constantly leaning out of the window. He also yawns frequently and drops off readily to sleep; he reads, but cannot concentrate on what he is reading, but turns the pages, leafing through to the end. Evagrius' description is accurate to the point of being comic. He encourages those suffering from the assaults of this demon to lighten up and laugh at themselves. This is important because this demon is 'the most oppressive'.[4] The word used here can also be translated as grievous, or, more vividly, 'heaviest'. Sloth is a weight that, once settled, is hard to shift. The demon of acedia does not target one particular part of the soul; it is characteristic of this demon that it is 'accustomed to enveloping the entire soul and strangling the mind'.[5] It is not surprising that the tempted monk is likely to respond instantly to invitations to visit the sick or to perform some act of service, but in offering service and visiting Evagrius warns that he is merely fulfilling his own need for distraction.[6]

What is much more important is to wrestle with the temptation itself.[7] Evagrius' practical advice concentrates on the spiritual warfare of those oppressed by the demon of acedia. First, the monk must stand firm and refuse to leave the cell. Seated in perseverance, the monk must 'valiantly welcome all attackers, especially the demon of acedia'.[8] Evagrius recognizes that the bored soul needs a challenge; to recognize the temptation to sloth as an armed enemy invading one's space with alien thoughts might help spark a spirit of active resistance. The strategy here is to prevent the all-enveloping nature of the temptation. 'This is the time', Evagrius says, 'to divide our soul in two. One part is to encourage; the other is to be encouraged.'[9] When the struggling ascetic is overwhelmed by listless gloom and distraction he should imagine a second self standing alongside offering support and encouragement. This second self is an expression of the soul's true freedom and potential, and while it can still be evoked in the imagination all is not lost. It is in this twofold state that the oppressed soul can return to prayer, using in particular Psalm 42, where this 'dialogue' within the soul is anticipated: 'Why are you saddened, O my soul, and why do you trouble me? Hope in God; for I shall confess him, the salvation of my face and my God' (v. 5).

Learning to deal with sloth means learning to recognize the soul's ambiguity and to work with it rather than against it. Evagrius teaches that to conquer sloth the monk must live every day as though ready to die the next day, while at the same time looking after the body as though he will have to live with it for many years.[10] The remembrance of death and judgement was another way of concentrating the mind on the importance of the present moment. Evagrius urges monks to 'remember your exodus',[11] which is both the death of the body and the liberation implied by death. In the present time of life before death, the cure for sloth is perseverance. The monk should set himself goals that can be realized and refuse to be deflected from them: 'Set a measure for yourself in every work, and do not let up until you have completed it.'[12]

The basic spiritual issue for the slothful person is that they expect to achieve union with God without too much effort. They assume that the integration they seek is something spontaneous, that once they get into the 'right' environment happiness, holiness and salvation will be theirs all in one go. The slothful person resents the discomfort of anxiety and inner conflict. They want to be at peace, they want to be 'at one' with themselves. But they are premature in their attempt at integration. Rather like the person who goes into psychotherapy to seek healing for emotional conflicts, and announces themselves 'cured' after only a few sessions, their withdrawal to the desert is a false 'flight into health'. It may be significant in this context that Evagrius teaches that acedia does not affect one particular part of the soul, but the whole soul. Surviving acedia involves a form of humility, a willingness to endure inner conflict and the worrying sense of being divided in oneself. Even this painful split within the self can be put to good use in fighting the false integration of sloth. The 'second self' that Evagrius tells us to conjure up imaginatively represents the part of the will which has not submitted to sloth, the part of the self which still has the energy and freedom to want to serve God.

Monks must not give in to the demon of acedia. Evagrius compares the struggle to keep going with the labour of polishing silver (he actually speaks of polishing money) – the effort of wrestling with sloth makes the heart shine, as polishing metal makes metal shine.[13] A shining heart is one that has recovered fervour, love and confidence in God. Struggling with sloth, in other words, renews the desire of the monk to love God, it rekindles the flame of love in the innermost person. Giving in to sloth, on the other hand, is to quell true feeling, 'the spirit of sloth drives away (beneficial) tears, and the spirit of sadness destroys prayer'.[14]

What this makes clear is that sloth is a kind of opting out of real life, a refusal to accept one's own humanity or to seek purpose and direction. It is what we would call apathy or indifference. This is very different from the *apatheia* which is the goal of the spiritual quest, that passionless freedom to which Evagrius would have us aspire. Apathy, in our sense, is enslavement to a view of the self that is untouched by space or time or necessity. It is an ultimate refusal to live. *Apatheia* on the other hand is freedom from being driven by compulsive fears or longings. The final fruit of apathy in our sense is death; the final fruit of monastic *apatheia* is love; the gentle, imaginative recognition and delight in the value of other beings as they exist in God, and of oneself as loved by God.

Sloth in the spiritual tradition

Sloth, acedia, sadness, laziness, moral and spiritual torpor – the states of mind grouped here shade into one another, and yet maintain distinctiveness. Laziness and sadness are clearly not the same thing. Evagrius distinguished sadness from sloth, but in the end the two states were combined under the name acedia. What the desert experience discovered was the spiritual danger of seeking perfection too soon. One of the best-known stories which reflect this is of John the Short who declared to his elder brother that he wanted to be 'free of trouble like the angels, doing no work and serving God unceasingly'. With this ambition he set off for the desert. After a week he went back to his brother:

> When he knocked on the door, his brother answered without open-
> ing it, and said, 'Who's there?' He said, 'It's John.' His brother replied,
> 'John has become an angel and is no longer among men.' But he went
> on knocking and saying, 'It really is John.' His brother did not open
> the door, but left him outside till morning as a punishment. At last
> he opened the door and said, 'If you are a man, you need to work in
> order to live.'[15]

This story may reflect a debate that continued for many years in the Church about the place of work, routine and discipline for followers of Christ. There have always been individuals, like those Thessalonian Christians whom Paul attacked, who have taken the gospel message of grace and salvation as an invitation to abandon daily work in anticipation of the life of heaven. The roots of this attitude may have been in the classical world of late anti-quity where a life of leisured contemplation was often seen as the ideal. Of course, it was an ideal very few were able to pursue; it required either a great deal of money or the adoption of a deliberately vagrant lifestyle. Some early Christian ascetics were virtually indistinguishable from vagrants, and acquired a bad reputation for their idleness and dishonesty. But there were some who were sincerely convinced that routine daily work was incom-patible with the call to prayer, people who took Paul's remark to 'pray with-out ceasing' (1 Thessalonians 5.17) literally, which left little time for work, or even sleep. (Some Christian groups apparently slept in relays to enable the work of prayer to be continuous!) One particular group, the Euchites (praying people), or Messalians as they were also called, were described as heretics by the historian Theodoret, Bishop of Cyrus. The Messalians put

great emphasis on the role of the Holy Spirit and on dreams and prophesies. Theodoret believed that they were infected by a plague of (spiritual)
'enthusiasm', which led them to reject manual labour as wicked. In
Theodoret's judgement their real problem was sloth, which was particularly
manifest in an indifference to the sacramental life of the Church.[16]
Theodoret's judgement was not entirely fair – the Messalians believed that
since the fall every individual's soul was in the grip of a personal demon
which could only be driven off by unrelenting and unceasing prayer. Even
baptism could not liberate the imprisoned soul. Their 'enthusiasm' in fact
was a frenetic desire for salvation, which might suggest the very opposite of
slothfulness.

The approach of such groups to the life of prayer was not generally
accepted. The encounter between such groups and the majority is encap-
sulated in a story about a group of Euchites who went to discuss their
lifestyle with the hermit Lucius. Lucius asked them what manual work they
did. They replied that they did not engage in any because of Paul's command to 'pray without ceasing'. So Lucius asked them whether they took
meals. On hearing that they did, Lucius asked who kept their continuous
prayer going while they were eating. Then he asked them if they slept, and,
again, who was responsible for the continuous prayer while they were asleep.
When they were unable to answer these questions Lucius offered them a
different interpretation of how Paul's command might be fulfilled – he
'prayed without ceasing' by offering repetitive prayer while he worked with
his hands.[17]

Many desert monks found that the life of prayer was plagued with
problems caused by their own restlessness. The great Antony of Egypt, for
example, was troubled by boredom and irritability – recognizable symptoms
of sloth – and prayed to God for healing.

> After a while he got up and went outside. He saw someone like him-
> self sitting down and working, then standing up to pray; then sitting
> down again to make a plait of palm leaves, and standing up again to
> pray. It was an angel of the Lord sent to correct Antony and make
> him vigilant. He heard the voice of the angel saying, 'Do this and you
> will be cured.'[18]

The story of John the Short, the visit of the Euchites to Lucius and Antony's
angel all reflect the way in which the pioneers of the desert began to
realize the need for rhythm and structure to cope with the passing of time.
They recognized that the desert could not provide an instant flight into
holiness. But it took longer to work out sustainable rhythms of work, rest
and prayer. In general the desert ascetics discovered that staying in one place
and performing regular, repetitive, simple work had an integrative effect on
the individual which enabled prayer to flow and controlled some of the
anxious thoughts which gave opportunity to temptation. The monk's cell
represented his firmness of purpose; it was the crucible in which he would
be transformed if only he persevered. 'A hermit said, "The monk's cell is
the furnace in Babylon in which the three children found the Son of God.

It is the pillar of cloud out of which God spoke to Moses." '[19] This is one of many sayings about the need for stability and endurance. Perhaps the best known is attributed to a brother Moses who advised an enquirer, 'Go, sit in your cell, and your cell will teach you everything.'[20]

What emerges from these stories is the recognition that sloth is dissipation; the gifts and abilities of the self are squandered by lack of focus and direction. When sloth strikes, prayer becomes impossible and the sense that the life of prayer might be worth living becomes less and less real. The experience of acedia then leads to the disintegration of the will. The temptation to give up is then overwhelming.

Evagrius' description of the character and effects of sloth is largely followed by John Cassian who was founding religious communities in France two decades after the death of Evagrius. He clearly recognized the relevance of Evagrius' teaching to those struggling with monastic life and echoes both his insights and his humorous descriptions, adapting them to mirror the life of the new monastic communities he was engaged with. Like Evagrius he observed that a monk afflicted with acedia develops a strong dislike for his cell, a contempt for his brothers and a constant sense that he is stagnating to no profit.[21] Cassian recognized the train of anxious and disturbing thoughts in which the monk becomes convinced that the only cure for the way he is feeling is to leave his cell and find someone to talk to, or go visiting the sick or dropping in on pious women who just might be feeling lonely and rejected.[22] Cassian develops Evagrius' insight that sloth might manifest itself in two quite different and apparently opposite ways. First, it could appear as an obsession with getting enough sleep, or an incapacity to resist sleep once the first yawn or sleepy thought strikes. On the other hand it could manifest in active behaviour which looks like its opposite, a drive to find short-term activity which puts some immediate gratification into long, empty hours. Cassian also, following up Paul's attack on the slothful Thessalonians, gives a lengthy description of the apostle's life, pointing out in particular his readiness to work for his living to support his missionary vocation.[23] Cassian claims that the monks in Egypt had learnt the central importance of manual work in the spiritual life, and that they worked not only to be self-sufficient, but also to meet the needs of the poor and those in prison.[24] It is idleness, Cassian claims, which is inhibiting the spread of monasticism in the West – the monks have become too dependent on the generosity of others. Manual work should remain central to monastic discipline, even when there is no economic need for it. To illustrate this Cassian speaks of a certain Paul, who was so remote from any town that it was not viable to sell his produce of palm leaves and kernels. In spite of producing more than enough for his own needs, and being unable to sell what he made, he still worked every day at weaving the palm fronds (most probably into baskets). Once a year, when he ran out of space to store the fruits of his labours, he burnt the entire year's efforts. By this example Cassian urges that manual work should be undertaken 'for the purification of his heart, the control of his thoughts, perseverance in the cell and the defeat and overthrow of *acedia* itself '.[25] In the final chapter of his treatment of acedia Cassian confesses that he had once been troubled by the malady himself, and was convinced that only a visit to Abba Paul could cure him. But another hermit, Moses, warned him that flight was no solution, he must endure, staying in his cell to resist and overcome.

Cassian's personal experience led him to value stability. He came to believe that growth in prayer requires a regular, disciplined and rhythmic lifestyle. He saw sloth expressed in the desire to wander from place to place, settling in a new environment at first with enthusiasm and then becoming disillusioned. He insists that there is no perfect environment and there are no perfect communities in which the individual could simply flourish without effort and endurance. It is the recognition that growth in stability in the life of prayer requires a measure of actual stability which led to the particular emphasis of the Rule of St Benedict. Benedictine monks take a vow of stability along with a vow of obedience and of continual conversion in all aspects of life, *conversatio morum*. Benedict knew he was both developing the tradition of the desert and starting something different. The monastic life could be abused, and in the Prologue to the Rule Benedict described two groups who, as he saw it, gave particularly bad examples. The Sarabaites improvise their own rules and live according to their whims, calling 'holy' anything that happens to please them. Even worse in Benedict's view are the monks he calls 'Gyrovagues' – who are really travelling spongers who move from community to community, enjoying others' hospitality and never putting down roots. A lack of stability was the cause of both distortions and both in different ways could be said to reflect the consequences of sloth, the refusal to endure. In the Prologue to the Rule, Benedict saw the way of life that he outlined as 'a school of the Lord's service' and implied that it was meant for beginners, who could not manage the heroic self-sacrifices of the desert pioneers. There is no mention of contemplation as the fruit and goal of ascetic practice. In fact there is very little about spiritual experience at all. The emphasis is practical, on doing not on feeling.

Above all the Rule offers a way of ordering time. It helps monks towards salvation by encouraging patience and perseverance. It is this very patience which enables the monk to have some share of the passion of Christ, and to inherit his Kingdom.[26] The aim of Benedict's way of life is the service of God, and the central feature of it is worship, the regular offering to God of prayer and praise. Prayer is balanced by manual work and study. The hours of sleep are not to be negotiated; they are prescribed. In Benedict's Rule there is no real space for what we might call leisure, the pursuit of individual interests or hobbies. There is certainly no time for relaxation, chilling out, gossip or a quiet drink with friends. The Rule seems designed to exclude the very possibility of sloth. Indeed, Benedict himself remarks that 'idleness is the enemy of the soul'.[27]

Benedict's monasticism can seem harsh from our perspective. But the point of it, as the contemporary Benedictine Joan Chittister says, is not rigour, but balance, which is perhaps harder.[28] The Rule is to help those who take it on to find a natural rhythm which is neither driven by urgency nor simply boring. Commenting on the Chapter 28 of the Rule, Joan

Chittister says, 'The function of the spiritual life is not escape into the next world; it is to live well in this one.'[29] Work and prayer are two sides of the same coin, and taken together create a life that is 'both holy and useful'. It is interesting that in this comment 'usefulness' is not excluded as part of the point of the spiritual life. This articulates a real break with the antique tradition of leisured contemplation being of value in itself.

Pope Gregory the Great, as we have seen earlier, did not categorize sloth as one of the seven principal faults. But he does recognize the spiritual issues connected with sloth and includes them in his treatment of sadness. These include rancour, cowardice, desperation, lack of self-care, restless thoughts and a straying of the mind towards other temptations, all of which could be summed-up as a basic instability of purpose.[30] In the different context of his *Pastoral Rule*[31] he contrasts the way in which a person in authority should deal with the slothful and the over-hasty. Here he treats sloth essentially as a form of laziness. The tendency to put off doing things when the time is right to do them often means that the slothful person finds it is too late – the tasks which should have been done eventually cannot be done at all (a common experience which is reflected in the General Confession in the Book of Common Prayer: 'We have left undone those things which we ought to have done'). As Gregory sees it, to allow sloth to gain a foothold is to allow torpor to develop into sleep, in which the individual gradually loses any desire to do things for God or to love and serve God. He or she is then vulnerable to temptation to fritter their life away in pleasure-seeking.

Here Gregory reflects over again his belief that a major consequence of Adam's fall is that we are hopelessly vulnerable to our own addiction to pleasure. We do not readily embrace the life of virtue. We are much more likely to be paralysed by the moral inertia which he describes as the sleep of sloth. The fact that we cannot find any lasting happiness by satisfying our craving for pleasure is a just punishment for our original fault. Our unhappiness is also meant to act as a scourge, driving us to recognize the desperate peril that goes with self-indulgence. The discipline of hard purposeful work is an essential part of the reform of character which Gregory believes is central to our salvation. Those who followed Gregory in the discussion of the vices which inhibit moral and spiritual life tended to take for granted his deep suspicion of pleasure and his earnest insistence on the need for constant striving to turn away from sin towards God. Sloth summarizes the human condition before or without conversion.

Thomas Aquinas connects sloth to sadness, quoting John of Damascus for whom sloth was a kind of 'oppressive sorrow'.[32] He discusses Gregory's treatment of sadness and also an attempt to distinguish between 'spiritual apathy' and 'despondency' by Gregory's contemporary, Isidore, Bishop of Seville. He finds neither of these treatments satisfactory. Sloth cannot be defined by laziness, because the opposite of laziness is hard work, whereas the opposite of sloth is joy. The sadness of sloth needs careful definition, and for Aquinas the key issue here is the relationship of sadness to God. Aquinas links sloth to a failure to keep the Sabbath day holy. The Sabbath is a time of rest, yet the slothful person fails to 'rest in God' in the sense of trusting God for their own good. Sloth is not merely a sadness *about* God. It is more specifically a lack of joy in the good that God offers. As an aside, Aquinas links the corrosive effect of sloth to that of acid, which is often cold to the skin. Sloth is a waning of the desire and belief in God's goodness, a coldness in the face of the good that God holds out to us. In that sense it is a refusal to love God with all one's heart and soul and mind and strength; a failure, in the end, of charity. So sloth was developed as a major mortal sin in the Western tradition. Aquinas' work formed the theological basis for the penitentials, which became standard manuals for the clergy after the decree of the Fourth Lateran Council in 1215 that the laity should confess their sins once a year. Sloth became depicted in the wall paintings of churches, one of the vices growing out of enormous trees of vice. In the sin tree at Hessett[33] sloth is portrayed leaning backwards, as though falling out of the tree. It simply has no energy to support itself.

All these developments of the tradition offer clarification of what is involved in sloth and why it might lead to personal disintegration, but there is some loss, as the Church takes the freshness and psychological acuteness of Evagrius' original description and schematizes it for mass consumption.

Evagrius, sloth and us

The evil thought that Evagrius describes as acedia has a long and complex history. As we have seen, at one end of its range of meanings it is indistinguishable from laziness, sloth in its most obvious form. At the other end it shades into an experience that we might feel comes close to what we would call depression. We now tend to see depression as an illness rather than a temptation; and, as depression, many struggle against it for months or years without apparently reaping the benefits of calm and joy that Evagrius predicts. Yet often even people whose depression does take the form of a real illness find ways through it which show that they have found new sources of strength and creativity. The endurance of depression can, in the end, be a useful experience, and perhaps Evagrius and his successors were not so far off the mark when they suggested that the sufferer should simply stay in the same place and resist temptation as far as possible. Often, for contemporary sufferers from depression there is little choice but to do just that.

In popular culture we tend to make a firm but different distinction between depression and sloth. Depression is undesirable, but sloth is often perceived as a positive good. We are encouraged to think of sloth as something we deserve, a good rest to reward all that hard work to which we are otherwise addicted, a time of chilling out, and passivity, to recover from our stress. Our belief that we are overworked gives us permission to seek leisure with a strangely driven intensity. Getting smashed on Friday night is the rightful prize for five twelve-hour days commuting to the office. If sloth has a negative connotation then it is surely that odd condition which affects hormonally challenged teenagers and keeps them in bed until midday. An irritation but nothing more sinister than that.

This turnaround of sloth from sin to virtue reflects two contradictory tendencies. The first is a mounting dissatisfaction with the moralism of the Western Christian spiritual tradition, and perhaps an instinct, among those who believe in God and try to pray, that human beings might be designed for something more relaxed and gracious than a spiritual regime of unrelenting penitence and self-improvement.

The second tendency is the deep lack of trust that there is any goodness being held out to human beings at all. In the absence of belief in God the human heart must make its own good, and the effort of this, let alone the lack of conviction that any good is ultimately lasting or reliable, is fertile ground for 'oppressive sorrow' to breed. Contemporary life in the Western world is driven by consumerism and the anxiety and insecurity that go with it. We do not have any sense of a lasting future – no one plans, builds or thinks with future centuries in mind. We do not rest in God, or anything else, and so the craving to 'opt out' of the ordinary becomes irresistible. There are various ways of opting out: we might seek to become extraordinarily powerful, rich or successful, or we might take endless holidays from the demands and obligations of communal life, or we insist on our primary right to privacy and 'family time', or we indulge our desires for comfort and pleasurable sensation. If there is ultimately no one to love, comfort and uphold us, then we must look to ourselves. Sloth justifies our self-interest and self-seeking and tells us, principally through our advertising media, that we deserve our rewards and that they are our right. It is perhaps no accident that one of the most frequently used contemporary phrases by which we say goodbye to one another is 'Look after yourself'.

There is something to be learnt here from Evagrius' conviction that acedia is an unwillingness to live within limits. Our contemporary society encourages us to believe that *any* limit to our desire, choice or experience is to be resisted. We are encouraged to live too much in our imagination, to desire the fruits of our labours before we have completed the labours themselves, to let ourselves become discontented with our present circumstances and to fantasize that a different, home, job, partner, church would make all the difference. Who hasn't sat in a schoolroom or at a desk or in a kitchen at ten o'clock in the morning, surveying what looks like a blank stretch of meaningless time until coffee, lunch or a midday glass of wine?

Sloth is a temptation, or false rationalization, to live as though space, time and necessity had no effect on us. It is to try to live as though we were not bodily, limited creatures who must find meaning and purpose in order to live. It may seem to be a temptation which is very far removed from contemporary experience. We live 24/7 lives, there is no natural rhythm of work and rest in the global economy. We are driven by desires to achieve and possess and by the fear that if we fail to do so we will not survive. So in a sense we know all too well the dangers of a slothful existence. It represents a failure to compete and succeed, a degradation of the will. This is why there is a tendency in today's society to be critical of those who cannot work, as though being without work is always the individual's fault. Scroungers, fraudulent claimants of social benefits, the work-shy, the dependent – these are some of the ways in which our media categorize people who do not live by the rules of our overworked society.

What Evagrius means by sloth touches us more deeply than we might think. For what he sees is that sloth is an attitude of mind and heart, a refusal to find purpose and meaning in the restrictions and requirements of daily living. Slothfulness is that fretful inability to inhabit our daily routine with any real sense of purpose. The search for distraction may take many forms: pathological sleepiness, flitting from task to task, wasting time, not finishing things, finding excuses to break the routine, micro-managing the work of others, endless lateness or turning up early for everything (especially meals), over-control of our children, allied to neglect of their real needs. Sloth can manifest as shopping therapy, pootling in a meaningless way round supermarkets, distracted by choice, flicking channels on television.

In a longer perspective sloth may involve a constant adding to one's load of small-scale tasks and responsibilities. By taking on more and more without thinking out how each particular task contributes to the whole, we begin to lose a sense of responsibility for our lives. We no longer have to work out what we really want to do, we no longer have to find the motivation of freedom and love which draws us nearer to God and to our true selves. Our life is measured out in things which occupy our minds for the short term without bringing us lasting satisfaction.

The demon of acedia reduces us to drudgery; either the desperate drudgery of watching the clock, or of having no time to do anything properly. Either way is to be less than human.

For those who retain belief in God an assault of sloth has a spiritual dimension which is additionally frightening. Sloth can be linked to spiritual depression in which the hope is bled out of life. Prayer seems a mockery. Churchgoing is tedious beyond belief, so we stay away, or treat ourselves to a holiday from commitment. Some wander from church to church, never staying long enough to get involved. The sense of belonging and mission and purpose which once gave zest to life seem empty. In their place is a round of trivial activities, a treadmill of distractions which seem without end or purpose, and in which we can make no decision or bring anything to completion. Even hanging in there and enduring seems an act of heroism beyond imagination.

Interestingly, Evagrius recognizes that the conquest of sloth brings about significant personal integration. No devils follow on from sloth. The person is left with a sense of peace and joy. Peace suggests harmony, an ability to be free and content within the constraints of time and place. And joy is gratitude, a pleasure and liveliness to be in the place where we actually are, doing the things that we actually do, loving the people we are called to love, and finding a rhythm of work, sleep and leisure that is healthy and life-giving. To come through sloth is not only to believe in the goodness that God holds out to us but to know it in body, mind and heart.

11

The thought of vainglory

The spirit of vainglory is most subtle and it readily grows up in the souls of those who practise virtue. It leads them to desire to make their struggles known publicly, to hunt after the praise of men. This in turn leads to their illusory healing of women, or to their hearing fancied sounds as the cries of the demons – crowds of people who touch their clothes. This demon predicts besides that they will attain to the priesthood. It has men knocking on the door seeking audience with them. If the monk does not willingly yield to their request, he is bound and led away. When in this way he is carried aloft by vain hope, the demon vanishes and the monk is left to be tempted by the demons of pride or of sadness who bring upon him thoughts opposed to his hopes. It also happens at times that a man who a short while before was a holy priest, is led off bound and handed to the demon of impurity to be sifted by him.[1]

Comment

Vainglory is an old English word which has fallen out of use. It is a literal translation of the Greek *kenodoxia*, which is a combination of the word for 'empty' and a word which means 'opinion', 'fame' and 'reputation' as well as 'glory'. This comes into Latin as *inanis gloria*, again, empty glory. The 'vain' of vainglory is related to the English word vanity. Evagrius sometimes suggests that vainglory originates in the irascible part of the soul;[2] at other times he indicates that vainglory and pride may be directly caused by demons fabricating dreams by night.[3] This association is connected to Evagrius' belief that the devils work by introducing mental images, fantasies which disturb the monk in the quest for stillness. Today vanity means conceitedness, especially about physical appearance. We have lost the more subtle sense of vanity as 'emptiness', though we still speak of an effort or initiative which bears no fruit being 'in vain'. When the Preacher of Ecclesiastes cried, 'Vanity of vanities, all is vanity' (Ecclesiastes 1.2), he was lamenting the emptiness, the ultimate nothingness, of all human achievement. There is no lasting basis on which human beings can glorify themselves. Yet the desire for fame and recognition is persistent. People want to know that they are 'worth it'. The person afflicted by vainglory longs to be admired by others. But this craving is bottomless, empty, first because it rests on the shifting sand of public opinion, and, second, because even the greatest of human achievements passes away through time. The desire for recognition can never be wholly satisfied.

Because of the particular bias of our own culture we might tend to link the thought of vainglory to the contemporary craving for 'celebrity' status. But though vainglory can manifest in very blatant ways, 'blowing its own trumpet' as it were, it can also be very subtle and hidden. Evagrius sees it as a particular temptation of the virtuous; it afflicts those trying to pursue a good life whether through practical work for others or through the adoption of an ascetical lifestyle. For such people vainglory is a secret desire, secret often from themselves. Nevertheless at root the hunger for recognition is related to the open craving for adulation which we see in contemporary culture. The virtuous often have the same longing for the attention and admiration of others. Evagrius would have listened to the inner thoughts of many of those pursuing a life of prayer and he knew how vainglory produces in such people appealing fantasies of extraordinary spiritual gifts and powers. The monk with vainglorious tendencies will see himself in his mind's eye surrounded by the needy and the sick, healing women with a touch or a word, setting the oppressed free from devils, always the focus of the prayer and the desperation of the needy. Vainglory draws the virtuous on to want more and more spiritual power. They see themselves giving spiritual direction and advice to others who ask them, or rather beg them, to seek ordination to the priesthood. When the individual modestly refuses to contemplate ecclesiastical office the fantasy has him being bound and led away to be forcibly ordained. The subtlety of this fantasy is that the monk keeps his virtue and modesty intact while attaining, at least in his mind, his true desire for fame. When the fantasy crashes the monk is left desolate, vulnerable to the further temptations of sadness or pride. The sadness comes from the bitter knowledge that the fantasy is unattainable. Pride then comes in and bolsters the wounded ego with the gratifying thought that even if the monk's secret dreams fail to come true, he is *really* worthy of all that they promised. A further fall is all too possible. The one who in his mind had become a holy priest is all too likely to fall into lust and shame.

Vainglory, then, is a craving for admiration which is often secret and always fed by fantasy, an inner conviction that one is more gifted, able, powerful or virtuous than others. Although Evagrius has argued that the conquest of acedia brings peace and joy, he here suggests that vainglory and pride can easily slip in once acedia has been vanquished. It is almost as though after a person has come through the bitter struggle with sloth, he or she then sits back and begins to admire what they have achieved. This is where the fantasies of writing a spiritual biography might come in, of making one's struggles public. No doubt the apparent motive for doing so would be to help others, but a more subtle, hidden motive could be to bask in the admiration of others.

Vainglory in the Bible

In the Bible vainglory can be blatant or subtle, as it is in our own experience. The Bible does not distinguish between vainglory and pride; the boasting and hunger for fame which is the expression of vainglory slips seamlessly into that self-sufficiency and self-worship which is ultimately condemned as pride. There are blustering tyrants like Nebuchadnezzar, who is satirized as a monstrous egotist (Daniel 3). Nebuchadnezzar builds a golden image of himself and commands his people to worship it. The point is obvious:

self-glorification is a form of idolatry; only God is worthy of worship. The story is told with humour and mockery, and followed by a harrowing account of Nebuchadnezzar's mental breakdown in which he is humbled before God. What is worth noticing here is that the Bible does not start from pride as the root of all the other sins (unless one reads the story of the forbidden fruit through the eyes of later Christian interpreters); pride tends to be seen as the final outcome of other sinful tendencies.

The biblical stories commend the humble, those whose lives point away from themselves. In the patriarchal narratives the central character is really God; the human characters become involved with God's purposes because they are called to make him known. The fame and reputation or notoriety of particular individuals is entirely related to the part they play in further-ing or hindering God's purposes. An interest in one's own particular physical or mental gifts leads to trouble. It is Joseph's 'long robe with sleeves', the gift of his doting father, which provokes the jealousy of his brothers. God tends to choose those who are not the most handsome, or the most strong, or the most obviously gifted. The patriarchal narratives set the pattern for the choosing of Israel. A group of oppressed slaves is to become the people of God. The pattern continues as the stammering Moses is chosen over the more fluent and plausible Aaron; the ruddy-faced David over his older brothers. 'The LORD does not see as mortals see; they look on the outward appearance but the LORD looks on the heart' (1 Samuel 16.7). The biblical approach to fame and reputation is perhaps best summed up in the ecstatic song of Mary of Nazareth: 'My soul magnifies the Lord, and my spirit re-joices in God my Saviour, for he has looked with favour on the lowliness of his servant' (Luke 1.47–48a).

Yet, for those who seek to serve God, the temptation to self-glorification is always present. Security and success lead to a hardening of heart when God's people begin to credit themselves with their achievements under God. Looking back with the hindsight of the experience of exile the writers of Deuteronomy warned the Israelites of the dangers of such complacency. The Israelites are wholly dependent on God for their escape from libera-tion in Egypt. They are not a great or powerful or numerous nation; their success is entirely due to God's choice of them and love for them (Deuteronomy 7.7). Their journey through the wilderness was a long training in dependence on God, and its trials, including that of hunger, were intended to humble them and make them reliant on God's word (Deuteronomy 8.2–3). God was bringing them into a land of great bounty, 'a land flowing with milk and honey', as well as supplies of water, wheat and barley, vines, fig trees, pomegranates and olive trees, with useful deposits of iron and copper (Deuteronomy 8.7–10). The people would prosper in the land, and build fine houses and increase in numbers. But with this would come temptation: 'Do not exalt yourself, forgetting the LORD your God who brought you out of the land of Egypt, out of the house of slavery' (Deuteronomy 8.14). They were not to forget the trials of the 'great and terrible wilderness' with its poisonous snakes and scorpions. Above all, they were not to start thinking of their relative affluence in the Promised Land as something they had achieved for themselves: 'Do not say to yourself, "My power and the might of my own hand have gained me this wealth." But remember the LORD your God, for it is he who gives you power to get wealth . . ."' (8.17). Complacency, in Deuteronomy, was the outcome of a lack of humility before God and it was inevitably accompanied by a turning away of the heart to other more visible gods who could be more easily placated and controlled. At the same time, this turning away from God would be accompanied by social injustice. It is because the land and its produce is an undeserved gift that the people must practise generosity: 'Do not be hard-hearted or tight-fisted towards your needy neighbour. You should rather open your hand, willingly lending enough to meet the need, whatever it may be' (15.7b–8).

The long journey of Israel through the wilderness is a training in humility and dependence on the invisible God. The people learn to function without an image of God and this seems to be intimately connected to their vocation to be a people who are not reliant on a glamorous or successful self-image. The question arises then of what reward is appropriate for God's people in God's service. The answer in Deuteronomy is clear-cut. There is curse and blessing, reward and punishment, depending on whether or not the people obey. Obedience, though, does bring a reward that the vainglorious would recognize. The people will, in fact, be feared and respected among other nations (28.10), and in this way they will be known as God's holy people. It is as though good reputation, even 'fame', is acceptable, as long as it is a by-product of the glorification of God and not a consequence of a grasping need for respect.

In the Wisdom writings of the Old Testament the theme of good reputation emerges again. Although humility under God is still a dominant concern, the desire to be well thought of by others is seen as a virtue: 'A good name is to be chosen rather than great riches, and favour is better than silver or gold' (Proverbs 22.1). Again, the concern for social respectability is regarded as legitimate. To be well thought of by others is a reasonable ambition. After his trials Job dies, rich and admired, surrounded by four generations of his loving family. Such an end is proof of God's blessing and reward for Job's patience and integrity.

The early Christians inherited Jewish attitudes blended with classical understandings of virtue and vice drawn from Hellenistic culture and philosophy. Modesty and humility are commended by St Paul. Yet he is painfully aware of an inner conflict with his own tendency to vanity. Though he was not an obviously successful figure in terms of high status, good looks or wealth, Paul did achieve considerable success in spreading the gospel of Jesus Christ among the Gentiles. In this he was a pioneer, but in a Church which was still developing its understanding of authority and leadership, it was not clear to Paul on what basis he might continue to encourage, reprove or warn his flock. One of the rhetorical devices familiar to him was to appeal to the superiority of his own experience. We see him fighting this temptation in his Letter to the Galatians, and again in his correspondence with the Corinthians. In his Second Letter to the Corinthians he seems to be throwing his weight about by claiming to have worked harder and suffered more than the arrogant group at Corinth which he is addressing. He recognizes the temptation behind his strategy and tries to get round it by claiming to be boasting only of 'the things that show my weakness' (2 Corinthians. 11.30). But then at the beginning of the following chapter, even though he knows 'nothing is to be gained by it', he launches into an account of his own mystical experiences, which he tries to soften by reporting in the third person, as though he is talking of someone else. He then describes how 'to keep me from being too elated' he received what he calls 'a thorn in the flesh, a messenger of Satan' and he repeats the phrase 'to keep me from being too elated'. He knows that 'being too elated' by his own achievements may feel wonderful at the time but may also spell potential disaster. This is valuable testimony, a witness to the paradoxes faced by those genuinely advanced in their Christian discipleship.

In the story of the temptations of Jesus the temptation to vainglory is represented by the second temptation in Matthew's Gospel (Matthew 4.5–6), which is placed third in Luke's (Luke 4.9–12). The devil spirits Jesus away to Jerusalem and puts him on the pinnacle of the Temple, urging him to throw himself down, providing a spectacular display as God would be bound to save him.

Jesus taught that there is no virtue or reward in performing pious acts in order to be seen by others. His typically playful example of such mis-directed piety is the person giving to the poor who calls attention to his charity by sounding a blast on a trumpet (Matthew 6.2). But giving to the poor should be a secret act, even from the self. The left hand is not to know what the right hand gives away (Matthew 6.3). The suggestion here may be that the left hand would take the gift back in some overt or sub-tle way if it 'knew' what the right hand had done. The point, though, is that virtue should be an act of trust in God, not a way of seeking recognition for oneself. Prayer is to take place in secret (Matthew 6.5) and should not be full of 'empty phrases' (6.7). Length of prayer is not the point; we cannot impress God by our efforts. Fasting, too, should be a secret dis-cipline. We are not to draw attention to ourselves (6.16ff.).

Jesus warned about the seduction of craving for special recognition. Luke writes of Jesus at a wedding banquet, noticing the jostling for the most prestigious places. He advises the disciples to avoid the shame of being removed from a high position to a less significant one by going first to the least attractive place (Luke 14.8–11). In the divine banquet those who exalt themselves will be humbled; those who humble themselves will be exalted. Ironically, the way to achieve exaltation is to practise humility.

Probably the most poignant picture of vainglory in the Bible is the parable Jesus told about the Pharisee and the tax-collector (Luke 18.9–14). The Pharisee prays 'with himself', thanking God that he is 'not like other people' whom he characterizes as 'thieves, rogues, adulterers'. He then recites a list of his virtues. He fasts twice a week, he gives away a tenth of his income. Yet it is not he, says Jesus, but the tax-collector who goes home justified, that is, righteous in the eyes of God. The tax-collector knows his unworthiness, and asks God for mercy. The parable exemplifies the way in which the Christian tradition develops earlier biblical insights. Real integrity cannot be based on a flawless self-image, but arises out of the opposite, out of pure dependence and humility. The parable reveals the ultimate emptiness of the Pharisee's prayer. It is based on a fantasy of his own superiority. Even the God to whom the Pharisee prays is expected to agree with the Pharisee's estimate of himself and to approve it. Such a god is an idol, manufactured out of the Pharisee's vanity. The real God is not one who is answerable to us. This is why Jesus is so critical of those who make their religious practices public. Those who fast ostentatiously so as to show others that they are fasting 'have received their reward' (Matthew 6.2b and 5b). Their egos are inflated, but spiritually they remain empty.

In the two gospel accounts which describe the temptations of Jesus in the wilderness, vainglory can be identified in the temptation to Jesus to make a spectacular display of his power by throwing himself down from the pinnacle of the Temple. For Matthew this is the second of three temptations; the last is to do with avarice, possessing all the kingdoms of the world and their treasures. But Luke puts the temptation to vainglory last, as if to suggest that this is an even more subtle and dangerous temptation than that of ownership of the kingdoms of the world, perhaps because its attack comes from within as much as from without. The person in the grip of vainglory is seduced by an empty image of their own importance; they are on the brink of that final delusion of grandeur, the isolation of pride.

What was really critical for the development of the Christian understanding of vainglory was the example of Christ's own humility before God. An early Christian hymn, quoted by Paul, speaks of how Christ, 'though he was in the form of God, did not regard equality with God as something to be exploited, but emptied himself, taking the form of a slave, being born in human likeness' (Philippians 2.6–7). The downward movement, from glory to humility, and even humiliation, is the divine route which brings us salvation. In our own imitation of that movement we must progress from a false image of our own worth to a true recognition of our own nothingness. This is the real significance of Jesus' teaching that those who exalt themselves will be humbled and those who humble themselves will be exalted. The humble person has no pretensions and does not require others to feed his or her vanity.

Vainglory in the life of Evagrius

Vainglory is a temptation to which the young Evagrius was prone. Palladius presents him as a brilliant young man, 'most skilled in confuting all the heresies',[4] and reports that he flourished in the imperial city. The historian Sozomen tells us that he was 'handsome in person and careful in his mode of attire',[5] suggesting that it was his attractive appearance that led to his disastrous romance and hasty flight from the city. Perhaps he enjoyed frequent visits to the gym, massage and bodybuilding, all of which would have been available to him in fourth-century Constantinople. The Syriac version of Palladius' *Life* says that he was 'ministered unto by slaves'.[6] The society Evagrius lived in as a young man was hierarchically ordered. Social relationships were based on patronage. Advancement depended on who you knew and on acquiring networks of influence that would facilitate your advance. The monastic protest against imperial society involved a rejection of this entire system. The search for worldly honour, status and esteem was held in contempt by those attempting to live an ascetic life. This was something Evagrius seems to have found extremely difficult. When he was staying with Melania and Rufinus in the monastery at the Mount of Olives, prior to taking up the monastic life, he lapsed into his old ways. Palladius tells us that 'the devil hardened his heart, as in the case of Pharaoh'. He changed back into his trendy clothes and reverted to what one can only imagine was his former talkative, gossipy self. Palladius says 'he was intoxicated with vainglory', though he also, more kindly, suggests that this was at least in part because 'he was young and full of uncertainty', a nice reflection of Evagrius' later recognition of how genuine vulnerability attracts and is exploited by demonic temptation.[7]

By the time Evagrius composed his treatise on asceticism, dedicated to the monk Eulogios, he had recognized the corrupting effect of the whole system of a social life based on the acquisition of 'honour', with the power of patronage and status that went with it:

> Virtue does not seek people's plaudits for it takes no delight in honour, the mother of evils. Human esteem, then, is the beginning of honour and its end is pride, for the person who demands honours exalts himself and such a one does not know how to bear contempt.[8]

But even in spite of his second conversion, which led to his taking the monastic habit, Evagrius did not get over his worldly life easily. This is shown in the advice he gives to those starting in the spiritual life. They are to beware of taking any pride in their dress as this gives a blatant invitation to the spirit of vainglory.[9] He also recognized that vainglory is the most worldly of the temptations: 'Vainglory involves fantasizing about social encounters.'[10] The networking of his old life, with the opportunities offered for gossip, influence and advancement, must have been in his mind. His withdrawal from such a life was still fraught with the temptation to fantasize about what he had lost. His initial encounter with Macarius the Great must have been a blow to his pride – he asked for spiritual advice from the older man just as any other aspiring monk might have done, only to be told to be silent until he was spoken to. This story suggests that the older monk probably knew of Evagrius' reputation as a successful and attractive theologian-about-town and that he struggled with his attraction to status and fame, and was seeing whether he could put him off by a display of typical Coptic roughness and bad manners.[11] If so, he failed, as Evagrius apprenticed himself to Macarius, and always afterwards counted himself as one of his disciples.

When he had been living the solitary life for some time, the Patriarch of Alexandria, Theophilus, tried to persuade him to become bishop of the region of Thmuis.[12] Although there was little doubt that in his earlier life

Evagrius would have been a strong candidate for episcopal office, and might well have enjoyed the honour and power of the role, at this stage in his spiritual life he was well able to resist the temptation. He fled to Palestine until the threat of promotion was over.

In his desert life Evagrius certainly was admired by others and many came to see him for spiritual direction of one kind or another. According to the Coptic *Life of Evagrius* he was visited by great numbers of pilgrims and found himself having to employ a manager to administer a budget for hospitality.[13] As his own spiritual life developed he was able to use his gifts not in order to enhance his own reputation but in order to give practical help to those struggling with temptation. His concerns had moved away from himself, and he no longer needed others to be the mirror in which he saw himself. What attracted people to him was his gift of discretion, or discernment as we more often put it. Discernment is an important word in the Christian spiritual tradition. It implies an understanding of the human heart, a recognition of individual differences that enabled Evagrius to tailor his advice to the individual without being diverted by the particular gifts or cravings that the individual presented to him. Discernment requires a certain detachment. It is all too easy in spiritual direction and counselling to be flattered or repelled by the needs and cravings of the other, and to fail to see them with real clarity and compassion. Evagrius was in demand, not only because he understood the ways of the human heart, but also because of the practical remedies for temptation that he developed, like the scripture verses in the *Antirrhetikos* that were designed to repel temptation. These practical aids could be taken up as much by the simple and uneducated as by the scholarly and articulate.

The capacity for discernment and the practical methods of resisting temptation were perhaps less likely to feed Evagrius' capacity for vanity than his more intellectual gifts. It is interesting to note that although he continued with his theological studies and his involvement in disputes with heretics, his contribution in these areas does not seem to have been much valued by others, even by his contemporaries. In fact his ability to express himself in prose with great precision aroused scepticism. One critic described him as a 'hewer of words who has led the brethren astray with his writings',[14] and Jerome was deeply critical of him.[15] He was, as we have seen, eventually condemned for heresy, along with Origen, the Christian biblical exegete he most admired.

The temptation to vainglory, however, can be very subtle, as Evagrius knew. The danger to monks was not over when they had learnt contempt for the status-seeking of the world. He was all too aware that when the mind of the hermit has attained a small degree of detachment from the passions, 'it then acquires the horse of vainglory and immediately rushes to the cities, getting its fill of the lavish praise accorded to its repute'.[16] There is a vividness and poignancy about that image of vainglory as a horse, tossing its mane, rushing on the spiritual beginner, to bear him off into the public realm where his craving for adulation can be satisfied. For Evagrius vainglory was 'an irrational passion, and it readily gets tangled up with any work of virtue'.[17] He also compares it to bindweed, which tangles itself round a growing tree, using the height of the tree to support itself while sucking life out of the roots.[18]

Real grief in the face of sinfulness (not the nostalgia which Evagrius depicts as the temptation to sadness) prevents vainglory from taking hold. Evagrius is very aware of how the practice of asceticism can lead to vainglory. The demons can get to work on moderate success in asceticism, spurring the novice on to competitiveness with others, living and dead.[19] The monk then fantasizes that he belongs among the great ascetics. The demons even manage to hide more lowly sins, like lust, from the monk's awareness, so that he assumes he has achieved great progress.[20] Evagrius also recommends that wise monks should avoid the temptation of discussing their spiritual lives with others in hope of receiving commendation.[21] Evagrius describes one monk who was attacked by demons praising him for his ascetic labours. He was able to repel them by reciting the psalm verse, 'Let them straightway turn to flight in shame, those who say to me "well done, well done"!' (Psalm 69.4).[22]

In general monks should not discuss their ascetical practices with others. 'The sharpest weapon of the beast is vainglory, which shoots down ascetic labours . . . As you conceal your sins from people, so too hide your ascetic labours from them.' [23] People who talk about their spiritual successes lose the fruits of their labour.[24] It is also important to continue to receive spiritual counsel.[25] These two safeguards protect against the admiration of others and, even more importantly, against admiration of oneself. The monk should think of his present life as a journey along a dangerous road 'full of thieves and brigands'.[26] Being dependent on the praise of others is like being constantly vulnerable to robbers; your treasures are on display for all to see. The monk must not 'sell' his labours for the esteem of others. Discussion of one's spiritual progress is only permissible when consulting a spiritual guide, when one is subject to another's scrutiny.

Evagrius sees vainglory as twinned both with pride and sadness:

> Strip down pride in yourself
> And put vainglory far away from you
> For the one who does not obtain glory will be sad
> And the one who does obtain it will be proud.[27]

The person tempted by vainglory is always vulnerable to disappointment if the honours they seek are not attained. If you long for admiration and the longing is frustrated, you are vulnerable to other, lesser temptations, chief of which here is the nostalgic sadness that you have not received the recognition which you believe your talents entitled you to. One thinks of what sometimes happens when a person is passed over for promotion and they cannot get over the 'nostalgia' for the position they had long imagined themselves occupying. On the other hand if secret ambitions are even partially fulfilled the individual may be assailed by pride. For Evagrius, pride is the most obvious consequence of vainglory, and the most dangerous temptation of all, as it separates the soul from God. But vainglory itself is a great survivor, as Evagrius recognizes in a delightfully humorous image: 'I have observed the demon of vainglory being chased by nearly all the other demons, and, when his pursuers fell, shamelessly he drew near and unfolded a long list of his virtues.'[28] Even when terrorized by other more obvious demons, vainglory pulls himself together, dusts himself down and *shamelessly* returns to recite his many virtues. Vainglory here is like the Pharisee in the parable, full of its own righteousness. It has no insight into itself; its virtuous self-image is not easily punctured. But such grandiosity, as Evagrius recognizes, is deflated by two things. The first is laughter. We instinctively know this. The satirical treatment of Nebuchadnezzar in the book of Daniel has its contemporary resonance; journalists and comics, at least in free societies, routinely poke fun at politicians and celebrities. This is not simply cruelty or disrespect; it comes from a healthy awareness that those in public life are prone to grandiosity. The other great antidote to vainglory is tears.

Macarius the Great, Evagrius' mentor who was initially so rude to him, had the gift of tears. Any temptation to vainglory he might have had was quenched by his deep grief for his own sinfulness. A story tells of how he resisted being made a guru to others. Macarius was old and the monks of Mount Nitria in Egypt longed to see him before he died. They offered to go to him in Scetis if the journey was too far for him. But he made the journey to them in response to their request. Then

> The elders asked him to speak a word to the brothers. But he shed tears and said, 'Let us pray and weep my brothers, before we go hence to the place where our tears consume our bodies.' They all wept; and fell on their faces, saying, 'Abba, pray for us.'[29]

Macarius would not allow himself to be treated as though he were a charismatic leader and demonstrated this by refusing to speak to those who had asked him to address them, choosing to demonstrate his solidarity with them by praying alongside them instead.

Vainglory is associated with one of the fundamental errors in prayer, the spontaneous habit of forming and clinging on to mental images and concepts of God: 'Vainglory is the origin of the mind's erring, when the mind is moved thereby, it makes attempts at circumscribing the divine in forms and images.'[30] Evagrius has often been criticized for his emphasis on image-free prayer, but in fact he did not commend this all the time. Luke Dysinger shows that in his comments on the psalms he commends the use of mental pictures in praise and petition to God.[31] He uses mental imagery himself, especially in describing the world of the demonic, as we see in his image of vainglory as a horse. He also commends the use of a very vivid form of meditation on hell and heaven to bring the novice monk to a place of stillness.[32] But at the same time he warns us that to think God is contained or circumscribed by an image is fundamentally idolatrous. The heart and mind at rest in God see nothing that can be seen.

What concerns him here is that there is a relationship between our mental images and concepts of God and the images and concepts that we hold about ourselves. Evagrius held firmly to the view that the true God must be beyond even images and concepts. At the same time his teachings suggest that our spiritual growth should lead us away from an inflated image of ourselves, or perhaps any image of ourselves, since to live from a self-generated image of ourselves is to restrict our openness to God. Evagrius is very aware of the way in which the human imagination produces fantasies from our memories and desires. Often these take a visual form – we see ourselves as we would like to be. The demons associated with vainglory have an ability to exploit this weakness. They produce dreams of spiritual success: power over demons, healing diseases, pastoring a little flock.[33] It is the spontaneously arising *image* of himself as a much-admired priest, ascetic or healer that leads the individual so easily astray. This is one of the reasons why for Evagrius true prayer needs to move away from both concepts and images and rest in God alone where there is refuge from both the depression (sadness) of not having achieved anything and the narcissism (vainglory) of spiritual vanity. It is God's impression on the soul that counts. Yet when God impresses himself on the soul the impression leaves no mark.[34] On the contrary, it is as though the presence of God liberates the soul to be itself.

In the end what really finishes off vainglory is the satisfaction of the monk's desire for God. Evagrius calls this contemplative knowledge. It is the real experience of the love and freedom of God flowing into the heart of the human person. The self-emptying of Christ in the incarnation is the pattern for the monk's emptying himself of vanity, craving for recognition and exaggerated self-esteem. This is what ultimately fills up the emptiness of the self, once the lesser temptations have been overcome.

Vainglory in the spiritual tradition

Vainglory was not an obvious temptation in classical culture. In the ancient world great rulers, philosophers, military commanders and statesmen were not expected to be modest. The 'triumph' accorded to a victorious Roman general was intended to be a stunning display of his prowess. Satisfaction in one's own achievements was more a virtue than a vice, and a very necessary virtue for any kind of leader or ruler. The autobiography of the first Roman emperor, Augustus, was grandly entitled *The Achievements of the Divine Augustus*. 'Greatness of spirit', magnanimity, was applauded.

At the same time there was an awareness among the philosophically inclined that an over-reliance on the praise of others could itself become a weakness. The truly great person was above others' praise or blame. The philosophy of Stoicism encouraged indifference to the opinion of others. Aquinas would later report that Cicero thought vainglory robbed people of spiritual freedom,[35] and Aristotle thought that the truly magnanimous person was indifferent to praise.[36] There was also a strong awareness in the ancient world of the transience of fame and the ultimate futility of worldly honours, however attractive and desirable they might appear. When conquering Roman generals held 'triumphs' to celebrate their return from war and to display their captives and booty, it was customary for a slave to whisper to the conqueror 'Memento Mori'. The tradition passed into the Christian world and at papal coronations a monk burns a paper in the sight of the new pope saying, 'Sic transit gloria mundi' ('Thus passes worldly glory').

Generosity and kindness were commendable in the great and the good, as long as they did not appear as weakness, which was unforgivable. The ancient world did not value humility. Humility was servility, an attitude appropriate to social inferiors, slaves, women and others who were dependent on the good will of others.

So the coming into the world of a Saviour who 'though he was rich, yet for your sakes he became poor' (2 Corinthians 8.9), brought about a completely novel approach to individual achievement and status. Vainglory, just because it is often linked to human achievements which are in themselves admirable, is one of the hardest temptations for virtuous human beings to come to grips with.

The ascetic movement began in earnest after the conversion of Constantine, at the point at which Christianity began for the first time to be respectable. It was obvious to many of the desert pioneers that respectability brought with it the most terrible danger. How could the Christian faith keep the integrity of its martyred heroes when it was becoming the faith of sinners as well as saints? The flight into the desert appeared to be a flight away from the vain pomps of the world, but of course it carried within it the hidden temptation to self-glorification. Visions and revelations were treated with suspicion. Some, of course, were valid, and these tended to be the disturbing ones. It was Evagrius' alarming encounter with an angel in a dream that compelled him to flee Constantinople in search of a saner way of life. Most visions, though, were thought to be of demonic origin. The desert pioneers, including Evagrius, often appealed to Paul's warning that the devil can appear as an angel of light, and the stories of the desert often reflect that insight.

> The devil appeared to a monk disguised as an angel of light, and said to him, 'I am the angel Gabriel, and I have been sent to you.' But the monk said, 'Are you sure you weren't sent to someone else? I am not worthy to have an angel sent to me.' At that the devil vanished.[37]

The antidote, as in this story, is humility. Evagrius also quotes a story of a demonic attack being repelled by the 'lightning-bolt' of humility.[38]

The temptation to vainglory was a real one for the more charismatic figures of the desert. Not all were invulnerable to the temptation to show off their spiritual prowess or to use it to hold power over others. One thinks of Simon the Stylite who famously lived for years on top of a pillar and wielded great influence over the Church in the mid fifth century. Bishops, theologians and rulers were ill-advised to act without seeking his counsel, even though, with the wisdom of hindsight, his example seems more a manifestation of spiritual exhibitionism than genuine holiness.

The subtlety of vainglory is noted by John Cassian who says that the old men and women ascetics of the desert compared it to an onion with its many layers.[39] However many layers you strip off there is always another underneath. There is no obvious behaviour which defeats it. If the temptation to vanity does not lead a person to extravagant dress, it will lead him or her to self-admiration in their sordid rags. If a person is tempted to show off in their praying and tries to prevent this by praying in secret, he or she may still be proud of having prayed in secret.[40] For the soul possessed by vainglory, even following the command of Jesus and shunning ostentatious religion, may not solve the problem. The hunger for admiration may be so strong that it causes a part of the self to detach and hang over the active, caring, praying self like a mirror. So the self admires the self, and has the reward it seeks by doing so. In Cassian's understanding, the craving for admiration can be so strong that if it cannot be gleaned from others it is often evoked from within.

In his Rule, Benedict of Nursia began with a call to attention, a call to prayer. Obedience is the road to glory, but it is a road which leads down before it leads up. At the heart of the Rule is the image of the ladder, Jacob's ladder, which leads from earth to heaven. Yet for Benedict the ladder is not to be climbed; it is a means of descent, 'Our proud attempts at upward climbing will really bring us down, whereas to step downwards in humility is the way to lift our spirit up towards God.'[41] Benedict sees the steps of the ladder as decisions which can take us closer to God. The sides of the ladder represent body and soul, the self in its integrity. Stepping down to find God is counter-intuitive, it resists our natural impulse to compete and achieve. Benedict outlines 12 steps down the ladder by which the aspiring monk comes into a lasting discovery that he is held and sustained by the love of God. They begin with attentiveness to God and include a laying aside of self-will, a readiness to be obedient, even to the point of suffering injustice, a readiness to be open about one's faults, a willingness to put up with less than perfect circumstances, a preparedness to see others as more significant than oneself and a restrained carefulness in conversation with others, particularly in laughter. It all sounds rather grim, but the purpose of the descent into humility is not to make oneself miserable but to come to genuine self-knowledge at the same time as helping to make life tolerable for others. The struggle to make the descent shows us all too clearly just how vulnerable we are to thinking we are superior to others, or more gifted, or even more wounded and special. So powerful are the instincts to set ourselves above or against others that we need to practise thinking of ourselves in a different way; not as another kind of set of achievements, but as a response to the call of God who loves us as we are with all our vulnerabilities and anxieties. The ladder of humility was intended to de-programme the monk from the expectations of an insecure, driven and violent society.

Benedict's Rule is a programme for living in the presence of God and of other people. Benedict, like Evagrius and Cassian, believed that the human person, though selfish and lazy, was capable of hearing the word of God and responding to it freely. Benedict founded his small communities on the principle that a life orientated towards God could bring a person fulfilment, not so much as an individual but as a person living alongside others.

Community life, as Benedict saw it, was fundamentally opposed to all forms of possessiveness and competitiveness. The Rule assumes that all are equal and should be treated with fairness. It was much admired by Pope Gregory the Great who was fascinated by the kind of paradox that Benedict presented in his ladder of humility. He, like Benedict, believed that a true ascent to virtue was only possible through a descent into humility. Any other kind of advance brought the danger of pride, and pride was critical for Gregory, as we shall see.

Gregory the Great departed from Cassian and Evagrius by downplaying the significance of vainglory. Instead of seeing vainglory as a step on the way to pride, he took pride to be the root of all sin with vainglory as its first shoot. That has many implications as we shall see in the next chapter. But it also meant Gregory had a rather different understanding of vainglory from that implied by Evagrius and Cassian. Where Evagrius and Cassian saw vainglory as blind to itself, Gregory thought vainglory does have some insight. For him, vainglory is aware of its emptiness. This means that it easily gives rise to envy of what others possess, as power and possessions are ways of filling its inner emptiness. The fruits of vainglory for Gregory are disobedience, boasting, hypocrisy, quarrelling, wrangling, discord and novelty seeking.[42] By making vainglory the origin of possessive envy Gregory is closer to the story of the temptation of Jesus as it appears in Matthew's Gospel, where avarice comes last, than the story as it appears in Luke's Gospel, where vainglory is the climax.

In these adjustments Gregory loses something of the subtlety and universality of the earliest tradition. In particular, what Gregory abandons is the insight that vainglory in some sense feeds on an image generated by the self, and destroys the self by doing so. It is the blindness of vainglory that makes it deadly, its lack of recognition of its own inner emptiness.

Thomas Aquinas follows Gregory in listing vainglory as a deadly sin that flows from pride rather than a temptation which leads to it.[43] For him, vainglory is the excessive pursuit of praise and admiration. This definition needs qualifying. Aquinas, with his usual common sense and moderation, does not regard a desire for excellence as a bad thing in itself. The praise that follows excellence is not in itself wrong. But vainglory is 'empty' because it looks for a degree of praise and admiration which is not in proportion to that which is due. Vainglory simply thinks too much of itself.

Aquinas, like Gregory, regards vainglory as a capital sin because it gives rise to other sins. If vainglory is seen as an attempt to display excellence to others this can be considered either in terms of words or deeds. If words are involved this implies boasting. If deeds, then it would tend to be what Aquinas calls 'a passion for innovation'. We live in a society which prizes innovation, but for medieval society it carried overtones of arrogance and assumed superiority. Aquinas also saw vainglory manifest in attempts to prove that we are not inferior to others. This can result in obstinacy, quarrelling — especially the kind of loud and noisy argument which others are intended to hear — or a refusal to obey the commands of those in authority over us.

Over time the lists of sins came to omit vainglory. Gregory's innovation of setting pride apart as the root of all the other deadly sins weakened vainglory and it eventually became hard to distinguish it from pride, especially once envy was established as a sin in its own right. The attributes of vainglory tended to merge with pride, so that pride became pompous and vain as well as cold and isolated. Some depictions of the deadly sins showed pride with some of the attributes of vainglory. For example, in the fifteenth-century murals of St Ethelbert's Church in Hessett, Suffolk, a fourteenth-century Pride is personified as a male figure, richly dressed and holding out his hands as though waiting for applause. And this in the end is what distinguishes vainglory from the ultimate sin, the sin of pride. Vainglory *needs* the applause it longs for. Pride, on the other hand, is beyond need.

Evagrius, vainglory and us

To get to grips with vainglory we need to distinguish it from the affirmation we all require for emotional and spiritual health. We only have to look at a baby looking with delight into the loving eyes of its mother or father to recognize the simple goodness of parental love. The baby's sense of self depends on seeing himself or herself mirrored back lovingly by the adults on whom he or she depends. This love cannot be pretended or forced; it is forged from the intimacy of sexual desire, pregnancy and birth. When we are at our most vulnerable we need to be at the centre of the universe in order to survive. In fact children who *do* receive such loving attention tend to find it easier to come to the mature recognition that they are not, in fact, the centre of the universe than those who have been deprived of it. Psychological theory suggests that a child who has not received positive reflection from his or her parents will be subject to narcissistic disorders in which vanity and controlling behaviour are a protection against wounds to self-esteem. So we need to distinguish between a healthy seeking of recognition for oneself, which also recognizes the humanity and giftedness of others, with an unhealthy craving for uncritical respect. This and the tendency to promote oneself at the expense of others are contemporary expressions of vainglory.

We live in a world which is fascinated by individual achievement, where fame and status are regarded as highly desirable. The gestures which are used to acknowledge applause tell their own story. A bow or a curtsey – a gesture of humility – used to be the formal gesture for receiving acclamation, followed perhaps by a few self-deprecating words. Now applause is often greeted with a punch into the air or a thumbs up sign, or by hands raised in a way which encourages more. The race for social visibility begins early. Ambitious parents try to imbue their offspring with a high sense of personal self-worth because they know that they need to learn to promote themselves in order to get noticed. We are right to be generous in praise and affirmation with children, but where these are given indiscriminately they cannot really be trusted, and children come to doubt themselves, to fear failure and refuse risk. Image is all-important and vainglory feeds on images. We are all much more visually aware than we used to be: cameras look at us, glass-fronted windows reflect us, we produce instant images through digital cameras and mobile phones. These can be used to threaten and control others by recording images of violence and messages of hate, which often seem to contain a pathetic plea for personal significance. Violent loners on killing sprees on school and university campuses, suicide bombers with their snarling self-righteousness seem driven to throw their lives away for an orgasmic moment of fame which they will never actually experience. Some will even see their lives as a sacrifice, as the fulfilling of a Messianic quest.

All this makes us a bit edgy, a bit nervous. We want to fit in, we want to be liked, or at least to pass as an OK sort of human being. This mild narcissism runs through our life, but it can become something much more serious. Those truly in thrall to contemporary manifestations of vainglory cannot contemplate the thought that there is any flaw in their image at all, any weakness that others might see, or anything of significance that cannot be seen, understood and manipulated in one way or another. The reaction to a frustration of their craving for control is rage. The unacknowledged and unrecognized vainglory of our contemporary culture produces an occupational hazard for those who preach, teach, care, act, broadcast, front institutions and so on.

Because the disconcerting truth is that vainglory really is empty inside. Vainglory disguises an inner deadness; the one who craves significance from others only comes to life in the gaze of others. Without the spotlight there is nothing there. So he or she doesn't just like the limelight; they need it, it is food and drink. Vainglory unmasked is a vampire, sucking the life out of others who typically do not realize they are being used. The fans, the groupies, the admirers, the members of the cult; they never quite realize how much the leader depends on their admiration.

We have seen how vainglory slipped out of the list of deadly sins, and one factor which may have contributed to this is precisely that it is the temptation to which the virtuous are most prone. As it is the professionally virtuous who do most of the teaching about sin it may have become rather too easy to ignore! Those whose Christian ministry is fed by a need for admiration are vulnerable to flattery which can take many forms. Invitations to dine with the rich and famous, to accept gifts of money, holidays and other favours, including the flattery of sexual suggestion, can all encourage and be encouraged by a sense of entitlement, the filling up of mind and heart by an over-agreeable image of the self. It is not unknown for popular, loved and attractive Christian ministers to end up having affairs with those they should be taking care of. The same is true of those in other 'caring professions'. Those who consciously or unconsciously work on their appearance to make themselves look a bit like Jesus (walking through the needy crowds, healing one with a touch, another with a word) are particularly vulnerable. The inner story of some of the great evangelical preachers, the devout and inspiring Catholic priests and religious, the much-loved pastors and teachers in churches, temples, synagogues and mosques suggests that the hunger for admiration runs very deep in those who love God and serve the faithful, especially in those with outstanding gifts. Religious life does not usually offer much recompense in the way of wealth or sexual satisfaction, and perhaps it is hardly surprising that those who devote themselves to virtue expect some sort of reward. The truth of how such rewards are sought and obtained is not often told by those who sought and obtained them, but it often could have been told by their spouses, their children or their subordinates!

The irony is that in spite of the prevalence of vainglory many people never really become enthralled to its seductions. This is because they do not really believe the publicity which goes with it. Told to have high self-esteem they manage never quite to believe in themselves; instructed to take care over their image they forget at a crucial moment. The failure to develop vainglory may be because they are prone to sadness, that depressed mourning for what is unattainable which Evagrius sees as vainglory's twin. On the other hand it may simply be because they are saner than average and are blessed with a realistic view of their own capacities which does not involve an overdependency on the admiration of others.

It is an unhelpful bias of our culture that we are so enraptured by our own image. Those with the highest self-esteem are not, in fact, the most creative members of society. They are more usually found in prison, clinging to a sense of innocence in which others are always to blame. But while we are rightly disturbed by pathological individuals we have to admit that we are all made vulnerable to the pursuit of glamorous appearances, to vaunting our specialness in one way or another. The importance of visual images in our culture also makes it harder for us to believe in invisible realities. God, heaven and virtue are concepts not easily comprehensible to minds as fluent in imagery as ours tend to be. We look for the most helpful image of God, the most plausible analogy of heaven, and for concrete examples of virtue. Seeing is believing; the challenge that Evagrius gives us to let ourselves drift free from mental images is something we find extremely difficult, and even frightening. We live in a visually attuned age. Yet Evagrius challenges us to consider whether sight is the best ally in our attempts to participate in the mystery of God. The danger is always in taking what the eye can see as being all there is, and this of course is exactly what vainglory encourages us to do: to mistake the surface of things for the substance.

12

The thought of pride

The demon of pride is the cause of the most damaging fall for the soul. For it induces the monk to deny that God is his helper and to consider that he himself is the cause of virtuous actions. Further, he gets a swollen head in regard to the brethren, considering them stupid because they do not all have the same opinion of him. Anger and sadness come following on the heels of this demon, and, last of all, comes in its train the greatest of maladies – derangement of mind, associated with wild ravings and hallucinations of whole multitudes of demons in the sky.[1]

Comment

Evagrius sees pride as the culmination of all the other temptations, the inevitable outcome of succumbing to what has gone before. Pride is the temptation to deny God, to fall into a kind of self-sufficiency, where the self replaces God as the active agent at the heart of life. This is a prelude to the disintegration of the self and leads to the chaos portrayed here as the free flight of raving demons. These unpleasant creatures populate the sky as though they are besieging the gates of heaven, claiming a victory which, fortunately, cannot ultimately be theirs. Pride is the final delusion, the belief that the self is autonomous and needs neither God nor other people in order to be fulfilled.

There can be no doubting that for Evagrius pride is serious, the most serious of the evil thoughts. But the order in which he describes the evil thoughts is important. Evagrius rarely describes pride in terms of the 'original' sin.[2] What is more typical for him is to see it as the culmination of giving in to earlier temptations. Pride is a refusal of relationship, and as such, it can afflict the would-be monk right at the beginning of the ascetic life. If a new monk needs food or clothing he should accept them from others. To refuse to do so is pride.[3] Pride grows alongside vainglory, and to avoid it those struggling to live virtuously must renounce all thoughts of praise. The search for honour encourages fantasies and ends in pride.[4] Evagrius' eight evil thoughts do not include jealousy, but he is aware that jealousy is a sour fruit that relates both to vainglory and to pride, whether as a cause or a consequence. Jealousy is 'the garment of pride', and the 'disrobing of humility'.[5] Humility is content to be needy and lowly in terms of possessions, power and status, but vainglory and pride are acquisitive of others' goods, powers and virtues. Finally, pride is opposition to God.[6] It prevents human beings from recognizing their true nature. As the key passage above shows, pride is stirred up when the individual is able to find a way of satisfying his or her craving for importance without any longer needing the active admiration of others. In fact those in the grip of pride regard all others as beneath them, as 'stupid', because they do not all hold the high opinion that they hold of themselves. As Evagrius accurately observes, when vainglory is not met by others' admiration the result is often either a retreat into sadness or a lapse into sins of lust. Either of these might be preferable to the inverted progress implied by pride. But for the person who has given in to pride there is no longer any reason for sadness on account of the opinions of others.

> Do not give your heart to pride
> and do not say before the face of God, 'Powerful am I';
> lest the Lord abandon your soul
> and evil demons bring it low.
> For then the enemies will flutter around you through the air,
> and fearful nights will follow you.[7]

Where egotism is complete there is no room for God. In this sense God abandons those who has abandoned themselves to pride. The sky is darkened with raving demons. The tragedy of those who have been overtaken by pride is that in their own eyes they have become a perfect mirror for themselves. There is no longer any need for God, nor any capacity to live in dependence on God. In fact there is no need for anyone else at all.

Evagrius learnt theology as a young man from the Cappadocian Fathers, three deeply influential thinkers who had a considerable impact on Christian life and thought in the fourth century. Gregory of Nazianzus ordained him a deacon, but Evagrius' theology draws especially on the thought of Gregory of Nyssa. From him Evagrius took the idea that the human soul is destined to be the mirror in which God shines.[8] To reflect God authentically the mirror of the soul must be pure from faults and rifts, clear of fantasies and the *logismoi* that arise from them, and united within itself. Such a soul has found that holy freedom which Evagrius calls *apatheia*. Basil of Caesarea also contributed to Evagrius' spiritual theology with his perception that the dawn of the authentic knowledge of God could be compared with the experience of light shining in the soul.[9] Evagrius himself says that 'the proof of *apatheia* is when the spirit begins to see its own light'.[10] He continues that once the faculties of the soul are awakened its capacity to see its own light is maintained even in the presence of the flickering images of dreams. It is also maintained when the normal practical business of daily life demands attention.

The human soul, then, is the place where God reveals himself. It can be compared to the place of God's revelation to the people of Israel on Mt Sinai:

> When the mind has put off its old self and shall put on the new one, born of grace, then it will see its own state in the time of prayer resembling sapphire or the colour of heaven; this state scripture calls the place of God that was seen by the elders on Mt Sinai.[11]

Scripture describes Sinai as a place of striking clarity, a perfect image of heaven: 'Under his feet there was something like a pavement of sapphire stone, like the very heaven for clearness' (Exodus 24.10). As we have already seen, the way to this knowledge of the mind as a place of God's revelation requires the progressive putting aside of all mental images:

> If someone should want to behold the state of his mind, let him deprive himself of all mental representations, and then he shall behold himself representing sapphire or the colour of heaven. It is impossible to accomplish this without impassibility, for he will need God to collaborate with him and breathe into him the connatural light.[12]

It is only in the greatest humility that the human mind can see itself as luminous, lit up with God. The revelation is not of the soul itself, it goes beyond any innate capacity that the soul might possess. It is the result of pure grace. Yet this grace is held within the purposes of God; God intends human beings to be transparent to him from all eternity: 'The state of the mind is an intelligible height resembling the colour of heaven, to which the light of the Holy Trinity comes in the time of prayer.'[13] The model for the praying Christian, and the source of grace, is Christ, because he alone understands the invisible, imageless, bodiless state of being which is the pure light of the Trinity.[14]

If the human soul really is destined to be the place of God's manifestation, then pride is the ultimate sin. For pride denies the true nature of the soul and understands humankind as enclosed within itself, God to itself. The introduction of pride as the final sin poses a final spiritual challenge. The destiny of the human soul is either to be in God or to be totally deprived of God. In other words, the soul is presented with a stark choice, either to be a mirror of God or a blank wall, enclosed in self-sufficiency. Such a soul may appear calm and complete but is in fact cracked and chaotic.

Evagrius sees the demonic world as fragmented. The demons go about in groups and sometimes compete with one another and sometimes collaborate. They are like bad weather, stormy, smoky, dark, restless. They do not appear to be organized under any single controlling intelligence. The point here is that Evagrius sees unity as a divine attribute and assumes that the demons are incapable of imitating it. In a letter Evagrius mentions the fallen archangel Lucifer,[15] but only in passing. The letter includes a consideration of the theological arguments in favour of the divinity of the Holy Spirit. There are those who claim that the Spirit is not divine, that his essence is changeable. But, no, Evagrius insists, changeability belongs to creatures. The Spirit can profitably be contrasted with Lucifer who manifested his creaturely and changeable status in his fall from heaven. The fallen angel is a prime example. Elsewhere he follows convention by describing Lucifer as the one cast out of heaven, 'the ancient evil' of pride,[16] and describes pride as 'the first offspring of the devil',[17] but he does not draw out any significant theological implications from this.

It is obvious that much of what Evagrius says of vainglory shades into what he says of pride: the two temptations are inextricably linked. But vainglory remains a very human temptation. It is essentially conceit, it feeds off admiration and needs the good opinion of others. Vainglory is nothing without its mirrors. Pride, on the other hand, is a temptation which really only comes into its own in relation to God.

Pride in the Bible

The Bible presents itself as the story of God's dealings with humankind, from the Garden of Eden to the consummation of all things. The theme of pride runs through it as a recurring refrain. The biblical attitude could be simply summarized: pride is rebellion against God, a refusal to accept the status of being God's creature. There is a recurring struggle going on between human belief in its autonomy and self-sufficiency and God's knowledge of the frailty of the human heart. The unfolding story of God's difficult relationship with humanity is told through the history of God's chosen people, who exemplify the problem as well as bringing forth its resolution in the person of Christ. God's holy people, chosen by God, redeemed from slavery in Egypt, drawn into covenant with him, are still constantly tempted to believe they can manage on their own, or, rather, with gods that they have created for themselves and which reflect their own desires and needs and aspirations rather than those of the living God. God's complaints about his people run through the Hebrew scriptures. They are instinctively rebellious, 'stiff-necked', that is, unwilling to bend to God's will, hard-hearted, ungrateful. God threatens them with punishment and calls them to return to him with love. Yet his people are weak, morally and spiritually, and easily distracted from the divine call. There is, if this great theme of the Bible is seen as a whole, a fundamental dissonance between the way human beings think they should live their lives and the way God calls them to do so. After Augustine, most Christian theologians in the Western part of the Church have assumed that pride was the first and primal sin which led Adam and Eve to disobey God's command and eat the fruit of the forbidden tree, though this has never been part of the Jewish understanding of the Garden of Eden story, nor was it the understanding of the early Christians.

Pride is serious though. The Bible sees pride not only in the life of God's people but also in those who oppose and persecute them. The pride of Pharaoh keeps the Hebrews enslaved in Egypt. Even when God assaults the land of Egypt with plagues, Pharaoh stubbornly refuses to let the people go, and when he eventually does relent he quickly changes his mind. The Philistine hero Goliath is portrayed as a proud but mindless thug, easily defeated by the skill of the unarmed shepherd boy David. The pride of other great rulers in the ancient world is mocked in the scriptures. Nebuchadnezzar, King of Babylon, makes a golden image of himself and commands his people to worship it.

Pride is condemned in the collected proverbs of Israel: 'Haughty eyes and a proud heart – the lamp of the wicked – are sin' (Proverbs 21.4). Pride is linked to arrogance and haughtiness, a rejection both of God and of other people. There is an important contrast here with vainglory. If those afflicted by vainglory long for adulation and admiration, pride is content with invisibility as long as it has unlimited power and control. It is the illusion of the proud that their evil deeds are not seen by God, that there is no justice which can touch them: 'In the pride of their countenance the wicked say, "God will not seek it out"; all their thoughts are, "There is no God"' (Psalm 10.4). Their wealth, their healthy, sleek bodies, their freedom from the worries and stresses that harm other people – all these become an object of the psalmist's envy: 'I was envious of the arrogant; I saw the prosperity of the wicked' (Psalm 73.2–5). The self-confidence of the proud slips into practical atheism; the proud simply run their lives to their own advantage without any sense of accountability to others or fear of human or divine judgement. 'And they say, "How can God know? Is there knowledge in the Most High?"' (Psalm 73.11). Although the psalmist is tempted to despair and to wonder whether attempts to live virtuously are in vain, he eventually concludes that the proud must in the end be subject to judgement: 'They are like a dream when one awakes; on awaking you despise their phantoms' (Psalm 73.20). Their arrogance is based on unreality; they will perish in their ignorance of God.

A particularly significant text for the early Christians was Proverbs 3.34. In the Greek translation of the Septuagint this reads as, 'God resists the proud, but gives grace to the humble.' In this version it is quoted both in the Letter of James and the First Letter of Peter, and later it inspired the opening of Augustine's *City of God*. Pride inevitably encounters divine opposition. It cannot last because it is inherently self-limiting. In this sense pride contains the seeds of its own downfall: 'Pride goes before destruction and a haughty spirit before a fall' (Proverbs 16.18). The contrast to pride is humility, as it is to vainglory. Again, Mary's song, the Magnificat, speaks of God as one who 'has scattered the proud in the thoughts of their hearts', who has 'brought down the powerful from their thrones, and lifted up the lowly' (Luke 1.51b–52).

There are hints in the Bible that pride has a supernatural origin. Evagrius believed there were whole armies of demons afflicting the human soul, and this widespread belief goes back to the ancient mythology embedded in the biblical writings. There are a number of occasions when the writers drew parallels between incidents of rebellion against God manifested in earthly power struggles and rebellion against God in the angelic world. For example, following the exile of the people of Judah in Babylon the prophet Isaiah looks forward to the destruction of Babylon (Isaiah 14.3–23). He prophesies that the proud city will pay for its arrogance against God's chosen people; its rulers will fall to the grave and be destroyed in the underworld. Caught up in the destruction is the angel Lucifer, who is here portrayed as the heavenly counterpart of the King of Babylon. The arrogance of Babylon, which has led to Judah's captivity, is played out in a similar act of arrogance in heaven. Lucifer, the brightest of God's angels, has attempted to climb into heaven and mount the throne of God. For this, he is thrown down to the underworld. So, the prophet claims, the fallen angel and the fallen king share the same fate. As Lucifer ends up in the realm of the dead, so Babylon becomes 'a possession of the hedgehog' (Isaiah 14.23), a watery waste, swept with the broom of God's destruction.

This way of thinking about the relationship between heavenly and earthly power is found elsewhere in the Bible. When the 70 disciples sent out by Jesus as missionaries return triumphant, Jesus claims that he has seen Satan fall like lightning from heaven. The victory of the gospel in earth is paralleled by a change in the heavenly order. The reign of pride against God is over. The Apocalypse, too, describes the defeat of the 'ancient serpent who is called the devil and Satan', who is thrown down from heaven to earth with a whole host of wicked angels and imprisoned in a bottomless pit. At the end of the millennium Satan is released for a while to continue his deceptions, but he is finally thrown into the lake of fire and sulphur to endure the torments he has inflicted on others.[18]

These examples simply make the point that there are strands in the Bible where pride is seen as being of demonic origin and as having a political and social dimension as well as being an issue for the individual. Pride is about control; it is about the kind of self-control that wrongs societies and wrongs the self. God longs for our willing obedience, but we are never forced to obey him. The forceful control of human beings is a demonic strategy; God wills our deepest liberation. Some early Christian thinkers, drawing on scriptural themes, believed that a heavenly rebellion against God had taken place before the creation of this world. This explained the Garden of Eden story. The serpent in the garden was in reality a fallen archangel. Since the fall human life is caught up in a war between God and the fallen angels who now rampage across the earth as demons. Pride is a sin directly aimed at God. It is also the greatest human weakness, making us susceptible to flattery and lies and the false dream of autonomy.

Pride in the life of Evagrius

As we have seen, there is evidence for vainglory in the life of Evagrius. In his teaching he insists that vainglory leads to pride if it is not exposed and cured. The two temptations are intertwined in his own spiritual development, as they often are. He probably saw pride as the fate from which he was saved by his obedience to the angelic vision he had in Constantinople. It would certainly have been possible for him to have disobeyed his call and continued his affair, even though his dream suggested that he knew this would bring him condemnation, at least of an earthly kind. It is not entirely clear when Evagrius first felt a call to some kind of monastic life. Some interpreters of Evagrius' life think he may have begun living as a monk under the direction of Basil of Caesarea, who made him a *lector*, a reader in the Church. The majority view, though, is that he did not accept the monastic habit until Melania persuaded him to. He was ordained a deacon by Gregory of Nazianzus, and his successor as Bishop of Constantinople, Nectarius, made him his archdeacon. As a young man he had an impressive range of connections with the intellectual elite of the Church in the imperial city. It was just at this point that his romantic entanglement occurred.

The temptation to live as though God had no claim on him re-emerged in Jerusalem, but what saved him was the persistence of Melania in making him tell her the real story of his departure from Constantinople. Challenged by her, he found that he simply could not deceive himself. Evagrius was able to see that he needed help from another person to find himself and his true path in life. The relationship with Melania was vital for Evagrius' spiritual development. His need for Melania at a critical point in his life brought him out of isolation and into a genuine recognition of the need for guidance from others. After taking the monastic habit he did not make the mistake of rushing into extreme solitude. His two years living in community in Nitria formed him in habits of prayer and self-examination which would sustain him when he eventually went deeper into the solitude of the desert. Such communal living helps deconstruct images of the self which are based on fantasy because living in community means discovering not only that others can be lovable, infuriating and demanding, but, more importantly, how one responds to lovable, infuriating and demanding others, and what is stirred up within oneself by their presence. What evidence we have suggests that this process was very hard for Evagrius. The Coptic version of Palladius' life suggests that even after he had received the monastic habit from Melania it took several attempts before he was established in monastic life. It was in the monastic community of Nitria that Evagrius lived alongside Coptic monks who lacked his educational advantages but lived holy and wise lives. Some of them gave him a hard time, being both suspicious of his learning and doubtful of his motives. Later, in Kellia, he had the experience of humiliation which is recorded in the *History of the Monks of Egypt*, when he attempted to offer an opinion and was crushingly told that his opinion did not count in the company of monks. All this could have defeated him, turned him in on himself and caused bitterness and resentment.

> Conversion and humility have set the soul up;
> Compassion and gentleness have made it firm.[19]

In fact the humiliations of communal life helped Evagrius to overcome a tendency to arrogance. He acquired a reputation for humility and gentleness of spirit. This was because he was prepared to learn responsibility, discovering how to contribute to harmonious living and practising restraint from gossip and anger and resentment; all of which are ways of drawing attention to the self and express that itch for self-sufficiency and control over others that leads to pride. Without such knowledge and self-knowledge no one was thought safe to embark on the hermit life.

In the Coptic version of the life of Evagrius by Palladius, Evagrius tells of a spiritual dream that he had one night in his cell. He was reading scripture with his lamp burning when,

> I fell into an ecstasy and I found myself as if I were in a dream in sleep and I saw myself as suspended in the air up in the clouds and I gazed at the whole inhabited world. And the one who was holding me said to me, 'Do you see all these things?' (For he had raised me up to the clouds that I might see the whole world at once.) I said to

him, 'Yes.' He said to me, 'I will give you a command. If you keep it, you will become ruler over all these things which you see.' He also said to me, 'Go, be merciful and humble and fix your thoughts correctly in God. You will be prince over all these things.'[20]

The command to be merciful and humble was important for Evagrius. He was certainly known as a gentle and compassionate guide. But what is interesting about this vision is how it echoes the temptation of Christ in the wilderness, when the devil showed him 'in an instant all the kingdoms of the world' (Luke 4.5–8). But where the devil promised Christ the kingdoms of the world in exchange for his submission, Evagrius is commanded to be merciful and humble and to fix his thoughts correctly in God. The promise that he will rule over all that he sees, in the context of Evagrius' theology, would have surely meant that he would acquire the fruits of natural contemplation, the knowledge of the manifold wisdom of Christ displayed in the creation.

Evagrius resisted the ascetic temptation to self-sufficiency and the pride that ensues. He kept in touch with Melania and the monastery on the Mount of Olives where he had found refuge. He wrote letters, made occasional visits and received others. He also took spiritual direction from Macarius the Great and from Macarius of Egypt and made aspects of their teaching his own, especially Macarius the Great's teaching on using simple, direct prayers in temptation, and on the proper use of anger to repel demonic attack. Evagrius may have been a solitary but he was a solitary who lived in dependence on others. In this he was following an established pattern of ancient Greek philosophy explored in the teaching of Aristotle for whom human beings were essentially social creatures. Virtue cannot be reached by thinking about it on one's own: it needs the active presence of others.

Evagrius recognized that the greatest danger to the person advanced in asceticism was to reach a point of such 'competence' in the practical aspects of withdrawal and self-discipline that one came to believe in the efficacy of one's own efforts, forgetting the essential truth that any genuine progress comes about as a result of the grace and mercy of Christ.

Pride and the spiritual tradition

In the ancient world the great and the powerful were expected to be proud. It was, in this sense, more of a virtue than a vice, a necessary accompaniment to courage and ambition. We too easily forget how deeply contradictory is the notion of a humble king, how bizarre it must have seemed to our early Christian forebears to worship a divinity who was humiliated and died to save all, regardless of their station in life.

Many of the stories and tales from the desert reflect the temptation to pride and the need for humility. 'A hermit said, "I would rather be defeated and humble than win and be proud."'[21] The remedy for pride was *compunction*, a pricking of the heart's swollen self-satisfaction which leads to tears and humility. The abrasiveness that we sometimes find in desert wisdom should perhaps be seen less as intended rudeness (though no doubt it sometimes was!) than as a weapon to reveal and puncture the temptation to pride. Theophilus the Bishop of Alexandria, who stirred up the row which ended with the expulsion of the Origenist monks from Nitria and Kellia, receives short shrift in this brief story:

> Once Theophilus of holy memory, the Archbishop of Alexandria, came to Scetis. The brothers gathered together and said to Pambo, 'Speak to the bishop, that he may be edified.' Pambo replied, 'If he is not edified by my silence, my speech certainly will not edify him.'[22]

Over the centuries pride has retained its place as the greatest of the temptations and thus the most serious of the sins. Evagrius certainly saw it in that light and he was followed in that view by his interpreter John Cassian. Between Evagrius and Cassian, their African contemporary Augustine, in his controversy with Pelagius and Julian of Eclanum, was formulating the way in which the Western Church would come to understand pride as *the* original sin.[23] In spite of Cassian's attempt to moderate Augustine's teaching, his general pessimism about the human capacity to respond to God became a key element in Western theology and spirituality. Augustine's dark perceptions about the human condition made sense in the fifth century, an age of increasing insecurity in the Western empire, when centuries of Roman civilization and culture were collapsing. His great work *The City of God* begins with what Augustine describes as a statement of the divine law, in the quotation from Proverbs which has passed into the New Testament as 'God resists the proud, but gives grace to the humble'. He contrasts this with a well-known line from the poet Virgil describing the vocation of Rome as 'to spare the conquered and subdue the proud'.[24] It was the pride of Rome, he suggests, which has led to its downfall; the city of God is hidden in the rise and fall of the empire. Its true citizens will only be known at the end of time. Meanwhile we live in a fallen and broken world in which salvation requires us to be broken, to have our pride purged and our guilt removed.

In spite of Cassian's difficulties with Augustine's teachings he had himself come to the conclusion that pride was the cause of the fall. He tells us that Adam and Eve's taking of the fruit was a prideful attempt to become like God by their own efforts: 'While he (Adam) believed that by the freedom of his will and by his own efforts he could obtain the glory of the Deity, he actually lost that glory which he already possessed by the free gift of the Creator.'[25]

Cassian further developed the tradition, as he had received it from Evagrius, in ways which would heighten the significance of pride as the deadliest of sins. The first of these ways concerns the role of Lucifer, the devil.[26] Cassian links the fall of Adam very directly to the fall of Lucifer. It was pride, as he saw it, which turned this brightest of angels into a devil. Lucifer is presented as an independent supernatural being who rebels against God. Cassian emphasizes the 'dazzling splendour and beauty'[27] of the archangel, and how he was, in a careless moment of contemplation, 'stricken by the dart of pride'. Lucifer's sin was that he came to believe that his radiance and virtue was self-generated and not the gift of God. God, therefore, was no longer necessary. This thought was the primal sin, and the inevitable outcome of it was that God did, in fact, abandon him to his self-belief. Hence his fall from heaven. Yet the pride of Lucifer continued in his demonic state. A false belief that they could acquire divinity by their own efforts was exactly the temptation with which he seduced Adam and Eve, assuring them that, if they ate the forbidden fruit, 'You will be like God' (Genesis 3.5).

Evagrius' host of demons skilfully represented the fragmentation of the world and showed how the demons encouraged further chaos and division. Cassian followed Evagrius in asserting that the fall of Lucifer was a fall into chaos and instability,[28] but his earlier concentration on the splendour and beauty of the archangel was perhaps a significant step in the creation of a dramatically persuasive figure who, in the sheer audacity of his pride, mimics the unity and integrity of God. Such a creation would have been inconceivable in Evagrius' more rigorous theology. Having brought in the theme of Lucifer as a central character in the cosmic drama, Cassian recognized that he had shifted the ground in his understanding of pride to the point where it became not only the culmination of sin, but the primal source of all sin. So, rebel though he was to Augustine's innovations, he accepted this essential point. He did so by an appeal to scripture. The key text which seems to recur endlessly in the discussion of pride, 'God resists the proud, but gives grace to the humble', was taken by Cassian to indicate that pride is the only one of the great faults in human nature which is directly opposed by God.[29] Evagrius, significantly, does not refer to this text at all. But Cassian claims a special status for pride. Whereas the other faults and sins can be mended by attention to particular virtues, 'this one truly pertains to God, and for this reason is fit to own him for its special opponent'.[30]

Furthermore, if pride was the cause of Adam's fall then it must be much more basic to the human condition than Evagrius had assumed. Significantly, Evagrius rarely mentions the Garden of Eden story. A brief reference to Satan appearing as the serpent focuses on Satan's deceitfulness rather than on his pride.[31] But after Cassian the normative interpretation of the Garden of Eden story was that Adam and Eve fell through pride. Pride, as Cassian describes it, no doubt with reference to the serpent, '*crept* back into the first born of mankind' and 'engendered both the weakness and the occasion of all vice'. Adam's fall mirrored the fall of Lucifer. He came to believe that 'he could acquire the glory of the godhead by his own free will and effort' and this meant that 'he lost even that glory with which he had been endowed by the grace of the Creator'.[32]

Cassian wanted it both ways, though, and he continued to place pride as the last of the vices as well as the primal sin: 'This plague may well be the last vice to be attacked, and is treated last, but it is first in origin and occurrence.'[33] In the context of spiritual formation, which was Cassian's chief concern, it remained important to treat pride last. Pride follows vainglory in assaulting those who are already advanced in virtue, and therefore have something to be proud about. But the lasting impact of Cassian's treatment of pride was to shift the weight of the developing monastic tradition in the West in the direction of Augustine's thought. By the time that Cassian was writing his *Institutes* and *Conferences*, Augustine had become recognized as a significant theological authority far beyond his own sphere of influence as Bishop of Hippo.

Benedict learnt much from Cassian and from the earlier tradition. The Rule is designed to root out attitudes of self-sufficiency and help form monks in a way of life of mutual dependence. The first word of the Rule is 'Listen'. We begin from a place of need and Benedict challenges us to accept and persevere in obedience. Religious life begins with turning from the pursuit of self-will. The life was 'the way of return to Christ',[34] the monastery a 'school of the Lord's service'.[35] Benedict overturned the Platonic notion that the willing soul ascends through stages of contemplation towards God. For him the spiritual life embraces the paradox that 'the peak of our endeavour . . . is to achieve profound humility'.[36] The image of Jacob's ladder is employed by Benedict to express this paradox. On the ladder, angels were constantly going up and down between heaven and earth. Monks were to resist 'proud attempts at upward climbing' and 'step downwards in humility'. Stepping down, then, is the way up, and Benedict proposes 12 such steps to establish the habits that enable the monk to come to the love of God, which casts out all fear. Benedict does not have much to say about pride; the enemy of the kind of life he proposes is more easily described as self-will. Yet it is clear that extreme self-will is a form of pride: a refusal of interdependence and a denial of creaturely status before God.

Gregory the Great accepted the idea that pride was the primal sin both from Augustine and from Cassian. He developed this with relish, seizing on the notion that pride has an energy and vitality of its own: 'Pride is the leader of the devil's army, whose offspring are the seven principal vices . . . pride is the root of all evil.'[37] Gregory thought of pride as generative, and so strengthened the notion that sin is something organic and living. As such the tentacles of sin are found in every aspect of the human person: in the instincts of the body, in the will and in our spontaneous thoughts.

This, of course, takes us far from the teachings of Evagrius. Spontaneous thoughts were not sins for Evagrius; they were expressions of vulnerability, ripples on the surface of the mind, to be observed and analysed and brought to Christ in prayer. By recognizing our vulnerabilities and bringing them into the presence of Christ we find healing and learn strategies to defeat the opportunism of the demons. But Gregory would not want to explore spontaneous thoughts in this way. Instead, he 'wants fervently to know and control each step of the heart: every footstep must be scrutinised, every feeling sifted through the febrile hand of discretion'.[38]

Thomas Aquinas reconsiders the whole argument of whether pride was the primal sin. He acknowledges that the central issue in the Garden of Eden was disobedience, he re-examines the claim of gluttony, and introduces the possibility that the real problem was the curiosity that the tempting devil aroused in Adam and Eve. He then considers whether one might identify lack of faithfulness as the first sin. Aquinas argues that the first sin must have arisen from the spirit rather than the body, and it was the overwhelming attraction of the knowledge beyond themselves which drew Adam and Eve into sin. This 'itch to know was caused by the inordinate appetite for superiority'.[39] The problem was not in wanting to be like God; that is, after all, human destiny, implied by our creation in the image and likeness of God. Nor was the problem in wanting knowledge. The problem was wanting the *forbidden* knowledge, knowledge beyond human measure. To have the knowledge of good and evil is, by implication, to have no need of God, no dependence on God, an abrogation of one's status as a creature.

Aquinas recognizes pride both as a specific and a general sin, the precondition and cause of all others. Pride is essentially an overstepping of boundaries. Proud people want to be more than they really are. Their offence is an offence against reason. The proud seek to dominate, to be like God. In this way pride is opposed both to the virtue of humility and to that heroic greatness of soul which presses on to glory despite feelings of unworthiness. 'Pride implies a certain uppishness' – it does not know its place. Aquinas goes on to argue that pride is distinctive among the sins in that it does not only contrast with the virtues of humility and courage, in some sense it opposes every virtue; it has the capacity to turn every virtue into a vice. But although he accepts that pride has a special status he is also cautious about the implications of this argument. There are serious vices which may not necessarily involve pride. Pride is deceptive. Whereas lechery may appear very serious and yet not be accompanied by pride, pride is more serious than lechery and may be so well concealed as to go unrecognized. Pride is complex; it manifests in different people in different ways. Nevertheless, behind them all is the 'craving for superiority which is immoderate because it is not in accord with right reason'.[40] The root of pride is the refusal to be subject to God and his rule. In support of this Aquinas quotes the sixth-century philosopher Boethius who makes the observation that 'while other vices flee from God, pride alone withstands him'. This should make us see pride as in a different category from the other sins; turning away from God may be the consequence of the other sins but it is the very essence of pride. So Aquinas concurs with the tradition that he has received from Augustine and Gregory. Yet one senses he does not want to romanticize this sin by giving too much weight to it. He does not refer to the fall of angels or to the Garden of Eden; he simply concurs with Gregory in seeing pride as 'the queen of the vices', who, having conquered the heart, delivers it into the hands of the seven deadly sins.

It may come as a surprise to discover that on first looking Dante appears to have no place in hell for the proud. Deepest hell is in fact reserved for various kinds of traitors. It consists of a frozen lake in various layers representing the relative seriousness of the betrayal involved. The final and lowest depth of hell is for those who betrayed their superiors. Brutus and Cassius are here, the two Roman senators who assassinated Julius Caesar, and here also is Judas, the betrayer of Christ. The theme of treachery is usually thought of as being quite different from that of pride; and yet in both there is the driving force of desire for self-sufficiency and independence. This deepest part of hell is cold; the burning fires of hell are higher up. What Dante is implying is that the final consequences of sin is a state of frozen rigidity. Two lost souls who are frozen together begin to weep as the poet/ narrator appears, but the frost immediately seals their eyes from the expression of grief. What is condemned is that frozen egotism of the spirit which allows for no relationship. For Dante this is betrayal of God, others and the self. But we can see how close this is to pride as the tradition has come to understand it. The devil, Adam and Eve and all of us become colder, more remote and more self-enclosed when we betray ourselves, others and God.

The proud in hell are beyond salvation; they live for eternity what they have become. But pride can be redeemed by repentance and the *Purgatorio* shows what this involves. The lowest part of purgatory is where the proud start from. Their ascent up the mountain is the longest because their sin is the deepest. The proud and vainglorious are purged by practising the contrary virtue of humility, and this involves them bearing the weight of their grandiosity and self-delusion in the form of heavy rocks on their backs. They are literally humbled, their eyes forced down, so that they can no longer 'look down' on others or admire themselves.

In medieval depictions of pride there is a certain conflation with vainglory. This is shown clearly in the sin-tree in the Church of St Ethelbert at Hessett. There are other examples in which pride is portrayed as a male figure. In a wall painting in the church at Little Horwood in Buckinghamshire, dating from about 1500, pride walks naked and on tiptoe, displaying his well-honed body to the world. Six scrolls emerge from the body with figures representing the other deadly sins. At St Peter's, Raunds, in Northamptonshire, pride takes a female form, a woman wearing a crown, 'Queen of vices', and dressed in style. She is surrounded by red dragons who are convulsively spewing out the other deadly sins.

Evagrius, pride and us

For Evagrius pride was the last of the *logismoi*, a spontaneous thought most likely to strike those advanced in virtue. Pride followed naturally from vainglory. If it was entertained and encouraged it could wreck the soul, bringing about a total disintegration of the personality. But thoughts, even this most evil of thoughts, were not themselves sins for Evagrius. Sin occurs only when we yield to the demonic voices which urge us to pay attention to the *logismoi* and when we begin to believe and act on them. To be seduced by pride gives the demons their greatest victory because it undoes the virtuous life from within. The proud person believes he or she has overcome all dependency. But to live as if this were true is to live from a lie.

It is hard for us to get an accurate perspective on pride because we use the term to refer not only to the cold arrogance which denies others, but to attitudes which are more innocent. There is what used to be called 'proper pride', which we could describe as self-respect or self-esteem. This is a form of a pride we would not want to condemn. We want people to have a sense of pride in themselves and in their real achievements. Gregory the Great might see shades of sinister self-love in this kind of pride, but it is hard to feel that there is anything wrong when a person's heart swells with pride on winning a race, getting married or graduating with a top first-class degree. It is good to feel pride in our children, our parents, our school or our ethnic and cultural history; such pride encourages continuity, loyalty and commitment. What makes these forms of pride tolerable is that they come with a sense of humility. A great achievement is rarely all one's own, there are others who deserve credit. The bridegroom takes pride in his bride, and is humbled by her choice of him which has lifted him into a new life beyond what he knew of himself. This is the kind of humble pride expressed in Mary's song, the Magnificat. Mary is proud *in God*: 'My soul proclaims the greatness of the Lord.' Mary's self-worth is given by God and she gives voice to it by renewing her dependence on God: 'He has looked with favour on his lowly servant.' Evagrius was commanded in his vision to be merciful and humble and to fix his thoughts in God. Humility is the antidote to pride.

Pride of a non-malevolent kind is also displayed in holding to important values, habits or behaviour in the face of threat or horror. Self-respect enables the self to hold together in times of extreme stress. It comes with a certain poise which can inspire others. The grieving widow makes herself up for the funeral, the person on trial shaves and dresses smartly to face judgement and sentence. This kind of pride is not arrogant. It gives away its specialness; it is warm and inclusive. Acquiring a sense of self-worth is an important step in the recovery of those who have been humiliated by others. Particular groups in society that have suffered hostility from others often find strength in publicly affirming their worth. Gay Pride and Black Pride are ways of salving the injuries of homophobia and racism and also challenging the attitudes behind such forms of enmity.

Yet even these innocent forms of pride can turn in on themselves and become a refuge for a partial or false identity. People can be caught up in ethnic or social pride in ways which prevent them treating others fairly. Pride in status is sometimes inherited and can encourage the perpetuation of inequalities. Pride can isolate an individual, making a person unable to ask for or receive help when they need it and others long to give it.

The kind of pride which is condemned by the tradition and has its origins in Evagrius' thought of pride is cold, isolating and domineering. It shows an inhuman desire for independence. Evagrius' insight that it grows from vainglory is surely often accurate. The difference between vainglory and pride is not always easy to discern; both can be identified with the psychological condition of narcissism. Narcissism is self-love, a fixation on the self as the source of value and worth. In its milder forms this is chiefly focused on body image, as in the original myth of Narcissus who dies of starvation after falling in love with a reflection of himself. This kind of narcissism is culturally acceptable today, and is in fact widely encouraged. Body defects must be corrected or airbrushed away from images. Botox treatments, implants, surgical fat removal and cosmetic dentistry flourish when the self is primarily valued as an image, a visible manifestation in the world. Damaging as this may be there is a deeper kind of narcissism which is less focused on body image and more on the acquisition of power. Aquinas' careful argument showing that what Adam and Eve really desired in the garden was the knowledge of good and evil is particularly important here. To lust after superior knowledge is an expression of the desire to dominate and control others. This is a temptation to which many succumb, whether it is the control-freak boss, who knows everyone else's job better than they do, the violent dictator who identifies his will with the destiny of his people, or the spouse who 'knows what their partner really wants'. Religious people are not immune from believing that they know best, even that they know the mind of God. Sometimes they assume too easily that when they speak on a public issue it is with a sure and certain knowledge of good and evil, which it is incumbent on others to respect and agree with. Those with a strongly secular agenda can display the same arrogant certainty.

In the West we are all children of the European Enlightenment, and take as rights freedoms that earlier ages would have found unimaginable. We assume freedom of religion, freedom of conscience, freedom of scientific enquiry and freedom of expression. If the Protestant Reformation broke some aspects of the institutional power of the Church, the Enlightenment redrew the map of the human self and encouraged us to see ourselves primarily as autonomous individuals, private enclosed selves.

When the self is seen in this way there is a danger that any challenge to its autonomy is seen as a kind of insult. Teenagers, testing out what it is to be an adult person, often conduct their first experiments in autonomy in rejecting the wishes of their parents. To an extent this is healthy and right; but we should also recognize that we are inculturating children into a society in which the more malevolent forms of pride are sometimes seen as virtuous. It is not good to encourage individuals into the kind of self-sufficiency which leads to contempt for others.

Pride affects us spiritually in a secular age because it almost *requires* us to disbelieve in God, at least in a God who holds authority over our lives and commands our obedience. The Enlightenment installed reason as the guardian of conscience and the arbiter of personal morality. Some Enlightenment thinkers took their inspiration from the ancient world and saw the exercise of reason as the way in which human beings participate in the mind of God. But the Enlightenment gave rise to a view of reason which has more to do with calculation than with the discovery of wisdom, a view in which knowledge is prized for what it can do and achieve rather than for the wisdom it can lead to.

Such an attitude to knowledge sets us at war with God on a new front: we find ourselves in quiet rebellion against any judgement of God or revelation which is not in accord with our opinions. We believe, of course, that these opinions are personal to us, although the fact is that most of our personal opinions have been instilled in us by parents, schools, religious teachers, pop culture and media. We have few effective ways of evaluating our values. We expect to be able to pick our values off the shelf and choose them as freely as we would a brand of baked beans. This is the result of centuries in which the world has been presented to us in the form of information to be absorbed and understood. We have learnt about all kinds of things but we have not become part of what we learn; rather, what we learn has become part of us, a possession to be utilized for our own advantage and advancement.

We have become rather suspicious of any notion of being formed or inducted into a traditional culture or way of life because we fear such an induction would rob us of our personal freedom. The texts and rites which have led communities through life are now seen as arbitrary, unnecessary and even damaging. There are Christian parents who are unwilling to 'impose' baptism on their children on the grounds that it would deprive them of their right to choose a faith for themselves. There are also those who have expressed a desire to renounce their own baptism, or, in the case of Jews, reverse circumcision on the grounds that it represents a form of assault on the freedom of the self. Pride is intertwined with these attitudes, the prideful belief that we exist to become who we wish to be, and that this can be achieved by an act of sheer will-power. The ancient world believed that character is honed and virtue acquired in community with others, and not as a choice of the individual self. Pride as self-sufficiency is at the heart of Western culture and makes our society vulnerable to the judgement of God.

One of the great challenges to the West in our time is the rise of Islam as a political and spiritual power in the world. The very meaning of Islam is submission, in the sense of submission to the will of God. The prostrations that accompany Islamic prayer express the constant surrender of the self to God's will, which is at the heart of Islamic spirituality. In the Islamic world the will of God is a thread that runs through the whole of life. Even small-scale, everyday decisions are made in a spirit of *binshallah*, 'God willing'. Such an attitude of humility before God runs counter to almost everything that the West has come to believe about people and God over the last five centuries. It represents a massive challenge to Western pride in its achievements, rationality and its beliefs about individual freedom and autonomy. Yet our exposure to Islam could be highly positive if it made us more self-critical, more conscious of the problematic nature of some of the freedoms we take for granted, more willing to recognize that our identity is not self-generated but received. The Western belief in its own superiority needs to be challenged by a call to humility, gentleness and compassion.

Part 3

TOWARDS A CURE

13

The mind's long journey to the Trinity

Like a morning star in heaven and a palm tree in paradise,
so a pure mind in a gentle soul.[1]

It has been the purpose of this study to rehabilitate Evagrius, and so to discover forgotten insights he brings us from the dawn of the Christian era. It was Evagrius' intention to offer diagnosis and therapy for the harmful passions which disturb people and have the potential to turn us away from God. By curing the passions we are set free to contemplate the manifold wisdom of Christ in the universe and eventually to participate in the life of the Trinity.

There are some obvious areas of difficulty for people of our age in getting to grips with some aspects of Evagrius' thought. In particular his anthropology is very different from ours, and yet with perseverance we can, I believe, still make use of his insights about what it is to be a human person.

Evagrius and the human person

We have to understand Evagrius' understanding of the human person in its context, and then draw from it what is insightful for ours. Evagrius thought human beings originated in the mind of God. He knew nothing about evolutionary biology; he could not have imagined the human species emerging from apes. But on the other hand he was not a modern creationist; he did not think that all there is to say about human origins is set down in the first chapters of Genesis. What he shares with us is a view that human beings are in a process of moral and spiritual development. Where he differs from us is in his Platonic view that the soul has three parts with different properties, which require distinctive therapies for their errant tendencies. Evagrius' theory of the passions is not where we might most naturally begin. The idea that our spiritual integrity is constantly under threat by harmful passions initially sounds very strange to us. We respect the energy generated by our emotions and instincts even when they are more unruly than we would like. We tend to think that disturbance and stress can be creative. We do not necessarily assume that a state of perpetual tranquillity, such as the *apatheia* Evagrius aspired to, is desirable. All these aspects of Evagrius' thought are troubling and make it difficult for us to know on what level he might still speak to us.

Evagrius believed that what endangered human beings was a failure to live 'according to nature'. This is where Evagrius stands in solidarity with a long tradition of classical Greek thought, which always understood human beings as part of an interconnected and rational universe. When Evagrius invites us to take positive steps towards the recovery of our natural life, perhaps we should listen and ask what our *natural* life is. More is being implied than simply biological life. We have to take account of what biological life has produced in us, which is not only selfish genes but ethical principles, including the capacity for self-sacrifice. Most human beings have always believed that, to be natural, our life must be in harmony not only with nature in general but with human nature in particular; furthermore, that any truthful account of human nature must always include some reference to the transcendent. This is the case even for those for whom religious beliefs are purely cultural phenomena. The fact that there are such phenomena needs to be taken seriously. Why should biology produce beings who can think of God as the fount of all being and of all virtue and strive to imitate God's goodness? In fact most people do still live their lives in reference to God or to the divine, and many others in reference to a spiritual and moral ideal. Beliefs and ideals are not the same thing, but they do both suggest that it is inherent to human beings to have values, and perhaps even to strive for virtue. We want to make sense of our lives by bringing ourselves into harmony with things we most value.

Evagrius invites us to desire *apatheia*, the quietness of spirit which enables us to love. As he sees it, this is the point at which we begin to participate in the restoration of the world. Many of us would like to learn to love, or to learn to love better. And many are also deeply concerned about the brokenness of the world and long for its healing. At this point we connect with what Evagrius can still say to us.

Evagrius and the human body

Evagrius was very hard on his own body and we probably feel repelled by his extreme asceticism. Yet his intention was to transform the body as the first stage in the restoration of creation. It is paradoxical to suggest this, but in some ways Evagrius had a more integrated view of the body and mind than we do. We tend to think of the body as an image of ourselves which we can manage from inside out, as it were. Evagrius on the other hand allowed the body a genuine life of its own, and seems to recognize that what we do with our bodies really matters because it affects the way we think and feel. The body in other words is the way to the soul, to what is most essential and most human about us. No one should conclude from Evagrius' writing that he thought the body unimportant. On the contrary, the body is providential because it moulds the life of the Spirit.

In the West our habit of assuming that we are 'inside' our bodies goes with an assumption that our bodies belong to us and are there for us to treat or mistreat as we will. It rarely occurs to us that what we do with our bodies has an effect on the people that we are and on our relationships with others. Yet we know how easily we collude with habits of body and mind which are bad for us. We get addicted to harmful patterns of behaviour. As Evagrius recognized, the *logismoi*, the spontaneous yearnings and impulses to which we are prone, if followed thoughtlessly, lead to various kinds of disintegration. The consequences of gluttony are obvious, lust can ruin relationships, anger puts up the blood pressure and leads to violence and hostility. None of this is surprising to us. Gluttony, lust and anger are thoughts which have a measurable effect on our bodies. To be healthy we need to be trained and to train ourselves to resist them. This too is an effort. We all have the instinct for sloth, for letting ourselves drift into a state in which serious effort is almost impossible. As Evagrius noted, sloth is the one evil thought which oppresses the whole person.

A disturbing reflection on contemporary Christian attitudes to the body is the virtual abandonment of any real concern about bodily posture in contemporary Christian worship. There is no sense that kneeling might itself be a kind of prayer, that by arranging our body in this way we might affect our minds and hearts. In fact kneeling to pray in church is often made difficult by the arrangement of chairs. Even sitting is not an attentive, alert sitting, but a casual sitting back as though in order to be entertained. Or perhaps we simply feel that kneeling is 'beneath' us. The assumption is that our inner attitudes to God are all that matter, and that prayerfulness can be evoked by music or speech. The position of the body and the expression of the body has no part in this. What we have to do is to make it as comfortable as possible while we get on with our worship with the rest of ourselves.

This is gross distortion of what it means to be a bodily self. The body is not just there to express the spontaneous desires and feelings of the moment; that is what the gluttonous, or lustful or slothful body does. Evagrius insisted that spiritual growth required certain decisions and restrictions on the life of the body. For him these were withdrawal, aloneness, stability, a rejection of sexual intimacy, wakefulness and a meagre diet. He would have used standing, kneeling, sitting and prostration to express the changing rhythms of prayer, attentiveness, praise, sorrow, intercession. It is through the body that we begin to understand who we are and what we are about; and move into *theoria physike*, the natural contemplation which is the birth of love. We may not be able to or desire to follow Evagrius in the particular ways prescribed, but we are deluding ourselves if we think we can live the resurrection life without training the body. The point is not that the body becomes the instrument of our will, but that the body helps transform the will towards God. If the body remains casually comfortable in prayer we remain detached onlookers; our participation in prayer remains partial and half-hearted. We know in theory that what we do with the body affects us psychologically, but we do not always recognize the creative potential of simple, formal bodily postures for forming us spiritually and strengthening our good dispositions and motivations.

The body also affects the way we see ourselves in relation to the rest of the world. If we treat our bodies primarily as the site for various pleasurable experiences we will also treat the rest of nature as a source of gratification. The natural contemplation to which Evagrius calls us is the spiritual prerequisite for any healing of our relationship with the natural world. As

Thomas Merton put it in his comments on Evagrius, '*Theoria physike* is a most important part of man's cooperation in the spiritualization and restoration of the cosmos. It is by *theoria* that man helps Christ redeem the *logoi* [meaning] of things and restore them in himself.'[2]

Evagrius and the passions

Overcoming the passions takes time and patience. Yet Evagrius was convinced it could be done, or at least attempted, with the help of divine grace, discipline and the support of spiritual guides. An example of how an approach like his has been tried with success in contemporary life would be the various 12-step programmes for overcoming forms of addiction.[3] These begin with the recognition of helplessness in the face of a destructive habit, they call on the help of a 'higher power' which may be God or the support of others. They work by retraining the individual both to understand the roots of their addiction and to find other ways of filling the inner emptiness that has caused the problem. It is often important to see that addictions are not only a form of bodily intemperance but also of latent anger, sadness and boredom. As Evagrius might have seen it, the *logismoi* that spur us to drink, smoke or overeat come with false rationalizations: before enrolment on 12-step programmes people are in denial about the extent of their addictive behaviour. Twelve-step programmes probably provide the most widespread form of spiritual guidance in the Western world. Those who take them are receiving a spiritual formation in understanding and struggling with the passions in a particular and acute form.

It is also possible to see that there is a relationship between the addictions that afflict individuals and our social and communal addictions that are putting a strain on the earth. We have recently started to speak of our 'addiction to oil' as a problem that needs to be solved. More is at stake here than the need to replenish a resource that is beginning to run out. Our whole way of being is under question and without the recovery of a spiritual vision of the cosmos it is difficult to see how humanity can flourish on the earth.

We have begun to express our ecological trespasses in the language of sin being used in church. But so far our understanding of the problem and our attempts to heal it are seen very much as a matter of the will. We look for words with which to confess our failure to be good stewards of the earth and we tend to end up with language which either blames others or is too bland to mean anything very much. A more thoughtful relationship with our bodies would help us to recognize that the authentic life of the Spirit requires us to see ourselves as an authentic part of nature. It is as a part of nature that we are to live out our relationship with Christ; we are here to discover the manifold wisdom of Christ in the creation of our world. Merton comments:

Things are not fully spiritual in themselves; they have to be spiritualised by our knowledge and love in our use of them. Hence it is impossible for one who is not purified to 'transfigure' material things;

on the contrary, the *logoi* [meanings] will remain hidden and he himself will be captivated by the sensible attraction of these things.[4]

The *logismoi* and the demons

Evagrius' demonology presents a problem to those of us who are disinclined to believe in demons. Yet it also brings helpful insights which can lead us beyond our limited understanding of sin and temptation. As I have shown, Evagrius sees a close connection between the eight thoughts and the demons. At times the demons seem to inspire the thoughts, at other times the words 'demon' and 'thought' are used almost interchangeably. Perhaps most typically Evagrius expects the thoughts to occur more or less randomly. Their occurrence may indicate the presence of demons, or may instigate an attack by demons. Either way there is a dynamic interaction between thoughts and demons. The two come together, trapping the aspiring monk on a pincer movement of temptation from both within and without.

Evagrius' theory that sin has a dual cause could be helpful to us as we consider the roots of personal and social breakdown in our advanced Western societies. There is a conflict in contemporary Western thought which tends to run along political lines. Social conservatives locate the origin of bad behaviour in the individual whereas liberals tend to see it as the outcome of social forces. When liberals are in the ascendant there is a tendency to speak of problems (such as the rise of obesity in the Western world) as though they were illnesses. Individuals are then seen as victims, patients, who require medical intervention. When conservatives are in the ascendant individuals are condemned for their moral failings, and shame and rejection are used to try to force those who err into conformity.

Evagrius offers us a template for drawing creatively on both these models. The language of demons could provoke us to reflect on those external forces which pressure people into destructive behaviour. On the other hand even the most demoralized individuals retain some moral agency; we are not simply victims to our own desires and whims. It is within the potential of the individual to resist external temptation. If I have been concerned to demonstrate that Evagrius has a therapeutic view of what is wrong with us rather than the forensic view which dominated in the West it is not because I think he neglects the importance of moral choice. The reverse is true: at every point in the subtle and shifting interactions between the thoughts and the demons, choice is possible – either to resist or surrender. What we perhaps need to take from him is his awareness that human moral behaviour is influenced both from within and from without. Our sins and mistakes, and our virtues too, have more than one cause and need healing on more than one level.

Christ and the human heart

The essential difference between Evagrius' perspective on sin and that of the later Western tradition is in his attitude to the human heart. Gregory the

Great believed that the human heart was invaded by the devil. Evagrius was quite sure that the demons could never understand its mysteries: 'The demons do not know our hearts, as some people think, for the Lord alone is the knower of hearts.'[5]

For Evagrius all that the demons are capable of recognizing are the unstable mental images and fantasies that hover in the heart, and it is these that they exploit. But in a very real sense they do not know what they are doing; they do not have access to the core of our being and have no rights over it. Evagrius never believed that we have vice written into us in the way that the later Western Christian tradition came to believe. We are not virtuous without a struggle, but we do have the potential to be virtuous as long as we recognize our need for God: 'We possess the seeds of virtue';[6] 'The seeds of virtue are indestructible.'[7] Even those who are in hell are not excluded from the possibility of bringing the seeds of virtue to fruition. The rich man, condemned for his failure to share with Lazarus, yet shows that the seeds of virtue are intact by the concern he still has for his brothers. 'To have mercy is the outstanding seed of virtue.' 'We come into life possessing all the seeds of the virtues.'[8] 'We were constituted as possessing the seeds of virtue, but not those of evil.'[9]

This is what Gregory and the Western spiritual tradition came close to denying. For Gregory, the devil has indeed found a way into our hearts and minds and we stand before God as strangers to ourselves and estranged from God. As the prayer of confession from the daily office in the Book of Common Prayer puts it, 'There is no health in us.' There is nothing that is good or sound, nothing that is capable of a free and spontaneous response to the goodness and mercy of God. Christ is Judge of humankind before he becomes our Saviour. There is an exquisite satisfaction for our sinfulness in the sacrificial punishment of the cross.

There is of course tremendous drama in this theology. In Catholic Christianity it powerfully confirms our most tragic intuitions about life, while offering hope that, by the grace of God and devoting ourselves to prayer, penance and good works, we might yet come through to salvation. The Protestant version of this is rather different, the hope offered is that by trusting Christ alone for our salvation and by a constant attempt to displace the sinful self we might find our salvation in Christ assured. In both Western Protestantism and Catholicism we have no hope apart from divine grace. This comes to us by the irruption of God into our world in the incarnation and by the sublime merits of Christ's sacrificial death. Many years ago a television producer said to me that he was not inclined to believe that Christianity was true because he did not accept that the world was crazy. Christianity only made sense in a world that is overwhelmingly terrible.

Because of the scale of our defeat by the forces of evil there is a sense in which Christ and the human heart are thought of as being permanently at war with one another. It might even be said that the devil knows us better than Christ because he is already *in* the human heart, whereas Christ is on the outside knocking, and hoping to be invited in. Holman Hunt's famous picture of *The Light of the World* depicts a wan-faced royal Christ knocking on the door of a ruined house. Salvation depends on Christ overcoming the guarded reluctance of the heart to admit him, sometimes by violence. This is given wonderful expression in John Donne's great poem:

> Batter my heart, three-person'd God; for you
> As yet but knock; breathe, shine, and seek to mend;
> That I may rise, and stand, o'erthrow me, and bend
> Your force, to break, blow, burn, and make me new.
> I, like an usurp'd town, to another due,
> Labour to admit you, but O, to no end.
> Reason, your viceroy in me, me should defend,
> But is captiv'd, and proves weak or untrue.
> Yet dearly I love you, and would be loved fain,
> But am betroth'd unto your enemy;
> Divorce me, untie, or break that knot again,
> Take me to you, imprison me, for I,
> Except you enthrall me, never shall be free,
> Nor ever chaste, except you ravish me.

Donne's theological assumptions in this poem derive from both Augustine and Gregory, but he goes beyond them to give voice to the particular preoccupations of the Reformation. From Augustine he locates the human problem in the heart divided against itself and barricaded against God. Yet reason remains, 'reason, your viceroy in me'. Gregory trusts reason as the only part of the self which has not betrayed the image of God. Yet the Reformers have no absolute faith in reason, here reason too is 'Captive'd and proves weak or untrue'. The human heart, human reason, the human self has no solidity in God; in fact the whole personality is 'betroth'd unto your enemy'. The only freedom comes from radical divorce, and that can only be achieved by God's violence in seizing the self from the enemy.

The eloquence of the poem makes it hard to criticize theologically. Many Western Christians, myself included, feel its echoes in their stumbling efforts to live as faithful disciples of Jesus Christ. We have been formed to see ourselves as rebels, proudly and defiantly resisting God. But the problem is that when the human heart is thought of as radically opposed to Christ, conversion is always fragile. How can we rely on ourselves to rely on Christ, if really, deep down, our hearts are given to the enemy? The spiritual life can easily become a constant and wearying attempt to keep vigilance against an internal foe, while the attempt to be true to Christ can result in what feels like a permanent assault on one's own inner life.

Self at the centre

In the tradition that Protestants and Catholics have inherited there is no real distinction made between temptation, sin and guilt. We are guilty of our thoughts. Instead of learning from them, of 'asking Christ' what they mean, as Evagrius suggests, we feel ashamed of them and bury them. The only place they have in church is the confessional, and though the practice of confession is a help to many, there are perhaps very many others who feel safer bringing their darkest thoughts and even deeds to a 'neutral' counsellor or therapist who can be trusted not to make moral judgements. But the option for a non-judgemental neutrality can ultimately bring its own problems. Insight into our weaknesses and failures is not in itself therapeutic unless it gives birth to a desire for a wiser and humbler way of living. For some this desire will arise spontaneously and be eagerly or soberly embraced. But it is possible to stay for years in the moral impotence of our own excuses and denials, endlessly treading the same ground without recognizing the need for conversion to God, or at least to the practice of virtue. In Evagrian terms this would be a form of sloth.

Yet sloth might seem preferable to the common tendency of Western culture to overdramatize sin. It has often been pointed out that the character of Satan in Milton's *Paradise Lost* is much more compelling than the other characters. We are fascinated by Faust and his pact with the devil. Don Giovanni is doomed, but he is seductive. Anyone who challenges God is a secret hero. It is surely to prevent the attractiveness of the forbidden taking us over that we have become over rigorous and moralistic. When Gregory the Great made pride the principal sin he ensured that self-hatred and self-diminishment became the only reasonable and moral responses to the fluctuations of human consciousness. While attempting to train the wayward self in the ways of virtue he ensured that the self was enthroned at the heart of the spiritual struggle. Paradoxically sin becomes interesting *in itself*, a subtle focus of self-interest and self-flattery.

The Western view of sin has undoubtedly contributed to the moral and creative energy of the West, particularly since the Protestant Reformation. Guilt and anxiety always have been powerful motivators. But the downside is obvious. Western Christianity, as its detractors often point out, presents an agonized, compulsive and judgemental face to the world which is neither attractive nor charitable. In the West the primacy of pride as the deadliest of sins dramatizes and even romanticizes our alienation from God and one another. The self is centre stage and Christ is the enemy of the self until the self is converted and captured for Christ. Christ then becomes the enemy of all that is not himself, the terrible judge who is secretly hated and feared. It occurs to me that Evagrius might have interpreted the Western emphasis on guilt as a demonic victory, convincing us that the life of prayer and virtue is simply unrealizable. The suspicion of the self that infects Western spirituality has led to a rebellion against the Church and an indifference to organized religion. Increasingly religion is seen as the enemy of our humanity, and those secular thinkers who attack Christianity are assured of an enthusiastic audience who see them as liberators.

So what would it be like if Evagrius' insights had prevailed? What would our churches be like if his attitude to sin had not been lost to the West? Would Dante still have written *The Divine Comedy*? Would Aquinas have produced his *Summa*? These are questions which cannot be answered. The nearest we can now get to an Evagrian perspective of sin is to see how his insights are still contained within the spiritual and liturgical life of the Orthodox Church, which, though it formally disowns him as a theologian, still transmits something of his vision to Orthodox Christians.

Orthodoxy and original sin

The Orthodox Church does not hold the Western view that the sin of Adam leaves each individual soul with a legacy of guilt. The Orthodox view is rather that the inheritance of Adam's sin is our mortality. We are born carrying a death sentence in our bodies; and the cause of our struggles and suffering in this life is the knowledge that we will all die. This is how the Orthodox understand Paul's teaching in Romans that 'sin came into the world through one man, and death came through sin, and so death spread to all because all have sinned' (Romans 5.12). Until the development of a distinctive Latin theological tradition with Tertullian, salvation was generally thought to imply immortality. The remission of sins was an important theme, but it was not the dominant one in the thought of the early Christian fathers. It is because our lives are dominated by death and the fear of death that we suffer from the conflict of desires that leads to sin. We struggle for survival; our bodily needs make us subject to the passions and turn us away from the divine life.

But the divine life still invites us to hope more deeply than our fears. God is still the creator of humanity and Christ is our Saviour and Friend. Our natural life is the immortal life that God still desires us to share. Baptism in Orthodoxy is seen in this light. Children are baptized not because they have sinned, nor because they need to be saved from original sin, but in order to endow them with immortal life, which is the one thing their natural parents cannot give them. Baptism is the sacrament of Easter. It is the resurrection of Christ that abolishes death and restores to us the eternal life that God created us to enjoy. Baptism not only endows us with immortality, but it also takes away the fear of death and so gives us strength to struggle with the passions. We no longer have to be anxious. Because death no longer has power over us, we are no longer subject to the addictions and compulsions of our bodies and souls. We are restored to the immortality for which we were created.

Sin and confession in the Orthodox Church

Evagrius did not think that sin was inevitable or that we inherited guilt from Adam. Sin, when it occurs, is always a free act. We choose to sin, it is an exercise of our free will. It is not a transgression of a penal code so much as a betrayal of friendship with God, a turning away from the baptismal gift of immortality in a wilful movement towards death and disintegration. What needs to be re-established is the truth of our relationship with God which is manifested in the resurrection. In the Orthodox Church there is provision for the personal confession of sins. This takes place in church and usually in the presence of an icon of Christ, the book of the

Gospels and the cross. The priest or confessor stands beside the penitent as witness and friend and invites the penitent to confess:

> Behold, Child, Christ stands invisibly here to hear your confession. Be not ashamed, neither be afraid, and hide nothing from me. Rather fear not to tell me all that you have done, so that you may receive forgiveness from our Lord Jesus Christ. Behold his icon is before us. And I am only a witness, that I may bear witness before him of all you tell me. If you hide anything from me, you shall have the greater sin. Take heed, therefore, that having come to the place of the physician, you do not depart unhealed.[10]

The invitation of the confessor is clear: it is a summons to absolute honesty in the presence of Christ, the aim of which is to re-establish friendship with God, a friendship which has never been broken from God's side. We are not to shrink back in shame, or to be so frightened of what we have done that we conceal it. In some Orthodox churches the priest does not give absolution, as is the pattern in Western Catholicism, but may give spiritual advice and a prayer for forgiveness. This will always be the case when the one hearing the confession is not a priest.

When priestly absolution is given, the penitent kneels and the priest lays his stole on the penitent's head. Sometimes a penance is suggested, not as a punishment, and not to offer satisfaction to God, but as medicine or therapy. Or if the issue is serious the individual may be required to abstain from communion until things are resolved.

What the Orthodox understanding of sin enables us to do is to recognize sin in ourselves in the context of a loving relationship which is never broken from God's side. It is the gift of Orthodoxy to demonstrate that everything human is accepted in the presence of God, and that God does not turn away from us. If there is any turning away it is from our side. The characteristic Orthodox understanding of judgement is not of a departure lounge from which the righteous are despatched to heaven and sinners to hell, having received the sentence of mercy or condemnation. Judgement is simply to be in the presence of God and to experience that either as transfiguring light or as annihilating fire. In this sense, we make hell for ourselves when we refuse to receive the friendship that God holds out to us.

Involuntary sin

The Orthodox Church also makes provision for something that we have never really allowed for in the West, the confession of involuntary sin. The assumption is that when priest and penitent stand before the icon of Christ the penitent will not pre-judge his or her own motivation, or attribute blame. They will simply open their heart and confess what hurts, shames and wounds their relationship with God. This means that those who have been driven into sin through the wickedness of others can bring their sorrow and anger to God without either accepting the blame for what others have done to them or having to justify or excuse themselves. There is a realism in this which is extremely important. What is to be said to a woman driven into prostitution by a violent man, or an adolescent who has been sexually abused and found it exciting, though he or she never wanted it to happen? The Western understanding of sin and confession has no way of dealing with this because the forensic approach means that sin can never be involuntary. When we come to the divine tribunal we have either infringed a divine commandment or we have not. If we have, we should confess and be forgiven; if we have not, we should forget about it. In recent years a form of liturgical confession was offered for use in the Church of England which suggested that

> we have sinned against you and against our fellow men,
> in what we have thought,
> in what we have said and done,
> through ignorance, through weakness,
> through our own deliberate fault.[11]

A confession of sinning through ignorance is about as near to the confession of involuntary sin as the Western Church can come. It met with criticism; many people could not accept that 'ignorance' could count as a sin. Those in favour of the phrase glossed it as meaning wilful and deliberate ignorance, like ignoring world poverty by refusing to take notice of the fact that people were starving. But in doing so, they opened the way for the word ignorance to be replaced by the more obviously culpable 'negligence'.

In Orthodoxy ignorance is not negligence. It is rather a state of need which begs for knowledge and enlightenment. This is exactly the kind of ambiguous area where human beings feel the need of God's understanding and healing and grace. It is not always clear whose fault it is when I find I am drawn to confess ignorance; the feeling of pain and loss and regret is much the same whether I was personally culpable or not. In the Orthodox tradition this is not a problem. Confession of sin and recognition of the weakness and need which are part of our mortality can both be brought to God, without needing to be too precise about where one ends and the other begins. At an Orthodox funeral it is customary to pray that the sins of the deceased may be forgiven whether they are voluntary or involuntary. Here is the recognition that the roots of sin in the *logismoi* make us vulnerable in a way that goes beyond our conscious will or consent. This does not mean that we are necessarily guilty of sin when our spirits are disturbed by some bad memory or grief, but it may mean that we are implicated in the sins of others in such a way as to require healing. Some rather agonized questions about guilt and forgiveness might be eased if we made room for some expression of involuntary sin, if we recognized that sin does not always arise out of choice, that we are not always sinning out of a hidden desire for significance as rebels against God. Ignorance and weakness are the ground out of which our deliberate sins grow. It is quite proper to articulate in the presence of God the state of the ground as well as express regret for the rank weeds that might arise out of it. This vulnerability is part of our nature as mortal beings and we should have no hesitation in bringing the truth of ourselves to God.

In this life, where we are still trying to manage our passions, we will experience God both as healing light and as purging fire. This should not disturb us; it is the state of our souls which is being revealed to us, a sense of guilt and inadequacy and even fear of God should provoke in us a deeper cry for mercy and a deeper awareness of God's glory. One of the most quoted maxims from an Orthodox teacher of recent times has been the words addressed to the Staretz Silouan which he understood as coming from Christ, 'Keep your mind in hell and despair not.' This is in invitation to recognize that the experience of prayer will bring us suffering as well as joy, and that this suffering is potentially helpful to us. In the West we often interpret good feelings at times of prayer as reassurance and bad feelings as a sign that we have done something wrong. The Puritan notion of 'keeping short accounts with God' is unhelpful advice if it leads us to think we are at any one time *either* in a state of a grace *or* a state of sin. Orthodoxy does not think in terms of spiritual 'states'. Our relationship with God is much more fluid and dynamic than that, like any other personal relationship. In a sense the Orthodox understanding of our relationship with God reminds us of Luther's definition of the redeemed Christian as *simul justus et peccator* – at the same time justified and a sinner. Yet this definition could also suggests that we exist before God primarily as two simultaneous states or modes, as though we were *objects* in God's eyes and not persons.

What is needed in the Western Church is a deepening of our interior language. There has been much talk of conscience in the tradition, but not so much of consciousness. When an individual begins psychotherapy or counselling they are invited to be honest, to express their thoughts and feelings without the fear of immediate interpretation or premature judgement. Why are we unable to see that this is what should be happening in our prayer lives?

Evagrius is surely right when he tells us to *observe* our disturbing thoughts, to notice their frequency and duration and record what precedes and follows them. We should grow accustomed to examining our thoughts and feelings, perhaps by picturing them as images passing on a screen, or recalling them as snapshots, sounds or sense-impressions. Self-examination of this kind is not, as it is sometimes feared to be, a self-referring, self-indulgent process. The mental act of observation shifts the centre of the self. We stand apart, even if only for a few moments, from the restless emotions and ideas that compete for attention in our daily life. This standing apart could be the beginning of *apatheia*, the recognition of a selfhood which is deeper and more open than the streams of thoughts and feelings which chase across the surface of the mind. The spiritual potential of this approach has been explored in recent years by the Jesuits in their rediscovery and reinterpretation of the teaching of their founder, Ignatius of Loyola (1491–1556). This is not the place to consider the contemporary revival of Ignatian spirituality, but one of the reasons for its current popularity is that it encourages people to observe their feelings and thoughts honestly and to an extent objectively. The spiritual freedom to which Ignatius calls people through his Spiritual Exercises is related to *apatheia*. It is a state not of passivity but of poise, where the will is free from self-protection and self-deception and able to accept the greater and more loving will of God.

Yet this awareness of a deeper self remains only a private awareness if it is not brought into the light and spaciousness of liturgical participation. The liturgy is scriptural and traditional; it provides the scaffolding and structure of the self's relationship with God. But just as important, it relates the individual self to others in such a way that these others become part of the self, not in a possessive way, but in a constitutive way. We are who we are because of those others with whose lives we are involved. Within the Christian Body we are invited to recognize that personal life does not consist so much in choosing to have particular relationships with people but in accepting that the relationships we actually have form us to be the people that we are. If we get even a hint of this in church, it may help us to be reconciled to other sometimes uneasy relationships which are nevertheless part of our history and part of our selfhood.

Confession and liturgical language

At the start of this study I wrote of my unease at our Western liturgical language of confession and absolution. I said that the words we use do not express what most of us now feel because we are no longer motivated by the fear of divine judgement. Because it is less plausible than it once was to believe in a God of wrath we have become careless and superficial in our attitude to sin and penitence. We have not understood that judgement is something we bring on ourselves. The result is that we either take refuge in structural notions of sin, which diminish our personal sense of responsibility, or, if we do have a disturbing sense that we are in the grip of harmful passions, we take our worries out of the church (where they might embarrass us) and into the more neutral 'safe' space of the non-judgemental counsellor.

If our liturgies were to reflect a therapeutic approach to sin, what would they be like? First, they would probably help us to recognize that sin is a personal choice. It is by abandoning Christ that we make hell for ourselves and each other, while God's voice is always to be heard in the call for salvation. The Orthodox Divine Liturgy of St John Chrysostom has no penitential rite of any kind that Western Christians might be familiar with. There is no communal grovelling and no priestly absolution of the kind we might recognize. Instead there is a constant and repeated cry for mercy which runs through the whole liturgy. This cry, this plea, is evoked not by digging about for things to accuse ourselves of, but simply by the recognition of God's glory. The more we see the glory, the more we know ourselves to be in need of healing.

In the more intensely penitential seasons, the Orthodox liturgy deepens the language of penitence, not by finding new and novel sins to get upset about but by encouraging us to recognize our sinfulness expressed through the various voices of scripture. So in Holy Week, a beautiful verse is sung as though from the point of view of the guest of Matthew 22.11–12, who was invited to the wedding banquet but came without a robe: 'I see thy bridal chamber adorned, O my Saviour, and I have no wedding garment that I may enter there. Make the robe of my soul to shine, O giver of light, and save me.'[12] On Holy Tuesday the story of Christ's curse of the barren fig tree provides the content for this *Ikos*: 'While there is still time return to soberness and cry: I have sinned against thee, O my Saviour, do not cut me down like the unfruitful fig tree; but, O Christ, in thy compassion take pity on me as I call on thee in fear', at which point the theme returns to the wedding banquet, 'May we not be left outside the bridal chamber of Christ!',[13] a cry which recurs again and again throughout Holy Week.

This first-person liturgical language which calls on biblical images and figures as types of the human person expresses the anguish of our condition in a way which positively prepares us for the recovery of salvation. It is not the polite bland generalized language of contemporary Western liturgy. Nor is it the self-accusation which struggles to be scrupulously exact for fear that some sin might be forgotten and so remain unforgiven. The language of the Orthodox liturgy is biblical and personal, but not individualistic. We are invited to see ourselves as we really are, sick and in need, in ways which are already wider and more inclusive than our individual experience would allow. The General Confession in the Anglican Book of Common Prayer approaches something like this when it refers to the parable of the lost sheep: 'We have erred and strayed from thy ways like lost sheep, We have followed too much the devices and desires of our own hearts, We have offended against thy holy laws . . .' It is memorable, but the reference is not carried through or developed in the way it might have been within the Orthodox tradition. Nevertheless it engraves on the memory and imagination the image of the straying sheep in the Bible and the anticipation of the Good Shepherd coming to find it and return with it rejoicing. It is personal and yet it transcends individualism. It offers a biblical image which acts as a scaffolding for our feelings, thoughts and reflections, and also helps to form those feelings and thoughts and reflections on a biblical model.

For Evagrius, the demons seek to undermine the self and thus keep us from Christ. What deflects them is the sound judgement that is formed 'in the tribunal of the heart'[14] as the evil thoughts are brought to awareness and their roots in the passions exposed. In 1961 the philosopher Hannah Arendt (1908–75) coined the phrase 'the banality of evil'. It was in the context of a study of the trial of Adolf Eichmann.[15] Eichmann was no one's idea of what a demonic figure should be. He was not in any way glamorous. No one would have seen him as a rebel against God, or even as a hater of humanity. He was a very ordinary man. Yet under Hitler he became an architect of the Holocaust, the powerful administrator of the gas chambers and the death camps. Hannah Arendt argued that the terrible evils of history are not committed by callous monsters full of hatred for humanity, or by the mad or the fanatical. What enables evil on the scale of the Holocaust is more a lack of imagination, an unwillingness to think or judge actions from a position of empathy with those who might suffer as a result. In doing so, I believe Hannah Arendt was expressing an Evagrian view of evil. It is not dramatic wickedness that keeps us from God, but little, ordinary tedious sins which keep us from God and from truth, the repeated giving in to shoddy thinking, the submission to empty fantasy rather than active imagination, and the false logic which if unrecognized and unchecked accumulates into the monstrous inhumanity that destroys the self and other selves.

Yet the Christ who inspired in the young Evagrius 'a certain longing for godly teachings', and who enabled him to endure years of 'starving and battling with foul thoughts' in his search for wisdom, still calls out to us to take his yoke upon us and learn from him. The yoke he offers is the baptized life, a pilgrimage under his guidance into the loving communion for which we were created, the Kingdom of the Holy Trinity. Evagrius believed that the living Christ is latent in every human person created in God's image and likeness, present in the self that comes to birth in baptism, calling from the future in the self that dies daily to sin and rises to new life in Christ. Evagrius' mentor, Gregory of Nazianzus, put this dynamic understating of Christian selfhood in these words:

> Yesterday I was crucified with Christ;
> today I am glorified with him.
> Yesterday I was dead with Christ;
> today I am sharing in his resurrection.
> Yesterday I was buried with him;
> today I am waking with him from the sleep of death.[16]

Notes

Part 1: Symptoms

1 Before the deadly sins: the relevance of Evagrius

1 *New Patterns for Worship* (London, Church House Publishing, 2002), p. 91.
2 Bamberger (tr.), *The Praktikos & Chapters on Prayer*, p. xciii (I have taken the liberty of putting this comment in inclusive language).
3 The term 'cracks in the heart' is from Andrew Louth's comments on Evagrius in *The Wilderness of God*, p. 52.
4 Bamberger (tr.), *Chapters on Prayer* 122, p. 75.

2 A brief history of sin

1 Hicks (tr.), *Lives of Eminent Philosophers* (Zeno) 110–13, pp. 215–17.
2 'Pity' is condemned because the compassion that a virtuous person might feel for another is regarded as irrational and disturbing.
3 Hicks (tr.), *Lives of Eminent Philosophers*, p. 219.
4 King (tr.), *Tusculan Disputations* 4.6, p. 339.
5 Staniforth (tr.), *Meditations*.
6 Sinkewicz (tr.), *Maxims* 2.2, in *Evagrius*, p. 230.
7 Fairclough (tr.), *Epistle* 1.1.33–42.
8 See Galatians 5.19–21, 22–23 and also Colossians 3.5, 8; 12.13a; compare with 2 Timothy 3.2–5.
9 Staniforth (tr.), *The Didache* in *Early Christian Writings*, p. 193.
10 Testament of the Twelve Patriarchs, *PG* 2.1039–150.
11 Sinkewicz (tr.), *Thoughts* 1 in *Evagrius*, p. 153.
12 Tertullian, *On Modesty*, *ANF*, vol. 4, p. 97.
13 Tertullian, *On Modesty*, *ANF*, vol. 4, p. 97.
14 Greer (tr.), *On Prayer* 9, p. 151.
15 Kelly, *Doctrines*, pp. 217–18.
16 Cyprian, Treatise VII, *On the Mortality*, *ANF*, vol. 5, p. 470.
17 Cyprian, *Epistle* 55, as cited by Kelly, *Doctrines*, p. 217n.
18 The Niceno-Constantinopolitan Creed, commonly and inaccurately known as the Nicene Creed.
19 Louth, *The Wilderness of God*, p. 52.
20 Bamberger (tr.), *Praktikos* 6, p. 16.
21 Augustine, *Contra Faustum*, XXII, xxvii, 'Dictum vel factum vel concupitum contra legem aeternam', *PL* 42.207–518.
22 Clark (tr.), *The Happy Life* in *Selected Writings*, pp. 168–9.
23 Augustine, *On Nature and Grace*, ch. 5, *NPNF* First Series, vol. V, p. 123.
24 King (tr.), *Tusculan Disputations*. See p. 9 above.
25 Gregory the Great, *Moralia* 31.45.87, *PL* 76.620.
26 Gregory the Great, *Moralia* 33.45.81, *PL* 76.621.
27 Gregory the Great, *Moralia* 26.17.28, *PL* 76.364.
28 Gregory the Great, *Moralia* 35.17.43, *PL* 76.775.
29 Straw, *Gregory the Great*, p. 124.
30 Gregory the Great, *Moralia* 24.11.32.

31 Straw, *Gregory the Great*, p. 122.
32 Gregory the Great, *Moralia* 9.38.61, *PL* 75.893–4. (See Straw, *Gregory the Great*, p. 157.)
33 Straw, *Gregory the Great*, p. 105.
34 Bieler (ed.), *Penitential of Cummean* in *The Irish Penitentials*.
35 Nineham, *Christianity*, pp. 60–1.
36 Sayers (tr.), *The Divine Comedy* 1, *Hell*, p. 85.

3 Evagrius lost and found

1 Sinkewicz (tr.), *Prayer* 60 in *Evagrius*, p. 199.
2 Casiday (tr.), *Evagrius*, p. 6.
3 Casiday (tr.), *On the Faith* 2 in *Evagrius*, p. 46.
4 Casiday (tr.), *Evagrius*, p. 8.
5 Sinkewicz (tr.), *Prayer* 60 in *Evagrius*, p. 199.
6 Sinkewicz (tr.), *Reflections Part 1 Gnostic Chapters* 4 in *Evagrius*, p. 211.
7 Budge (tr.), *Of Eucarpus*, ch. xxx, in *Paradise*, p. 263.
8 Casiday (tr.), *Evagrius*, p. 26, quoting from article written by von Balthasar in 1939 and now available as 'The Metaphysics and Mystical Theology of Evagrius', *Monastic Studies* 3 (1965), pp. 183–4. Casiday regards von Balthasar's judgement as 'monstrously unjust'.
9 Bamberger (tr.), *Praktikos*, Preface by Jean Leclercq.
10 Luibhéid (tr.), *Conferences*, Introduction by Owen Chadwick, p. 4.
11 See n. 30.
12 Dysinger, *Psalmody and Prayer*, p. 196.
13 Casiday (tr.), *Evagrius*.
14 Casiday (tr.), *Evagrius*, p. 31, quoting Martin Parmentier on *The Great Letter* of Evagrius.
15 Casiday, *The Great Letter* 17 in *Evagrius*, p. 67.
16 Hebrews 5.12–14; 6.1–2; 1 Corinthians 2.1–8.
17 *Praktikos*, Introduction 9, here as cited by Casiday, *Evagrius*, p. 32.
18 Casiday, *The Great Letter*, in *Evagrius*, p. 69.
19 *Les six centuries des 'Kephalaia Gnostica', édition critique de la version syriaque commune et édition d'une nouvelle version syriaque avec une double traduction française* (Paris 1958). *Patrologia Orientalis*, vol. 28.
20 Meyendorff, *Byzantine Theology*, p. 67.
21 Bamberger (tr.), *Praktikos*, Introduction, p. xxvi.
22 *The Seven Ecumenical Councils*, *NPNF* Second Series, vol. XIV, pp. 318–19.
23 Dysinger, *Psalmody and Prayer*, p. 194, on the *Scholia on Proverbs*, where Evagrius explains that even the rich man of Luke 16.28, in his concern for his brothers, shows that there is a possibility of learning mercy and compassion from 'this place of torment'.
24 Socrates, *Ecclesiastical History*, VI.7, *NPNF* Second Series, vol. II, pp. 142–3.
25 Casiday, *Evagrius*, p. 16.
26 Luibhéid (tr.), *Conferences* 10.3, pp. 126–7.
27 Socrates, *Ecclesiastical History*, VI.7, *NPNF* Second Series, vol. II, pp. 142–3.
28 Socrates, *Ecclesiastical History*, VI.7, *NPNF* Second Series, vol. II, p. 142.
29 Jerome, *Letter 133*, *NPNF* Second Series, vol. 6, p. 274.
30 Sinkewicz (tr.), *Foundations* 9 in *Evagrius*, p. 10.
31 Dysinger, *Psalmody and Prayer*, p. 16.
32 Casiday, *Evagrius*, p. 18.
33 Casiday, *Evagrius*, p. 21.

34 Casiday, *Evagrius*, p. 20.
35 John Moschos, *The Spiritual Meadow*, cited by Merton in *An Introduction to Christian Mysticism*, p. 97.
36 Luibhéid and Russell (trs), *The Ladder of Divine Ascent*, p. 166.
37 Meyendorff, *Christ in Eastern Christian Thought*, p. 122.
38 Meyendorff, *Christ in Eastern Christian Thought*, p. 122.
39 Dysinger, *Psalmody and Prayer*, p. 196.
40 Bamberger (tr.), *Praktikos* 2, p. 15.
41 Bamberger (tr.), *Praktikos* 3, p. 16.
42 Sinkewicz (tr.), *Reflections* 22 in *Evagrius*, p. 213.

4 The spiritual teaching of Evagrius

1 *Antirrhetikos*, Prologue, translated by Luke Dysinger in an online translation: <http://www.ldysinger.com/Evagrius>.
2 *Gnostic Chapters* II.25, as quoted by Merton in *An Introduction to Christian Mysticism*, p. 100.
3 Sinkewicz (tr.), *Praktikos* 50 in *Evagrius*, p. 106.
4 Driscoll (tr.), *Ad Monachos*, p. 15.
5 Driscoll (tr.), *Ad Monachos*, p. 62.
6 Sinkewicz (tr.), *Praktikos* 8 in *Evagrius*, p. 96.
7 Thomas Merton notes (*An Introduction to Christian Mysticism*, p. 102) that the irascible Jerome has never been suspected of attaining to *apatheia*!
8 Gregory of Nyssa, *Homilies on the Song of Songs*, as cited by Merton, *An Introduction to Christian Mysticism*, p. 102.
9 Prayer Book of the Scottish Episcopal Church, 1912.
10 Cassian, *Conferences*, NPNF Second Series, vol. XI, pp. 265–371.
11 Cassian, *Conferences*, NPNF Second Series, vol. XI, p. 370.
12 Cassian, *Conferences*, NPNF Second Series, vol. XI, p. 368.
13 Cassian, *Conferences*, NPNF, Second Series, vol. XI, p. 368.
14 See page 43.
15 Bamberger (tr.), *Praktikos* 48, p. 29.
16 Sinkewicz (tr.), *Eulogios* 13.12 in *Evagrius*, p. 39.
17 Bamberger (tr.), *Praktikos* 50, p. 29.

Part 2: The diagnostic tool kit

5 The thought of gluttony

1 Attributed to Synesius of Cyrene (375–430), translation by A. W. Chatfield.
2 *Praktikos*, SC, 508–10.
3 Bamberger (tr.), *Praktikos*, Introductory Letter, p. 14.
4 Ward, *The Desert Fathers* 4.60, p. 30.
5 Ward, *The Desert Fathers* 4.53, p. 28.
6 Ward, *The Desert Fathers* 4.6, p. 20.
7 Ward, *The Desert Fathers* 3.47, p. 27.
8 Ward, *The Desert Fathers* 3.19, p. 22.
9 Clement of Alexandria, *The Instructor* 2.1, ANF, vol. 2, p. 238.
10 Ward, *The Desert Fathers* 1.4, p. 3.
11 Meyer (tr.), *Lausiac History*, p. 113.
12 Sinkewicz (tr.), *Foundations* in *Evagrius*, p. 10.
13 Sinkewicz (tr.), *Foundations* in *Evagrius*, p. 5. 'Even if you have only bread, salt and water, you can with these gain the reward of hospitality.'

14 Ward, *The Desert Fathers* 5.40, pp. 26–7.
15 Sinkewicz (tr.), *Thoughts* in *Evagrius*, p. 178.
16 Bamberger (tr.), *Praktikos* 17, p. 21.
17 Dysinger, *Psalmody and Prayer*, p. 122.
18 John Chrysostom, *Commentary on Matthew 13*: 'By the body's incontinence was Adam expelled from Paradise', *PG* 57.209.
19 Bertram (tr.), *Institutes*, 5.6, p. 72.
20 Cassian, *Conference of Abbot Serapion* 5.11, *NPNF* Second Series, vol. II, p. 343.
21 Bertram (tr.), *Institutes*, 5.23.
22 Bertram (tr.), *Institutes*, 5.7: 'More appetising food which promotes physical health does not hinder bodily purity if taken in moderation.'
23 Bertram (tr.), *Institutes*, 5.15–16, pp. 78–9.
24 Barry, *St Benedict's Rule* 4, p. 14.
25 Barry, *St Benedict's Rule* 39, p. 47.
26 Barry, *St Benedict's Rule* 40, p. 40.
27 Barry, *St Benedict's Rule* 49, p. 60.
28 Gregory the Great, *Moralia* 31.45.88, *PL* 76.556–7.
29 Gregory the Great, *Pastoral Care* 3.19, p. 147.
30 Gregory the Great, *Moralia* 30.18.60, *PL* 76.556–7.
31 *Summa Theologiae* 2a2ae.148.4.
32 For a treatment of this theme and examples, see R. M. Bell, *Holy Anorexia* (University of Chicago Press, 1985).
33 Peers (tr.), *Dark Night of the Soul* 1.6 in *Complete Works of John of the Cross*, p. 343.
34 Assuming that he left the monastery at Nitria in 384/5 and died in 399.

6 The thought of lust

1 *Praktikos, SC* 510–12.
2 Sinkewicz (tr.), *Foundations* 1–2 in *Evagrius*, pp. 4–5.
3 Sinkewicz (tr.), *Eulogius* 13 in *Evagrius*, pp. 38–9, and 18, p. 45.
4 Sinkewicz (tr.), *Evagrius*, p. 22.
5 Sinkewicz (tr.), *Eight Thoughts* 2 in *Evagrius*, pp. 76–8.
6 Sinkewicz (tr.), *Exhortation to a Virgin* 54 in *Evagrius*, p. 135.
7 Sinkewicz (tr.), *Eight Thoughts* 2.19–20 in *Evagrius*, p. 78.
8 Sinkewicz (tr.), *Eulogius* 18 in *Evagrius*, p. 45.
9 Sinkewicz (tr.), *Thoughts* 16 in *Evagrius*, p. 163.
10 Sinkewicz (tr.), *Foundations* 5 in *Evagrius*, p. 6.
11 Meyer (tr.), *Lausiac History*, p. 111.
12 Budge (tr.), *Paradise*, vol. I, Book ii.14, p. 223.
13 White, 'Gregory the Great: *Life of Benedict*' in *Early Christian Lives*, p. 168.
14 Bamberger (tr.), *Praktikos* 54, p. 31.
15 Sinkewicz (tr.), *Eight Thoughts* 2.7 in *Evagrius*, p. 76.
16 Sinkewicz (tr.), *Eight Thoughts* 2.8 in *Evagrius*, p. 76.
17 Bamberger (tr.), *Praktikos* 51, p. 30.
18 Armstrong (tr.), *Life of Plotinus* 1, p. 4.
19 Bamberger (tr.), *Praktikos* 55, p. 31.
20 *Antirrhetikos* 2.35. Author's translation based on Luke Dysinger's reconstruction of the Greek.
21 *Antirrhetikos* 2.49. Author's translation based on Luke Dysinger's reconstruction of the Greek.
22 Ward, *The Desert Fathers* 4.41, p. 27.
23 Ward, *The Desert Fathers* 5.4, pp. 33–4.

24 Ward, *The Desert Fathers* 5.29, p. 43.
25 Ward, *The Desert Fathers* 4.68, p. 31.
26 Ward, *Desert of the Heart*, p. 46.
27 Bertram (tr.), *Institutes* 6.
28 Bertram (tr.), *Institutes* 6.4.
29 Bertram (tr.), *Institutes* 6.7.
30 Bertram (tr.), *Institutes,* 6.5.
31 Cassian, *The Third Conference of Abbot Chaemeron* 6, *NPNF* Second Series, vol. II, p. 424.
32 Augustine, *City of God* 14.23–4, *NPNF* First Series, vol. II, pp. 279–80.
33 Augustine, *City of God* 14.24, *NPNF* First Series, vol. II, p. 280.
34 Gregory the Great, *Moralia* 31.45.88, *PL* 76.621.
35 Barry, *St Benedict's Rule* 7, p. 22.
36 Barry, *St Benedict's Rule* 22, p. 31.
37 Aquinas, *Summa Theologiae* 2a2ae.153.2.
38 Aquinas, *Summa Theologiae* 2a2ae.153.3.

7 The thought of avarice

1 *Praktikos*, SC 512–13.
2 Sinkewicz (tr.), *Praktikos* 35–6 in *Evagrius*, p. 104.
3 Leviticus 27.30; Numbers 18.26; Deuteronomy 14.24; 2 Chronicles 31.5.
4 Meyer (tr.), *Lausiac History*, p. 113.
5 Driscoll (tr.), *Ad Monachos* 18, p. 44.
6 Sinkewicz (tr.), *Foundations* 8 in *Evagrius*, p. 9.
7 Sinkewicz (tr.), *Thoughts* in *Evagrius*, p. 157.
8 Sinkewicz, *Thoughts* in *Evagrius*, p. 157.
9 Driscoll (tr.), *Ad Monachos* 25, p. 45.
10 Sinkewicz (tr.), *Thoughts* 8 in *Evagrius*, p. 158.
11 Roth (tr.), *On Wealth and Poverty*, p. 55.
12 Ward, *The Desert Fathers* 6.1, p. 53.
13 Ward, *The Desert Fathers* 6.5, p. 54; Sinkewicz, *Praktikos* in *Evagrius*, p. 113.
14 Ward, *The Desert Fathers* 6.21, pp. 58–9.
15 Bertram (tr.), *Institutes* 7.3, p. 108.
16 Bertram (tr.), *Institutes* 7.4, p. 109.
17 Bertram (tr.), *Institutes* 7.7, p. 109.
18 Bertram (tr.), *Institutes* 7.7, p. 111.
19 Bertram (tr.), *Institutes* 7.30, p. 123.
20 Barry, *St Benedict's Rule* 12, pp. 39–40.
21 Leo the Great, *Letters* 4.4, *NPNF* Second Series, vol. XII, pp. 3–4.
22 Zimmerman (tr.), *Dialogues* 4, p. 269.
23 Gregory the Great, *Moralia* 31.45.88, *PL* 76.621.
24 Sinkewicz, *Eulogius* 17 in *Evagrius*, p. 44.
25 Aquinas, *Summa Theologiae* 2a2ae.118.2.
26 Bruce H. Wilkinson, *The Prayer of Jabez* (Colorado Springs, Multnomah Press, 2000).
27 Bamberger (tr.), *Chapters on Prayer* 129, p. 76.

8 The thought of sadness

1 *Praktikos*, SC 514.
2 Sinkewicz (tr.), *Thoughts* 12 in *Evagrius*, p. 61.

3 Sinkewicz (tr.), *Eulogios* 7 in *Evagrius*, p. 34.
4 Sinkewicz (tr.), *Eight Thoughts* 17 in *Evagrius*, p. 83.
5 Sinkewicz (tr.), *Eulogios* 7 in *Evagrius*, p. 34.
6 Sinkewicz (tr.), *Eight Thoughts* 11 in *Evagrius*, p. 82.
7 Sinkewicz (tr.), *Eight Thoughts* 23 in *Evagrius*, p. 84.
8 Sinkewicz (tr.), *Eight Thoughts* 24 in *Evagrius*, p. 83.
9 Bamberger (tr.), *Praktikos* 95, p. 40; Ward, *The Desert Fathers* 1.5, p. 3.
10 Sinkewicz (tr.), *Foundations* 9 in *Evagrius*, p. 9.
11 Cassian, *Institutes* V.32, *NPNF* Second Series, vol. X1.
12 Benedict, *Rule* 3.3, *PL* 77.53–54.

9 The thought of anger

1 *Praktikos*, SC 516–18.
2 Driscoll (tr.), *Ad Monachos* 10.
3 This discussion owes a good deal to Dysinger's *Psalmody and Prayer*, especially pp. 124ff.
4 Lee (tr.), *Timaeus and Critias* 38.70, pp. 97–8.
5 Budge, cited by Bamberger (tr.), *The Praktikos & Chapters on Prayer*, p. xlv.
6 Ward, *The Desert Fathers* 16.2, p. 172.
7 Bamberger (tr.), *Praktikos* 24, p. 23.
8 Bamberger (tr.), *Praktikos* 42, p. 27.
9 Meyer (tr.), *Lausiac History*, p. 113.
10 Dysinger, *Prayer and Psalmody*, p. 51.
11 Dysinger, *Prayer and Psalmody*, p. 129.
12 Gregg (tr.), *Letter to Marcellinus*, pp. 101–29.
13 Gregg (tr.), *Letter to Marcellinus*, pp. 101–29.
14 Ward, *The Desert Fathers* 4.28, p. 24.
15 Bamberger (tr.), *Praktikos* 25, p. 23.
16 Gregory the Great, *Moralia*, 5.45, *PL* 75.724, as cited in Aquinas, *Summa Theologiae* 2a2ae.158.5.
17 Casey, *Pagan Virtue*, p. 11.
18 Casey, *Pagan Virtue*, p. 21.
19 Ward, *The Desert Fathers* 4.22, p. 23.
20 Ward, *The Desert Fathers* 7.33, p. 71.
21 Bertram (tr.), *Institutes* 8.1, p. 125.
22 Bertram (tr.), *Institutes* 8.21, p. 136.
23 Gregory the Great, *Moralia* 31.45.89, *PL* 76.622.
24 Gregory the Great, *Moralia* 31.45.88, *PL* 76.621.
25 Aquinas, *Summa Theologiae* 2a2ae.158.8.3.
26 Sayers (tr.), *Divine Comedy*, 1 Hell, Canto 7.112, p. 113.
27 Sayers (tr.), *Divine Comedy*, 1 Hell, Canto 7.121, p. 113.

10 The thought of sloth

1 *Praktikos*, SC 516–18.
2 Louth, *Origins of the Christian Mystical Tradition*, p. 105.
3 Eaton, *The Psalms*, p. 326.
4 Sinkewicz (tr.), *Praktikos* 28 in *Evagrius*, p. 102.
5 Sinkewicz (tr.), *Praktikos* 36 in *Evagrius*, p. 104.
6 Sinkewicz (tr.), *Eight Thoughts* 6 in *Evagrius*, p. 84.
7 Driscoll (tr.), *Ad Monachos* 54–6, pp. 50–1.

8 Bamberger (tr.), *Praktikos* 28, p. 24.
9 Bamberger (tr.), *Praktikos* 27, p. 23.
10 Bamberger (tr.), *Praktikos* 29, p. 24.
11 Driscoll (tr.), *Ad Monachos* 54, p. 50.
12 Sincewicz (tr.), *Eight Thoughts* 18 in *Evagrius*, p. 85.
13 Driscoll (tr.), *Ad Monachos* 55, p. 60.
14 Driscoll (tr.), *Ad Monachos* 56, p. 51.
15 Ward, *The Desert Fathers*, 10.27, p. 94.
16 Theodoret, *Ecclesiastical History* 4.10, *NPNCF*, p. 114.
17 Ward, *The Desert Fathers* 12.9, pp. 131–2.
18 Ward, *The Desert Fathers* 7.1, p. 60.
19 Ward, *The Desert Fathers* 7.38, p. 72.
20 Ward, *The Desert Fathers* 2.9, p. 10.
21 Bertram (tr.), *Institutes* 10.2, p. 145.
22 Bertram (tr.), *Institutes* 10.2, p. 145.
23 Bertram (tr.), *Institutes* 10.7, p. 148.
24 Bertram (tr.), *Institutes* 10.22, p. 148.
25 Bertram (tr.), *Institutes* 10.24, p. 160.
26 Barry, *St Benedict's Rule*, Prologue, p. 5.
27 Barry, *St Benedict's Rule* 48, p. 57.
28 Chittister, *Rule of St Benedict*, p. 133.
29 Chittister, *Rule of St Benedict*, p. 132.
30 Gregory the Great, *Moralia* 31.45.88, *PL 76.621*.
31 Davis (tr.), *Pastoral Care* 3.15, pp. 134–6.
32 Aquinas, *Summa Theologiae* 2a2ae.35.
33 See p. 32.

11 The thought of vainglory

1 *Praktikos, SC* 520–6.
2 Sinkewicz (tr.), *Thoughts* 8 in *Evagrius*, p. 158.
3 Sinkewicz (tr.), *Thoughts* 28 in *Evagrius*, p. 173.
4 Meyer (tr.), *Lausiac History* 38.2, p. 111.
5 Sozomen, *Ecclesiastical History*, *NPNF* Second Series 6.30, p. 368.
6 Budge (tr.), *Paradise*, p. 225.
7 Meyer (tr.), *Lausiac History*, p. 112.
8 Sinkewicz (tr.), *Eulogios* 3 in *Evagrius*, p. 31.
9 Sinkewicz (tr.), *Eulogios* 23 in *Evagrius*, p. 50.
10 Sinkewicz (tr.), *Vices* 6 in *Evagrius*, p. 64.
11 Budge (tr.), cited by Bamberger (tr.), *The Praktikos & Chapters on Prayer*, p. xlv.
12 Socrates, *Ecclesiastical History*, *NPNF* Second Series 4.23, p. 109.
13 *The Coptic Life* 17–18, as cited by Casiday (tr.), *Evagrius*, p. 11 and notes p. 206.
14 Budge (tr.), *Paradise*, p. 264.
15 Jerome, *Letters* 133, *NPNF*, Second Series, p. 274.
16 Sinkewicz (tr.), *Thoughts* 15 in *Evagrius*, p. 163.
17 Sinkewicz (tr.), *Eight Thoughts* 7.1 in *Evagrius*, p. 85.
18 Sinkewicz (tr.), *Eight Thoughts* 7.2 in *Evagrius*, p. 85.
19 Sinkewicz (tr.), *Eulogios* 33 in *Evagrius*, p. 58.
20 Sinkewicz (tr.), *Eulogios* 33 in *Evagrius*, p. 58.
21 Sinkewicz (tr.), *Eight Thoughts* 7.10–13, 19 in *Evagrius*, p. 86.
22 Sinkewicz (tr.), *Eulogios* 19 in *Evagrius*, p. 46. In other translations the Bible reference is Psalm 70.3.

23 Sinkewicz (tr.), *Eulogios* 14 in *Evagrius*, p. 41.
24 Sinkewicz (tr.), *Eulogios* 14 in *Evagrius*, p. 41: 'Set the seal on the spices of your ascetic labours, lest unfastened by your tongue they be stolen by esteem.'
25 Sinkewicz (tr.), *Eulogios* 15 in *Evagrius*, p. 42.
26 Sinkewicz (tr.), *Eight Thoughts* 7.14 in *Evagrius*, p. 86.
27 Driscoll (tr.), *Ad Monachos* 61, p. 51.
28 Bamberger (tr.), *Praktikos* 31, p. 24.
29 Ward, *The Desert Fathers* 3.9, p. 14.
30 Sinkewicz (tr.), *Prayer* 116 in *Evagrius*, p. 106.
31 Dysinger, *Prayer and Psalmody*, p. 170.
32 Sinkewicz (tr.), *Foundations* 9 in *Evagrius*, p. 9.
33 Sinkewicz (tr.), *Thoughts* 28 in *Evagrius*, p. 173.
34 Dysinger, *Prayer and Psalmody*, p. 38: 'The highest of the *noemata*, the thought of God himself, by its nature leaves the mind unstamped, because it is incorporeal.'
35 Cicero, *De Officiis* 1.68, as cited in Aquinas, *Summa Theologiae* 2a2ae.132.2.
36 Aristotle, *Ethics* iv.3, as cited in Aquinas, *Summa Theologiae* 2a2ae.132.2.
37 Ward, *The Desert Fathers* 15.68, p. 165.
38 Sinkewicz, *Eulogios* 25 in *Evagrius*, p. 53.
39 Bertram (tr.), *Institutes* 11.5, p. 164.
40 Bertram (tr.), *Institutes* 11.4, p. 164.
41 Barry, *St Benedict's Rule* 7, p. 21.
42 Gregory the Great, *Moralia* 31.45.88, *PL* 76.621.
43 Aquinas, *Summa Theologiae* 2a2ae.132.

12 The thought of pride

1 *Praktikos*, SC 532–4.
2 An occasion where he does is in *Exhortation* 1.6, Sinkewicz (tr.), *Evagrius*, p. 218.
3 Sinkewicz (tr.), *Foundations* 4 in *Evagrius*, p. 6.
4 Sinkewicz (tr.), *Eulogios* 3 in *Evagrius*, p. 31.
5 Sinkewicz (tr.), *Vices* 8 in *Evagrius*, p. 65.
6 Sinkewicz (tr.), *Vices* 9 in *Evagrius*, p. 65.
7 Driscoll (tr.), *Ad Monachos* 62, p. 52.
8 Gregory of Nyssa, *Song of Songs*, PG 44:824.
9 Davies (tr.), *Basil of Caesarea*, p. 108: 'The spirit which is not scattered on the outside and diffused by the senses into the world, returns to itself, and sets out from there to be one with God; and then, brilliant and resplendent with divine beauty it begins to forget its own nature . . . it concentrates its whole being on attaining eternal goods.'
10 Bamberger (tr.), *Praktikos* 64, pp. 33–4.
11 Sinkewicz (tr.), *Thoughts* 39 in *Evagrius*, p. 39.
12 Sinkewicz (tr.), *Gnostic Chapters* 1.1 in *Evagrius*, p. 211.
13 Sinkewicz (tr.), *Gnostic Chapters* 1.4 in *Evagrius*, p. 211.
14 Sinkewicz (tr.), *Gnostic Chapters* 1.1 in *Evagrius*, p. 211.
15 Casiday, *On the Faith* 2 in *Evagrius*, p. 55.
16 Sinkewicz (tr.), *Praktikos* 2 and *Thoughts* 19 in *Evagrius*, pp. 95 and 166.
17 Sinkewicz (tr.), *Thoughts* 1 in *Evagrius*, p. 153.
18 For a detailed discussion of the relationship between earthly events and heavenly powers in the New Testament, see Walter Wink's *Naming the Powers* and *Unmasking the Powers*.
19 Driscoll (tr.), *Ad Monachos* 53, p. 259.

20 Quoted by Driscoll (tr.), *Ad Monachos*, p. 260. The translation from the Coptic is by Mark Sheridan.
21 Ward, *The Desert Fathers* 15.74, p. 166.
22 Ward, *The Desert Fathers* 15.42, p. 158.
23 See pp. 20–1 above.
24 Virgil, *Aeneid* 6.853: 'parcere subiectis et debellare superbos'.
25 Bertram (tr.), *Institutes* 12.8 p. 177.
26 It is perhaps worth noting that neither Evagrius nor Cassian had any appreciation of the original relationship between the fall of Lucifer and the fall of the oppressive historical powers which provided its original context. They are not unique in this – patristic exegetes had no great interest in the historical settings of the scriptural accounts.
27 Bertram (tr.), *Institutes* 12.4, p. 174.
28 Bertram (tr.), *Institutes* 12.5, p. 175.
29 Bertram (tr.), *Institutes* 12.7, p. 176.
30 Bertram (tr.), *Institutes* 12.7, p. 176.
31 Sinkewicz (tr.), *Eulogios* 17 in *Evagrius*, p. 44.
32 Bertram (tr.), *Institutes* 12.5, p. 175.
33 Bertram (tr.), *Institutes* 12.8, p. 177.
34 Barry, *St Benedict's Rule*, Prologue, p. 1.
35 Barry, *St Benedict's Rule*, Prologue, p. 4.
36 Barry, *St Benedict's Rule* 7, p. 20.
37 Gregory the Great, *Moralia* 31.45.
38 Straw, *Gregory the Great*, p. 22.
39 Aquinas, *Summa Theologiae* 2a2ae.163.3.
40 Aquinas, *Summa Theologiae* 2a2ae.162.4.

Part 3: Towards a cure

13 The mind's long journey to the Trinity

1 Driscoll (tr.), *Ad Monachos* 107, p. 60.
2 Merton, *An Introduction to Christian Mysticism*, p. 125.
3 Alcoholics Anonymous was the first and best known of these.
4 Merton, *An Introduction to Christian Mysticism*, p. 126.
5 Sinkewicz (tr.), *Thoughts* 37 in *Evagrius*, p. 179.
6 Sinkewicz (tr.), *Thoughts* 7 in *Evagrius*, p. 158.
7 Dysinger, *Scholia on Proverbs 5.14* in *Psalmody and Prayer*, p. 194.
8 Dysinger, *Scholion 3 on Psalm 125.5* in *Psalmody and Prayer*, p. 194.
9 Sinkewicz (tr.), *Kephalaia Gnostica* 1.40 n. 14 in *Evagrius*, p. 268.
10 The Book of Needs, vol. 1: *The Holy Mysteries* (South Canaan, Penn., St Tikhon's Monastery Press, 2000).
11 An Order for Holy Communion: Alternative Services, Series 3 (1971).
12 Mattins for Monday in Holy Week, Mother Mary and Ware, *The Lenten Triodion*, p. 514.
13 Mother Mary and Ware, *The Lenten Triodion*, p. 525.
14 Sinkewicz (tr.), *Eulogios* 13.12, in *Evagrius*, p. 38.
15 Arendt, *Eichmann in Jerusalem: A Report on the Banality of Evil* (Harmondsworth, Penguin Books, 1963).
16 Gregory of Nazianzus, *First Theological Oration* 4, NPNF Second Series, vol. VII, p. 203. This version is taken from *Common Worship: Daily Prayer* (London, Church House Publishing, 2005), p. 76.

Bibliography

In the extracts from the *Praktikos* at the beginning and end of each chapter of Part Two, where I consider the eight thoughts in turn, I have used the Greek Text of the *Praktikos* directly. I have used the Latin text of Gregory the Great's *Moralia* 31.45.81ff. The translations offered here are thanks to Dr Jo Spreadbury. Elsewhere I have used English translations as indicated.

Greek text of the *Praktikos*

A. and C. Guillaumont (eds), *Évagre le Pontique: Traité Pratique ou le moine*, Sources chrétiennes 170–171 (Paris, 1971). Referred to here as *SC*.

Greek quotations and citations from other patristic texts are generally from the text as edited or reproduced by J. P. Migne, *Patrologia Graeca*, and referred to here as *PG*.

Latin quotations and citations of patristic texts are generally as edited by J. P. Migne, *Patrologia Latina*, and referred to here as *PL*.

English translations

Works of Evagrius

Bamberger, John Eudes (tr.), Evagrius Ponticus, *The Praktikos & Chapters on Prayer*, Cistercian Studies Series 4 (Kalamazoo, Mich., Cistercian Publications, 1981).

Casiday, A. M., *Evagrius Ponticus*, The Early Church Fathers Series (London, Routledge, 2006).

Driscoll, Jeremy (tr.), *Evagrius Ponticus: Ad Monachos*, Ancient Christian Writers (New York, Paulist Press, 2003).

Sinkewicz, Robert E., *Evagrius of Pontus: The Greek Ascetic Corpus*, Oxford Early Christian Studies (Oxford University Press, 2006 [2003]).

Translations of other texts

The *Ante-* and *Post-Nicene Christian Fathers* series, in spite of their nineteenth-century provenance, still provide the standard translations for many patristic texts (Edinburgh, T&T Clark; Grand Rapids, Mich., Eerdmans, reprinted 1989). Referred to as *ANF* and *NPNF* First Series and *NPNF* Second Series.

Armstrong, A. H., 'Plotinus', Porphyry, Loeb Classical Library (Cambridge, Mass., Harvard University Press, 1966).

Barry, Patrick, *St Benedict's Rule: A New Translation for Today* (York, Ampleforth Abbey Press, 1997).

Bertram, Jerome (tr.), St John Cassian, *The Monastic Institutes* (London, The St Austin Press, 1999).

Bieler, L. (ed.), *The Irish Penitentials* (Scriptores Latini Hiboriae), vol. V (Dublin Institute for Advanced Studies, 1975).

Budge, E. A. W., *Paradise of the Holy Fathers*, Part 1 (London, Chatto & Windus, 1907).

Chittister, Joan, *The Rule of St Benedict* (New York, Crossroad, 1998).

Clark, Mary T. (tr.), Augustine, *Selected Writings*, Classics of Western Spirituality (New York, Paulist Press, 1984).

Davies, Oliver (ed.), *Gateway to Paradise: Basil the Great*, tr. Tim Witherow (New York, New City Press, 1991).

Davis, Henry (tr.), Gregory the Great, *Pastoral Care – Regula Pastoralis*, Ancient Christian Writers no. 11 (Westminster, Md., Newman, 1950).

Fairclough, H. Rushton (tr.), Horace, *Epistles* 1.1, 33–42 Loeb Classical Library (Cambridge, Mass., Harvard University Press, 1926).

Gilby, Thomas, et al. (tr.), Thomas Aquinas, *Summa Theologiae*, 16 vols (London, Blackfriars, 1964–1981).

Greer, Rowan A. (tr.), Origen, *On Prayer*, Classics of Western Spirituality (New York, Paulist Press, 1979).

Gregg, Robert C. (tr.), Athanasius, *The Life of Antony and the Letter to Marcellinus* (New York, Paulist Press, 1980).

Hicks, R. D. (tr.), Diogenes Laertes, *Lives of Eminent Philosophers*, vol. II, Loeb Classical Library (Cambridge, Mass., Harvard University Press, 1965).

King, J. E. (tr.), Cicero, *Tusculan Disputations*, Book 4, Loeb Classical Library no. 41 (Cambridge, Mass., Harvard University Press, 2nd edn 1927).

Lee, Desmond (tr.), Plato, *Timaeus and Critias* (Harmondsworth, Penguin Classics, 1965).

Luibhéid, Colm (tr.), John Cassian, *Conferences*, with Introduction by Owen Chadwick, Classics of Western Spirituality (New York, Paulist Press, 1985).

Luibhéid, Colm and Russell, Norman (trs), John Climacus, *The Ladder of Divine Ascent*, Classics of Western Spirituality (New York, Paulist Press, 1982).

Mary, Mother and Ware, Kallistos, *The Lenten Triodion* (London, Faber, 1978).

Meyer, Robert T. (tr.), Palladius, *The Lausiac History*, Ancient Christian Writers no. 34 (London, Longmans, Greer & Co., 1965).

Peers, E. Allison (tr.), *The Complete Works of St John of the Cross* (Wheathampstead, Anthony Clarke, 1978).

Roth, C. P. (tr.), 'St John Chrysostom, *On Wealth and Poverty* (New York, St Vladimir's Seminary Press, 1984).

Staniforth, Maxwell (tr.), Marcus Aurelius, *Meditations* (Harmondsworth, Penguin Books, 1964).

Staniforth, Maxwell (tr.), (rev. Andrew Louth), *Early Christian Writings* (Harmondsworth, Penguin Books, 1987).

Sayers, Dorothy L. (tr.), Dante, *The Divine Comedy*, 3 vols (Harmondsworth, Penguin Classics, 1949).

Ward, Benedicta, *The Desert Fathers: Sayings of the Early Christian Monks* (London, Penguin Books, 2003).

Ward, Benedicta, *The Desert of the Heart: Daily Readings with the Desert Fathers* (London, Darton, Longman & Todd, 1993).

White, Carolinne, *Early Christian Lives* (Harmondsworth, Penguin Books, 1998).

Wortley, John (tr.), John Moschos, *The Spiritual Meadow* (Kalamazoo, Mich., Cistercian Publications, 1992).

Zimmerman, Odo John (tr.), *Saint Gregory the Great, Dialogues*, vol. 39 (New York, The Fathers of the Church, 1959).

Other works

Casey, John, *Pagan Virtue: An Essay in Ethics* (Oxford, Clarendon Press, 1992).

Chitty, Derwas J., *The Desert a City* (New York, St Vladimir's Seminary Press, 1995).

Dysinger, Luke, *Psalmody and Prayer in the Writings of Evagrius Ponticus*, Oxford Theological Monologues (Oxford University Press, 2005).

Eaton, John, *The Psalms: a Historical and Spiritual Commentary* (Edinburgh, T&T Clark, 2003).

Kelly, J. N. D., *Early Christian Doctrines*, A&C Black (5th edn, London, Continuum, 1977).

Louth, Andrew, *The Origins of the Christian Mystical Tradition* (Oxford University Press, 1981).

Louth, Andrew, *The Wilderness of God* (London, Darton, Longman & Todd, 1981).

Merton, Thomas, *An Introduction to Christian Mysticism*, ed. Patrick F. O'Connell, Monastic Wisdom Series, no. 13 (Kalamazoo, Mich., Cistercian Publications, 2007).

Meyendorff, John, *Byzantine Theology* (London, Mowbray, 1974).

Meyendorff, John, *Christ in Eastern Christian Thought* (New York, St Vladimir's Seminary Press, 1975).

Nineham, Denis, *Christianity, Medieval and Modern* (London, SCM Press, 1993).

Straw, Carole, *Gregory the Great: Perfection in Imperfection* (Berkeley, Calif., University of California Press, 1988).

Wink, Walter, *Naming the Powers* (Minneapolis, Minn., Fortress Press, 1984).

Wink, Walter, *Unmasking the Powers* (Minneapolis, Minn., Fortress Press, 1986).

Wink, Walter, *Engaging the Powers* (Minneapolis, Minn., Fortress Press, 1992).

Index of biblical, ancient and medieval sources

Index of modern authors

Index of subjects

Aaron 144
Abel, murder 116
Absalom (King David's
  son) 77
absolution 186
accidie (acedie), sin of 125,
  128
acedia see sloth
Adam: fall 4, 71; sin
  185; sinful inheritance
  14–15; *see also* fall
addiction, 12-step
  programmes for
  overcoming 127, 180
addictive behaviour 127
adultery 15, 16, 78;
  biblical attitudes to 77
adults, mid-life crises
  created by nostalgia 113
agape, Evagrius'
  understanding 53
Ahab (king of Israel)
  92–3
alcoholics, anger 127
Alcuin, on gluttony 21
Amnon (King David's
  son) 77
Ananias and Sapphira
  (early Christians),
  avarice 96, 97, 98
Ancient Persia, beliefs on
  good and evil 12
ancient world: attitudes
  to vainglory 152–3;
  character in 174;
  understanding of sin
  and virtue 9–11; views
  on anger 121–2
anger 18, 19, 111, 179;
  Aristotle's views 119,
  121–2, 124; Augustine
  of Hippo's views
  124; biblical views of
  116–18; Cassian's views
  123; Dante's views 125;

English medieval
  church art 32; Evagrius'
  views 109, 115–16,
  118–21, 123, 126–7;
  Gregory the Great's
  views 23, 121, 124,
  125; Jesus Christ's
  teaching 124; linked
  with sadness 105, 114;
  the permanently angry,
  Dante's views 30;
  reconciliation after 118;
  righteous anger 116;
  as silent fury 122; and
  the spiritual tradition
  121–5; Thomas
  Aquinas' views 122,
  124–5; as viewed in
  the ancient world
  121–2
Anselm of Canterbury,
  on penitential systems
  26–7, 28
anthropomorphism,
  condemned by
  Theophilus of
  Alexandria 43
Antony of Egypt 18, 97,
  120, 135
anxiety 89; as lack of
  trust in God 131;
  related to gluttony 67;
  as the soil for avarice
  91, 95
apatheia 8, 48, 160–1,
  178, 188, 189; anger
  destroys 115; Cassian
  interprets as *purity of
  heart* (*puritas cordis*)
  54; differentiated
  from apathy 133–4;
  disturbance by anger
  120; Evagrius' views
  44, 52–3
apathy, as sloth 133–4

Apollo, temple of
  (Delphi) 11
apophaticism 42, 158; and
  the appreciation of God
  161; necessity in prayer
  151; Western fears of
  56
apostasy 15, 16
appetite, control essential
  to prayer 66
Aristotle 86; analysis of
  the vices 30; on anger
  119, 121–2, 124;
  condemns usury 97;
  deadly sin tradition
  associated with 10;
  on humanity 166;
  on magnanimity as
  opposed to vainglory
  152
Arius 36
Arsenius (monk), fasting
  66
asceticism: bodily
  asceticism 9–10; end
  33; as protest against
  the Roman empire 57;
  views of anger 123;
  see also desert ascetics
ataraxia 120
Athanasius 20, 120, 121
atonement: Anselm of
  Canterbury's views
  26–7; theology xi
Augustine of Hippo: on
  anger 124; *The City
  of God* 163, 167; on
  deadly sins 20–2; on
  the divided will 25; on
  divisions in the heart
  183; influence on
  Gregory the Great 70;
  influence on Thomas
  Aquinas 170; on pride
  162, 167, 168; on